Reporting the Arab–Israeli Conflict

For journalists and reporters, the allegation of hegemonic practices constitutes a most serious condemnation. It supposes that the media is working in the interest of the political establishment to create a false consciousness. However, starting with Raymond Williams's refined definition of hegemony, Tamar Liebes shows how hegemony is an almost unwitting process that supports the status quo and the establishment. *Reporting the Arab–Israeli Conflict* illustrates how this "soft hegemony" is manifest in the everyday workings of the media, and all the more so when the media are on one side of a serious conflict.

In considering the reporting of the Arab–Israeli conflict and the 1991 Gulf War, Liebes demonstrates how national journalism supports the dominant ideology. This unintentional assimilation is the result of shared values, the inaccessibility of the other side, the preference for celebrating success rather than exposing failure, and a wish to be popular with the public. The author shows how journalists abandon their watchdog role, however unintentionally, to support "our side," especially in time of war. *war reporting*

Reporting the Arab–Israeli Conflict: How Hegemony Works demonstrates how readers and viewers are implicated in this process by virtue of their expectations and their inability to decode the press critically. Illustrations are provided of how conflict may be otherwise depicted, for example by artists and front-line participants, as well as how media-literate readers can learn to read between the lines.

Tamar Liebes is Director of the Smart Institute of Communication at the Hebrew University of Jerusalem. She is the author, with Elihu Katz, of *The Export of Meaning* (1993).

ROUTLEDGE RESEARCH IN CULTURAL AND MEDIA STUDIES

Series Advisors: David Morley and James Curran

Reporting the Arab–Israeli Conflict

How Hegemony Works

Tamar Liebes

London and New York

First published 1997
by Routledge
11 New Fetter Lane, London EC4P 4EE

Simultaneously published in the USA and Canada
by Routledge
29 West 35th Street, New York, NY 10001

Reprinted 2001, 2002

Routledge is an imprint of the Taylor & Francis Group

© 1997 Tamar Liebes

Typeset in Times by Routledge
Printed and bound in Great Britain
by Intype London Ltd

British Library Cataloguing in Publication Data
A catalogue record for this book is available from the British Library

Library of Congress Cataloguing in Publication Data
A catalogue record for this book has been requested

ISBN 0–415–15465–0

Contents

Acknowledgments

A major part of the original research reported in this book has been supported by funding from the Spencer Foundation. Support has also been received from the Bertelsemann Foundation and the Smart Institute of Communication at the Hebrew University of Jerusalem.

Particular thanks are due to Rivka Ribak, who assisted throughout the collection of data and the analysis of decoding the news within families, and is a co-author of earlier versions of chapters 7 and 9; to Shoshana Blum-Kulka, who collaborated in the study of the framing of the intifada by Israeli soldiers, and was a co-author of the original version of chapter 10; and to Theodore Glasser who co-authors a later version, in progress, of chapter 4. In addition, I consulted colleagues at many points in the study. My greatest debt is to Elihu Katz, whose generous advice was of great value throughout, and who took part in conceptualizing the chapter on peace ceremonies. I should also like to thank Michael Gurevitch, Theodore Glasser, Sonia Livingstone, Peter Lunt, Daniel Dayan, and finally all those who took part in the field work.

An earlier version of chapter 5, entitled " 'What a relief' – When the press prefers celebration to scandal," appeared in *Journal of Political Communication*, 1994, 11, 35–48.

An earlier version of chapter 7, entitled "A mother's battle against the news: A case study of political socialization," co-authored with Rivka Ribak, appeared in *Discourse and Society*, 1991, 2, 203–22.

An earlier version of chapter 8, entitled "Decoding TV news: The political discourse of Israeli hawks and doves," appeared in *Theory and Society*, 1992, 21, 357–81.

Portions from chapter 9, entitled "In defense of negotiated readings: The decoding of intifada news," originally appeared in *Journal of Communication*, 1994, 44, 108–24, co-authored with Rivka Ribak.

An earlier version of chapter 10, entitled "Managing a moral dilemma: Israeli soldiers in the intifada," co-authored with Shoshana Blum-Kulka, originally appeared in *Armed Forces and Society*, 1994, 21, 45–69.

Chapter 1

Introduction
How hegemony works

To say that the Israeli press represents the Arab–Israeli conflict from where "we" stand seems redundant. We have learned that any report on reality expresses the reporter's point of view, that conflict makes it physically and psychologically difficult to get to the other side, that journalists have to tell stories which are relevant and familiar to their public, and thus that journalists, willy-nilly, are servants of their culture. Might this be what we mean by hegemony? The question applies not only to journalists, but to all interpreters and commentators – researchers included. Somewhere along the line "we" researchers – no less partisan in our personal commitments – should clarify where the reporting of conflict from "our" side may no longer be excused as "technical" but should be labeled hegemonic, and try to delineate how this hegemonic process works.

When analyzing the workings of the press we have in mind the ideal of an independent, critical, "watchdog" press, against which we judge journalists when we find that they work, probably inadvertently, to enhance the powers that be. And war, or the threat of war, exacerbates this tendency.

The allegation of hegemony would constitute a most serious condemnation of the press had the term retained its original straightforward connotation of working in the interest of the political establishment to create a false consciousness. But, as Raymond Williams reminds us, social science has advanced beyond this crude definition of hegemony with its "trivializing explanations of 'manipulation' and 'corruption,'" and has substituted the much more subtle definition of the internalization of "a lived system of meanings and values" of a dominant culture through which people experience reality and see themselves.

This refinement of the concept of hegemony means not only that hegemonic processes are much more sophisticated and pervasive, "saturating" our lives (Berger, 1972), but also that anything is suspect. It makes it difficult, perhaps impossible, to distinguish between the two models of the press – one hegemonic, the other critical – inasmuch as ideas or contributions which seem to be alternative and oppositional may still operate within a specific ideology, and may be limited, neutralized, and incorporated by it. By the same token, what may be labeled hegemonic at first glance may yet supply us with alternative readings "between the lines."

The challenge to the analyst, according to Williams (1977), is to examine how specific formations of domination occur. The power of his theory of hegemony is in its capacity to talk of culture as a lived dominance "thus stitching experience, politics, and ideology into the study of everyday life" (ibid., p. 110). We apply this notion of lived hegemony to everyday media representations of conflict following Williams's recommendation, in an attempt "to develop modes of analysis which do not reduce works to finished products." (ibid., p. 114), that is, to examine the "careers" of texts and their producers, and, in parallel, to look at consumers in order to identify the changing meanings of these texts, their functions, and the ways in which they are negotiated. Thus we may discern texts which own a "finite but significant openness."

Granted that both journalists and readers operate, inevitably, within some hegemonic confines, and that all of us are caught up in the process. Yet it is also true, nevertheless, that the hegemonic process is active, constantly changing, coopting opposition but leaving cracks for some active elements of new ideas to come through. Our object is to peer through some of these cracks. We would like to go outside ourselves, if possible, to observe reflexively the way in which the Israeli press covered various moments of the Arab–Israeli conflict – before, during, and after the intifada.

The local coloring of the dominant culture varies, of course. While in British society – Williams's model of hegemony – popular culture reflects class dominance, in the USA it is the naturalized acceptance of capitalist ideology. In Jewish-Israeli society hegemony probably applies best to the consensual acceptance of Zionist ideology, which the Arab–Israeli conflict helps to sustain. In what follows, we attempt to break down the concept of hegemony into its components, and to illustrate the ways in which it works in the practices of the Israeli press and electronic media, and in the decodings by their readers and viewers – that is, in reporting and reading from "our" side. The challenge is to show how the Israeli press unwittingly remains within the realm of the hegemonic culture, even while taking on an increasingly critical stance, and adhering to the norm of independence.

"SOFT HEGEMONY"

Textual analysis of coverage of the conflict in the press and the electronic media, interviews with journalists, and with readers and viewers, all point to four hegemonic constraints on the reporting of conflict. First, conflict enforces technical limitations on seeing the two sides, pushing reporters and viewers inadvertently to one side. Second, even without conflict, journalists and publishers see themselves as actors within the Zionist movement, not as critical outsiders, a commitment which in conflict gains legitimacy, and may be expressed *jorircliHeisept* unequivocally. Third, there is a particular difficulty in criticizing anything that involves the military as, semiotically, the Israel Defense Forces (IDF) signifies the anti-diaspora ideology of Zionism. Fourth, the public effectively sets limits on the capacity of the press to criticize the establishment; it cannot afford to alienate its clients.

Thus, to begin with, there is the unwitting reporting from "our" side of the conflict, because conflict means that you simply do not have access to the other side, that you are blinded by the hurt caused to your own side, that you feel misunderstood by the world, and end up acting as missionary. And these processes spiral, as the conflict continues, feeding on themselves.

This consolidation of "our" point of view may be effectively demonstrated by the ongoing press coverage of the intifada, the Palestinian uprising. During the first weeks of the intifada, reporters interviewed Palestinian victims and witnesses in order to put forward their point of view on Israel Television news. As clashes between protestors and army went on, "they" disappeared from the screen, leaving behind only a threatening mass of stone-throwing demons, faces obliterated behind their *kaffias.* This was not a policy decision but a process in which the various constraints that operate in the routines of the reporting of conflict conspired to construct a hegemonic, dichotomous picture. As clashes continued, Palestinians became less accessible to reporters in the field; travel to the "territories" became risky, your car could be smashed, there were soldiers and road blocks on the way, and "their" witnesses would be reluctant to talk to an Israeli reporter anyway, even if you got there.

Thus, within a few weeks, the Palestinian image was frozen (with active contribution of the Palestinians themselves) into that of "the other." This meant that in the endlessly recycled intifada story on Israeli media "their" point of view was missing. "They" were only shown archetypically in the role of terrorists. The daily suffering of "their" ordinary people was absent from the screen. Daily incidents of stone throwing became "routine," and stopped "counting" as news; only exceedingly violent incidents, or ones in which Israelis were hurt, were reported. Hegemony took over without anybody noticing.

If this first slide into the hegemonic process is unwitting and unselfconscious, a second force is the witting, almost self-conscious, awareness on the part of Israeli journalists that, conflict or not, they are Zionists. As such, they have a responsibility toward the new, fragile, and struggling society of which they are part, which gathers salience at moments in which the society seems to be under acute threat.

And this commitment is shared, of course, with the journalists on the other side. No more would an Israeli journalist of the older generation deny that he or she has a commitment toward Zionism than would a Palestinian journalist deny that his or her mission is to play an active role in the creation of a Palestinian state. In fact, in pre-state Mandatory Palestine, Hebrew journalism was often practiced by would-be politicians, with steady commuting between the two professions (Goren, 1979).

This is not to say that formal mechanisms of control, such as military censorship on matters of security, do not exist. But censorship alone cannot explain the cooperation – some would say, cooption – of the Israeli press, which, for months, sometimes years, refrained from reporting stories of Jewish immigration from unfriendly countries (which might have stopped the immigration altogether, had it become public knowledge). Such stories could be (and were) leaked to foreign correspondents, but not without feelings of guilt.

While "we" see ourselves as participating in a social revolution, it is easy to see how the other side is betraying its own professional duty to "objectivity," that is, to understanding our side too. Thus, ironically, only fifty years after the Hebrew press operated in the service of Zionism against British rule, the Israeli army censorship suppressed Palestinian newspapers for "unprofessionally twisting genuine news articles to the needs of nationalist incitement." For the Palestinian editors this type of reporting constitutes the "mobilization of the people to national consciousness" (Shakow, 1995).

While it is easy to think of journalists during the process of nation building as committed to the cause, and proud of being part of the political elite who lead the revolution, we should remind ourselves that even in established Western democracies there is commitment to the collective. This becomes apparent as soon as the society is involved in conflict in which men may die. During World War II, for example, NBC reporters decided against reporting the incident in which General Patton slapped a hospitalized soldier. They did so in order not to harm morale, explaining that "every mother would figure that her son is next."

The belief expressed by these reporters in the statement that "we're Americans first and reporters second" holds even in lesser conflicts – such as the Gulf War – in which there was no immediate danger to the society. Once President Bush declared war on Saddam Hussein, going as far as to label him a new Hitler, all public debate in the US came to a halt (Hallin and Gitlin, 1993). In Israel, when Saddam shot his missiles into the center of Tel-Aviv, a docile and trusting press handed over the radio and television transmission to the military as soon as the alarms were sounded, relinquishing responsibility for supplying the public with accurate information. After the fact, it became clear that the missing information might have been crucial to the public's safety (Katz, 1992).

This complete faith in the military should be seen in the context of the cultural position the Israel Defense Forces occupy in the new Jewish state, a position which constitutes a third constraint on reporting the conflict hegemonically.

Ideologically, Zionism is juxtaposed to Jewish existence in exile; as such it has made the idea of the IDF into a central symbol in the civil religion of Israeli society, far beyond its instrumental importance (Limor and Nossek, 1995). The military embodies the transformation of the Jew from a physical weakling and economic parasite, with no territory or political independence, into a tough pioneer, fighting to gain and preserve political independence. In the wake of the Holocaust, Israelis are brought up to be good soldiers, never again to be led as sheep to the slaughter.

The creation of shared symbols was essential for the Israeli polity inasmuch as there was an urgent need to replace the traditional religious values which kept Jewish communities alive in diasporic existence. Skipping over 2,000 years of "slavery" to connect directly to the independent ancient state of Judea, Israel became a warrior state, its sacred pantheon of heroes populated by twentieth-century generals, who continue in the direct line of the ancient Israelite generals who fought against the Greek and Roman conquerors of the land of Canaan.

The ideological centrality of the military in Israel means that the society is, in fact, more hegemonic in the classic sense, i.e. more intrusive, more demanding. Gaining a critical perspective on the way "we" handle the conflict is often read as a casting of doubt on a sacred value of the dominant culture. It seems only a step away from the more radical perspective of a critical theory, which dares to question whether the continued salience of the Arab–Israeli conflict may not operate to maintain the centrality of the military and, thus, that the garrison state may itself be a hegemonic device to preserve social integration in an otherwise fragmented society (Russett and Shye, 1993).

The fourth constraint that conspires to hegemonize the press are its clients. As elsewhere, journalists know their public, and are loathe to cross the lines which may offend them. While it may be acceptable to act as watchdog in regard to internal political issues, that is hardly the case in a security crisis. In crisis, the public wishes to share in the selective perception of reporters *vis-à-vis* the other side. Moreover, for the television audience, press *reporting* on what one is seeing from one's own side constitutes an obvious constraint on reception in that the public has access only to the *mediated*, redundant, journalistic construction of the conflict. Thus, the starting point for viewers can only be the most dramatic, or violent, events, which juxtapose a personalized "us" with a depersonalized "them" in black-and-white framing. All these mechanisms of press and television mediation combine to make it easier for socially dominant security "hawks" to defend their own position than for the "doves," who believe in compromise. Thus the cycle of hegemony is reinforced. Public expectation of journalism peaks in the face of a terrorist event, the threat of war, and the breaking out of war. There is a desire for an emotional togetherness, a national rallying against a common enemy, for the communal celebration of victories, and for the coronation and mourning over heroes. This is a moment in which journalists – ordinarily isolated, sometimes disdained – overcome their alienation, to gain some longed-for popularity by joining the community and crossing the line between "observing" and "participating" (Hallin, 1994). The Gulf War constituted a recent reminder of the public's protectiveness of its right *not* to know in times of crisis, when knowing might mean losing confidence in the leadership.

Arguing for a hegemonic framing of the Arab–Israeli conflict by press and public at the time at which these lines were written is somewhat like freezing a frame at the moment of its transformation. By now, the practices of Israeli reporters and readers are in the process of accelerated change. Both the politics of the conflict and the politics of press and electronic coverage are slowly but surely being revised. The forces which converge to make this a liminal moment for viewers are the cumulative trends toward de-collectivization, individualization, and depoliticization, in which television probably played some part. Tired of the conflict, viewers want to see more soaps, and less news. For the press this process of cultural change is exacerbated by the aggressive commercialization and brutish competitiveness of the major newspapers, and by the revolution in communication technologies, which transformed Israel from a media environment of one-channel public television into a new multiplicity of channels which are global (transcending the nation-state culture) and segmented (cutting through it) simultaneously (Katz, in press). Finally, and not unrelated to the changes in the cultural climate, Israel's politics is undergoing dramatic transformation, with the heretofore unthinkable recognition of the Palestine Liberation Organization (PLO), and a new readiness for compromise with Syria. Even if this is only a crack in the window of opportunity, it is a good moment for looking back at the dynamics of the conflict, with the hegemonic aura which it radiated diffused.

This book first examines the workings of a loyal press (chapters 2 to 6), and then looks at how encoding by the press constrains decoding by citizens (chapters 7 to 9). At the same time, alternative channels may well express views of the conflict which, more or less intentionally, break through the "them" and "us" mold (chapters 10 to 12). The various chapters reflect the substantive and theoretical issues which were prominent at the time of their writing (over the last five years), albeit complicated, willy-nilly, by changing external circumstances, changing norms of press behavior, as well as changing emphases in the field of communication research.

Chapter 2 starts with the various turns hegemony has taken in the history of the Israeli press and electronic broadcasting, in which Israeli journalism has moved through a succession of stages, characteristic of the role of the press in nation building. It charts three historical transformations: (1) from a revolutionary press fighting for the Zionist national movement against colonial British rule to a socially responsible press, loyal to a nascent, yet insecure, state; (2) from a highly political but ideologically bound party press to an independent commercial press speaking to pluralistic audiences; and (3) from a commercial press with a professional mission to an increasingly monopolistic press, with new masters, committed to profit and entertainment. The itinerary of the electronic media, from public to private broadcasting, follows parallel lines. The chapter shows how the Israeli press evolves from worst to maximal conditions for press independence. But a close look at its history reveals the seeds of the subtler version of present-day hegemony, especially in regard to the coverage of the conflict.

Chapter 3 contextualizes this coverage in terms of the actual salience of the conflict in Israeli society and the way in which it is used for preserving national integration. It describes the centrality of news in Israeli public broadcasting, the Israeli public as obsessive news consumers, the media presentation of the intifada, and the kind of conflicts which the intifada news story resembles.

Moving from the broadly drawn macro-lines of historical development, chapter 4 examines the relationship between social and professional commitments from the point of view of the journalists themselves. It shows how today's journalists reconcile the conflict between a free press and the needs of national security in the process of negotiating with military censorship. We try to understand whether the journalists' claim that the censor can only prohibit the publication of stories which they would not publish anyway is not a clue to their cooption, i.e. to their sharing in the deep-seated concerns of post-Holocaust Jewish Israeli society.

Our own reading of news texts, in chapter 5, illustrates how formal censorship may indeed be unnecessary for the hegemonic process to work, unwittingly. Analysis of the framing mechanisms deployed in the case of the coverage of a terrorist attack shows the reluctance of the press to play watchdog even in relatively minor cases, even where there are no victims on "our" side.

The point of chapter 6 is to show that Israeli journalists are not unique in reacting to a security crisis as involved participants rather than detached observers. Take, for example, the case of the American press, which activated similarly hegemonic framing in the reporting of "their" Gulf War. By contrast, the same American journalists had no problem in seeing the moral issues that arose in "our" war, the intifada in this case, which, though centuries apart technologically, also involves extremely uneven forces, and could easily be questioned from the perspective of public opinion.

Moving on to analyze how encoding constrains decoding, the second section joins television viewers in their "living-room wars." In these chapters we explore the ways in which prime-time evening news is used as a focus for political socialization by Israeli families. Conversations during the viewing, and discussions (initiated by us) directly following a broadcast, indicate how television's framing of the conflict affects viewers, and how much it can be bent in different situations.

Zeroing-in on the dynamics of argument in one divided family, chapter 7 looks at the losing battle of a mother who attempts to convince her daughter that "not all the Arabs are bad." The meta-assumption, common to both mother and daughter, that news represents the norm, or the normal, not the exceptional or the deviant, is shown to work for a them-or-us view of conflict. Generalizing from all fifty-two case-studies, chapter 8 shows how television news reinforces what social psychologists call the attribution error. It demonstrates how viewers who see the conflict as a zero-sum-game find it easier to "prove" their position in light of what they see on television than do viewers who believe in the possibility of compromise. Thus, some decodings survive the argument better than others (Noelle-Neumann, 1985).

Broadening the social circle to include Israeli Arabs, who represent the other side *within* Israeli society, chapter 9 points out that television news privileges extremists on both sides. For Jewish hawks, viewing Palestinian terrorists on the screen reinforces their image of reality, while the truth for Palestinian nationalists is deduced from what is absent from the screen. That *moderates* in both groups have to struggle to create more complex ways of seeing, constitutes the focus of the discussion.

Viewing the conflict through alternative channels means substituting the "them and us" frame for a much more complex, sometimes oppositional, view. Chapter 10 is based on face-to-face interviews with Israeli soldiers, serving in the intifada, some of whom find themselves (often reluctant) participants in, or misunderstood victims of, television's reporting. The dissonance between training to fight an enemy and finding oneself in the role of policing a civilian population motivates some of them to relate their own version of the conflict.

Presenting their own views as artists, a number of Israeli film-makers, often ideologically motivated, make an intentional effort to humanize and personalize the demonized presence of the Palestinian in the news. Chapter 11 analyzes several such filmic attempts to cause viewers to empathize with Palestinians. It shows how transforming the image of Palestinians can undermine the best of intentions because in spite of allegations that the media are "hostile" (to "us"), news is mostly perceived as "real" while film is regarded as "only fiction" (in which the individual artist is easily suspected of ideological manipulation). More sophisticated criticism argues that oppositional representations end up being hegemonic anyway, as attempts to make the Palestinian heroes seem like "us" mean depriving them of their cultural "otherness." Paradoxically, this claim seems convincing, especially as the structural analogies between Israelis and Palestinians fighting for national independence in the same landscape are striking.

Last, there are oppositional images of the other on the television screen itself, in those moments which constitute a liminal opportunity for changing frames: what Dayan and Katz (1993) call "transforming events." President Sadat's visit to Jerusalem, broadcast live to the world, is the archetypical example of these historic openings. Taking Sadat's visit as a model, chapter 12 observes the peace ceremonies of 1993–5. The Oslo Accord started another round of television diplomacy, in an effort to achieve peace with the Palestinians and with Jordan. This time it is a television series, not a one-time live event, with public reconciliation ceremonies alternating with secret negotiations, and with melodramas of terrorism in which "us" and "them" revert to the familiar roles. Media events, then, are not what they used to be. Even if we may be less naive about them, they show how hegemonic framing can make room for a more sympathetic portrayal of the other. Chapter 12 reports on the year in which Palestinian leader Yassir Arafat came to settle in Gaza, and Jordan's King Hussein agreed to appear in public to shake the hands of Israeli leaders, in an era in which alternative framings are publicly tried, modified, discarded, and reevaluated.

Chapter 2

Bedfellows

The evolution of a committed relationship over time

Shortly after the founding of the State of Israel, in the early 1950s, a young journalist by the name of Uri Avneri became the editor of a weekly called *Haolam Hazeh* (This World). In the decades that followed, this weekly was considered Israel's only truly oppositional popular newspaper. Situated outside of the consensus of mainstream Zionist ideology, poignantly critical of government policies, disclosing information considered harmful to Israel's image, its "cheap" aggressive commercial selling strategies (marked by half-naked girls on its back cover) made it easy to dismiss in Israel's puritanical society of the 1950s.

Forty years later, we asked Avneri what gave him the chutzpah to take liberties with the instructions of the military censors, to shoulder the responsibility for harming the newborn, vulnerable, isolated, state in those early years.[1] The answer was unhesitant. The other press editors, Avneri said, were all middle-aged, pre-state veterans. Having witnessed the miracle of the creation of a Jewish-Israeli army, they were filled with awe when confronting a uniformed army officer with the official title of military censor. Avneri, who was 25 years old at the time, and his 21-year-old reporters, belonged to a different generation. They were young men who grew up in British Palestine, and had just survived the battles of the 1948 War (of Independence). As field-officers they looked down on a non-combatant desk-officer, considering themselves much greater experts on the kind of information which constitutes a "real" security risk. Ironically, the censor himself must have thought the same. His respect for the authority of combat soldiers meant that Avneri's relationship with the censors was informal and chummy. Avneri, thus, may have been an *enfant terrible* of the Israeli press, but one who nevertheless belonged to the heart of the consensus.

The relevance of the phenomenon of Avneri to our argument is that even this most subversive voice in the Israeli press had its roots in a deep commitment to the mission of Zionism, granted his own version of it. Two generations later he was still not justifying his lack of respect for censorship in terms of the duty to a free press and professional norms. Remaining within the dominant belief that press freedom *should* be restricted, Avneri excuses the relative freedom of his weekly only by arguing that he himself was the better judge of what would really be harmful.

As this example illustrates, in spite of major institutional, cultural, and generational changes, the Israeli press coverage of the conflict has stayed within hegemonic confines.

In what follows we will look at the institutional and cultural transformations that the Israeli press has undergone throughout its relatively short history, arguing that though the present-day press is more independent institutionally, and its editors less personally related to the political establishment, it is no less committed to the dominant group in terms of its framing of the conflict.

This may be the place to note the distinction between the definition of hegemony as operating in the interests of the dominant group and the ideological *content* that this entails. While press hegemony means loyalty to the interests of the establishment, circumstances may modify, revise, or even make drastic changes in the establishment's outlook. This jibes well with Williams (1977), who sees domination as a process rather than as a permanently achieved state, identifying three kinds of cultural forces "discernible at any one point and within any one historical juncture" (ibid., p. 121). These are the dominant, residual, and emergent forces, which correspond respectively to the present, the past, and the future.

This raises the issue of the tricky relationship between the survival of the dominant group and these changing cultural forces. An acceptance of this model implies that future survival of the ruling elite depends on the way in which it manages its relationship with these cultural forces whether externally imposed or self-imposed. It may try to hold on to the dominant ideology and manage to squash or to postpone the emergent one, or it may promote or adopt an emergent ideology (which may take the form of trying to preempt a revolution, as in the case of Gorbachev). Of course, in either case the attempt may fail, and the old leadership may be deposed. The role of the press is crucial in these delicate maneuvers, whether in reinforcing the dominant ideology, or in anticipating emerging trends, in interpreting them, and in mobilizing support for the change, which will insure establishment stability or mark its downfall.

This notion of hegemony as a dynamic process provides a perspective within which to examine the historical context of the relationship between the dominant group and the press in Israel. Such an examination shows how the relationship evolved from an explicit partnership in which independence was normatively limited to an independent status in which criticism becomes legitimate, threatening hegemonic control. And yet, even in these best of circumstances, institutionally and normatively, both the printed and the electronic press operate within hegemonic constraints, granted a much subtler hegemony. In the continuation of this chapter we show how the seeds of these hegemonic practices may be traced to the historical beginnings.

Since the beginning of Zionist Jewish settlement in the country, this relationship has undergone three transformations. First, with the founding of the State of Israel, the Hebrew press had to transform itself from a revolutionary organ committed to the Zionist movement to a Western-type watchdog press, expected to criticize its former masters. Not surprisingly, this could not be done before the passing-away of the first generation of editors of the Hebrew press. For these pre-state veterans of the struggle for independence, the new government consisted of the very same leaders alongside whom they had fought against British rule. They could certainly be trusted to act responsibly, and the newly born state deserved all the protection it could get.

When the founder generation stepped down the Israeli press began to transform itself from a highly political but ideologically bound party press, preaching to the variously converted, to a commercial press operating under conditions of independence from party and government. This second transformation also means aiming to reach large pluralistic audiences, but at the same time catering to a de-ideologized public. However, the continued dominance of the Arab–Israeli conflict, marked by a succession of wars, operated to preserve the close links between press and government.

While the second transformation marks the beginning of a trend of shying away from political debate for fear of losing the audience, the third transformation marks the continuation of this trend, in which news values are defined by the market, giving hegemony a new cultural meaning. Characterized by increasing competition, including the upsurge of local papers and a new abundance of television channels, the press is moving – both in form and in content – toward "televisualization" and entertainment. Moreover, cross-ownership by press barons means that two or three families own a variety of other businesses including shares in the new commercial television, thus threatening the capacity of the press to protect the public against the abuse of its interest, constructing a new kind of hegemonic environment.

In the following examination of these transformations, the sources of today's residual press culture take on a new meaning within the context of the pre-state colonial period.

THE MOVE FROM A PRE-STATE, ANTI-COLONIAL, MOVEMENT PRESS TO A POST-STATE, WESTERN-TYPE PRESS

A movement press

The relationship between the press and the political leadership was never as equal, harmonious, and above board as during the pre-state period. At that time (1917–48), it was a voluntary yet fully binding relationship in which both the leaders of the Zionist-Jewish community in Palestine and the editors of the Hebrew press took part in the struggle against British Mandatory Rule. The Hebrew press of this period was a self-professed active participant in the struggle for a Jewish homeland, in the face of an increasingly hostile colonial government.

Though there was a Hebrew-language press in Palestine already in the 1880s, it was the arrival of a new Jewish immigration – Zionist, mostly socialist, and ideologically committed – which transformed it into a militant and ideological press. The new immigration was inspired by the British, who, having conquered Palestine, replaced the corrupt Ottoman empire with what was considered an enlightened colonial regime, and declared a policy favoring the creation of a homeland for the Jewish people in the country. As this policy collapsed, and the struggle for freedom gathered momentum, the editors of the Hebrew press accepted the directives from the Zionist leadership in everything that had to do with the fight for independence.

In any case, the journalists themselves were often the political leaders of the movement, or frustrated politicians, sometimes commuting between the two careers.[2]

A formal bond

The measures which the colonial British government undertook against the Hebrew and Arabic press may serve as a clue to the degree to which they were perceived as a threat, or, alternatively, to the effectiveness of the two in promoting the interests of their respective political masters. Thus, the British Mandatory government struck sometimes against the Arab national-movement press, and, at other times, against the Zionist press. In 1933, in retaliation for the part played by the Arab press in inciting the Arab population to acts of terror, the British issued a censorship order. Later, as the gradual abandoning of the policy of a Jewish National Home in Palestine became the object of increasing attacks in the Hebrew press, the British issued further rules, including sanctions against newspapers which ignored them.

It was the battle against British government censorship that pushed the Hebrew press into creating a *formal* bond with the leadership of the Zionist movement. The agreement between the two consisted of setting up an "Editors Committee" of the Hebrew press, which, in effect, would operate as the ideological arm of the Zionist movement in its struggle against colonial rule. In return for influencing public opinion in the spirit of Zionist policy the editors gained regular access to secret information of the Zionist leadership, could be present when decisions were made, agreed to keep "damaging" information from the public, and, on occasion, to collectively respond to what was considered false or harmful information published by the British government. This bond remained the basis for a symbiotic relationship between the press and the Zionist leadership – in time, the political leadership of the State of Israel – until recent years.

The incident which triggered the creation of the Editors Committee, in February 1942, was a failed attempt by the military arm of the Jewish community – the Hagana – to smuggle an illegal boat of Jewish refugees from Nazi Europe into the country. The Hebrew press mobilized collectively to assist in the self-censoring of information which was "damaging" to the Hagana. This spontaneous reaction led to the agreement to form a committee, and to the long history of formal collaboration between the press and the Zionist leadership. A most dramatic demonstration of the committee's effectiveness *vis-à-vis* the British was the collective action taken (in November 1943) following an incident in which a British policeman shot at Kibbutz members during an arms search. The British official justification of "a mass hysteria" was countered with the Hebrew press version of the story, which ignored the censor's orders. Government measures against individual papers brought on a collective strike, celebrated with the demonstrative burning of a government leaflet, telling the official story, in the streets of Tel-Aviv (Goren, 1979).

With such heroic beginnings, the committee continued on a much less impressive course for over two generations, becoming a symbol for a collaborative press, that invites cooption by the Israeli government, and prefers a paternalistic attitude toward its public.

Understandable as this might have been in the pre-state phase, after 1948 the liberal norms of a democracy demanded the development of a critical view toward the same leadership the press had been serving until then. But real-life transitions are more complicated. Surprisingly, with the founding of an independent state, only one of the editors suggested that the committee dismantle itself. It did not. This is not difficult to understand either, in view of the perception of Israel as vulnerable, still in need of the protective self-censorship on matters of national security, broadly defined. Implicit in the continuation of the committee is the idea that a fully independent watchdog press could await an indefinite future period of normalization.[3]

Thus, the very same institution that fought against the censorship of the British Mandate, now, regularly briefed by government sources, operated to prevent the publishing of information.

Recent years mark the diminishing influence of the Editors Committee. The slow death of the committee is due to changes in media technologies, to the coming of age of a new generation of editors who do not have a personal commitment to the political establishment, and, with it, to the resignation from the committee by editors who prefer fighting censorship in court in the name of the public's right-to-know to voluntary self-censorship.

THE MOVE FROM AN IDEOLOGICAL PARTY PRESS TO A POPULAR COMMERCIAL PRESS

Two shifts in the character of the Israeli press – a shift from a formal institutionalized bond between press and government to a press which defines itself as independent and professional, and a shift from an ideological party press to a popular "objective" commercial press – mark significant changes in the dominant culture. Thus, less bound by a signed agreement or by commitment to inflexible ideological lines, the press is seemingly less hegemonic. But as the study of the popular Western press has shown, institutional independence and professional norms are no guarantee against hegemonic practices, especially when it comes to war (Alexander, 1981; Hallin, 1994). Thus, it is not that surprising that an examination of the norms and practices adopted by the popular press and media in Israel shows that hegemony has only taken on a new expression under the guise of professional objectivity, particularly in regard to the conflict.

Ideological commitment was the basis for both the mobilization of the Hebrew press in the common cause of fighting British Mandatory Rule as well as for the individual commitment of each of these newspapers to the party it represented within the Zionist consensus. In parallel with the switch from commitment to the "movement" to a relative independence, the Israeli press made a switch from an ideological party press to a privately owned popular press.

In the pre-state era party newspapers occupied the central space. Among the eight Hebrew newspapers which joined the Editors Committee only two – one, an elite paper (*Ha'aretz*), the other, a popular paper (*Yediot Aharonot*) – were privately owned. All the other were party papers, which gave voice to different parties within the Zionist movement (Caspi and Limor, 1992). Of those only *Davar*, subsidized by the Labor party, still survives, under an acute threat of closing down. *Yediot* has become the most popular paper in the country, read by 70 percent of the population, and *Ha'aretz*, with about 50,000 readers, remains the most prestigious, its financial base secured by a network of local weeklies.

True, political party control meant that the editors and senior journalists were nominated by the party establishment and that the reporting, interpretation, and op-ed commentary were mobilized to party needs. But, while this goes against the accepted conventions of neutrality and objectivity, it does include a sense of mission and a political liveliness which is sadly missing in the pages of its more objective successors.

The disadvantage of this newly acquired freedom lies, then, in the paradox of an ideologically free commercial press, which has finally received the freedom to discuss political issues, finding itself facing a de-ideologized public who are tired of these exact issues, who demands more life-style, sports, and entertainment. Thus, ironically, just when the ideal conditions for an open debate seem to have been achieved there is in fact less, not more, political debate. This paradox brings to mind Alexander's (1981) finding according to which the European party press constitutes a much livelier forum for the discussion of public issues than does the independent press in the US, which, in its quest for economic competitiveness, shies away from potentially unpopular topics.

The new depoliticized blandness means that the press is making life easy for the political establishment by leaving all the crucial decisions to its uninterrupted consideration. But the blame does not lie only with the public. The journalists themselves are party to it at least inasmuch as they practice their trade in accordance with the professional definitions of the popular Western press in general. The definitions of professionalism, neatly summarized by Curran (1991), share the characteristics of relying heavily on authority sources, and of conducting an extremely constricted quest for the truth, limited only to its technical proceedings (as in framing political campaigns as horse-race news, not as democratic inquest). In addition, the European model of reporting to which Israeli-style journalism belongs, dictates assuming the part of passive mediation between competing interpretations of the world (Hallin and Mancini, 1984) while, in fact, playing a much more active role. Reporters, who do not try to tell a "closed" story like their US counterparts, act, in effect, as arbitrators of promoting the particular agendas which serve the interests of one party, and work against the interests of another. Although Curran himself does not use the term, these combine to create hegemonic representation.

There is no doubt that, concerning the conflict, each one of these practices acquires a particular effectiveness in the service of hegemony. Thus, turning mostly to establishment sources means uncritically accepting the government view – "conceptzia" – of the security situation, tending not to publish oppositional views. Before the Yom Kippur War, for example, making room for other views may have contributed to raising doubts among policy makers, and preparing for the possibility of an attack. Likewise, staying on the technical level in reporting the success of particular military measures does not leave room to ask about the ideological aims which those measures are supposed to facilitate.

But these professional norms in themselves are overshadowed by increasing commercialization. In the US, Hallin (1994, p. 179) tells us, economics has eroded the barrier between journalism and the profit making business of selling audiences to advertisers. And this is likely to bring into question both the notion of journalism as a public trust and the existence of the common public culture that news once provided.

Israel has not yet progressed quite as far down that road, but similar trends are at work in the latest transformation of the press and the electronic media which we are currently witnessing.

THE MOVE FROM A COMMERCIAL PRESS WITH A MISSION TO A TABLOID-FORM COMMERCIAL PRESS

Recent years have seen the Israeli press and electronic media embarking on a new, unabashedly profit-oriented binge, further weakening its ability to perform as a watchdog press. The need of private, unsubsidized press, including new commercial radio and television channels, to survive in an increasingly competitive environment, as well as the motivation of the owners to make as much profit as they can, is threatening to bring a profound change in the nature of Israeli journalism, modifying some hegemonic constraints, strengthening others, and introducing new ones.

In this new phase, the institutional environment of Israel's printed press has changed dramatically with the upsurge of local papers, the concentration of newspaper ownership in the hands of two or three families, who have also branched into other areas of related business, such as book publishing, popular music, computers, and the like, and the press owners establishing themselves in the role of editors. On the air, the monopolistic, BBC-like, one public television channel has turned into a multiplicity of television channels, with a new commercial (supposedly publicly controlled) Second channel, and a (supposedly regional) cable network (see chapter 3). Public Broadcasting has had to adapt to the new rules of the game, becoming a player in the competition on ratings. The press baron families, for their part, threatened by the loss of advertisers to this new aggressive commercial medium, hurried to become part owners of the companies which won the franchise for commercial television.

This commercial take-over of the press, coupled with its concentration in the hands of the very few, which stretched to a cross-ownership that controls the news in print and on the air, has a number of implications for hegemony. First, the larger the commercial empire, the more danger of press owners limiting the freedom of their own journalists to criticize economic bodies with whom they are connected. Second, the harsh competition between advertisers has the same effect of curtailing the freedom of journalists in order not to deter (potential or actual) clients. Third, getting the franchise for commercial television and keeping it means direct dependence on the government, which also has direct bearing on the amount of revenues franchise holders may make, as well as on the introduction of advertising. Fourth, cross-ownership means a new capacity to monopolize, and therefore censor, information. If the owner of a certain popular paper prevents publication of news that harms his economic interests, the other press channels will not address it either, whether as a direct result of cross-ownership, or because the various owners may protect one another's interests.

How does this new ecology of the press and media environment, in which a residual cultural sense of mission and commitment to the collectivity vie with the new weariness of wars and of longing for individual fulfillment, affect press framings of the Arab–Israeli conflict? Are the new informal interviewing style and sometimes vicious criticism of politicians and army generals signs that hegemony has finally been invaded?

Not quite. The answer seems to be, rather, that a new version of hegemony is at work, characterized by a "normalization" in which political issues are slowly being pushed aside (marginalized), perceived as relating to the traditional collective rather than to emerging individualistic culture. Editors' and producers' perceptions of the public are directing news in the direction of tabloid-news, press norms are being overshadowed by the demand to tell fast, neatly packaged, visualized stories, which appeal to the emotions rather than to the rational consideration of readers. The popular printed press adopts televisual forms, dominated by color photographs, headlines screaming with melodrama, commentators' texts restricted to a few lines, and pornographic advertisements placed right under pictures of the funeral of a former Chief of Staff. Politicians on talk shows are encouraged to replace debate over policy with scandal and melodrama, and to substitute family gossip with political positions, in the increasing blurring of the boundaries between news and entertainment.

A recent story may illustrate the ethical dilemmas with which the press and the electronic media in Israel are struggling today. A publisher-cum-editor of a major tabloid filed a law suit against a city weekly which had accused him of employing a reporter to investigate the affairs of advertisers of a competing tabloid *not* in order to inform the public but so that the information could be used for the purpose of intimidating the advertisers to switch their allegiance. In the course of the police investigation that followed it was discovered that the publisher had also tapped the phone of his top political correspondent in order to control, perhaps subvert, his conversations with his sources. The correspondent resigned from his job.

Ironically, at the same time as this affair made the headlines, the Press Council, a self-regulating body of the press, was endlessly debating changing the definition of the journalist's duty to publish information which is of "public interest" to information which carries interest "for the public."

Unlike the classical type of hegemony which resides in the near-symbiotic relationship between the press and the political establishment, the publisher's scandal poses the journalist him- or herself as a victim to the hegemony of capitalism in which press and media are commercialized, and a journalist's professionalism is subverted in the interests, purely business ones, of media owners. The publisher has moved one step ahead of the Press Council, which was struggling to adjust itself to the dictates of its new masters. While the Council was busy debating the definition of the press – as a profession, working in the interest of the citizen, and therefore entitled to decide what the public should know, or as a business serving its own interest and, therefore, having to treat the public as consumers who decide what they "want" – the publisher made it clear that the journalists may be subject to a new type of censorship, ruthlessly enforced. While lack of favor with the political establishment may mean losing useful sources, lack of favor with owners may mean losing one's job.

The next chapter takes us back from the period in which producers regard "bad news," such as news of the conflict, as something which might distract viewers from their (carefully cultivated) desire to consume, to the time, not so long ago, in which Israelis were united around one channel, and news of the conflict was its prime concern.

Chapter 3

Foregrounding conflict
Broadcasting conflict and national integration – the Israeli context

THE LATENT FUNCTION OF CONFLICT

The State of Israel was born into the Arab–Israeli conflict and has existed in its shadow throughout its history. There can be no doubt that the conflict was, and still is, the central preoccupation of the society. This means, for example, that resources are allocated to defense at the cost of social development, and to raising warriors at the expense of scholars. In the lives of individuals the reality of conflict takes the form of Katyusha raids, terrorist attacks, a constant threat of war, and the near certainty of war once a decade. For young people, being Israeli citizens implies a much greater commitment to the collective than in all Western countries (in the form of long compulsory army service, and years of reserve duty).

While there can be no doubt that the conflict remains a major existential threat to Israelis, it is also clear that it serves the latent function of acting as a hegemonic constraint. As surveys over time have shown, during periods in which the Arab–Israeli conflict becomes less acute, two other structural conflicts in the society erupt – the tensions between Israelis of Western and Oriental origin, and between the religious and non-religious communities (Levi, 1992). This disruptive potential within the society suggests that the external conflict serves to protect Israel from possible internal rifts of an ethnic and cultural nature, and functions to preserve social integration. When Israel has to unite against its enemies, unity is enhanced.

BROADCASTING AS FOCUS FOR THE SURVEILLANCE OF CONFLICT

The keen interest of Israelis in the news derives to a large extent from the predominance of the conflict. Forty years of hovering on the edge of war have socialized them to fear unexpected outbreaks of violence, whether in the form of terrorist attacks, Israeli retaliations, deaths of soldiers by accident or in action, threats of war, sometimes the outbreak of one (whether started by us or by them), even missile attacks during somebody else's war.

In a small country of four million adults national news becomes
One is forever in fear of personally recognizing one of the ch
involved – as witness, participant, sometimes victim.

The function of surveillance over conflict was allocated to broadcasting
from the outset. During its first two decades, radio news was in charge,
scanning the horizon for any lurking dangers, and serving as the central
focus for national integration, as did the BBC in its time (Scannell and
Cardiff, 1991). When television joined in the wake of the Six Day War, the
job was divided between the two. Radio, still the faster medium, provided
round-the-clock newscasts, while television conditioned its viewers to
convene around the family set at 9 o'clock sharp for the ritual viewing of
Mabat Lahadashot, the daily news magazine. As the more accessible of the
two media, radio news is regularly broadcast on public buses, and is
commonly attended to in total silence at moments of crisis; it is used by the
army for fast mobilization of its reserve forces, it stands in for the outdated
alarm system on the rooftops when it is time to enter the air-raid shelters
(the "sealed rooms" in the Gulf War version). This last role means that radio
has acquired, at least temporarily, an additional audience in the form of the
Israeli ultra-orthodox community. During Saddam Hussein's missile attacks,
rabbis allowed their flocks (which normally stay away from such lowly forms
of communication) to acquire radios. While television took over the
ceremonial medium of national integration, radio adapted itself by switching
to open-ended programming, always interruptable by the latest news of
conflict, thus maintaining a functional role in times of emergency, sending
regards from soldiers away from home to their families, instructing the
people in northern Kiryat Shemona to spend the night in shelters,
summoning soldiers to their reserve units by reading out the appropriate
slogans for exercising an emergency mobilization, or for enacting a real one,
when war is looming, or has started.

The central role of radio and television in the surveillance of the conflict
may be better understood in the context of the institutional structure of
broadcasting in Israel.

THE STRUCTURE OF BROADCASTING

The history of Israeli broadcasting starts underground. *Kol Yisrael* (Voice of
Israel) began broadcasting illegally during the last years of British
Mandatory Rule, as a means of mobilization for the national struggle.
With the founding of the state, radio was moved to the Prime Minister's
office to act in the service of government information (Caspi and Limor,
1992). As Israel was still vulnerable, still fighting for the full realization of
Zionism, and the political establishment was used to secrecy from the time
of British Mandatory Rule, the public received only restricted "unharmful"
information via radio. Nevertheless, radio became the main medium of

communication in the country, instrumental in building the new Zionist-Israeli cultural identity (mainly by teaching Hebrew to the masses of new immigrants). Only in 1965 did Israel Radio draw on its mandatory heritage, becoming an independent Public Authority, modeled on the BBC. While officially accorded a much more independent status, Israel Radio remained under constant pressure "to behave," and its directors preserved the notion of social responsibility, focusing mainly on information and enrichment, not on entertainment. At the period in which Israel Radio branched out into a number of channels, it also lost its centrality in the society, in part due to the strengthening of the IDF Radio Station, which started its own news and current affairs programs, but mostly due to the founding of public television, following the Six Day War.

Interestingly, the opposition to the introduction of general television lasted for some twenty years (1948–1967) and the first television seen by Israelis (in 1966) was an educational channel, transmitting school broadcasts only. There was the fear that newly developed Israeli culture and language, still in need of nurturing, would be swamped by imported, mostly American, junk; that the high level of book reading (marking Israelis as "the people of the Book") would decline; that national integration would be weakened; and that politics would become less ideological, that is, less oriented to issues, more to charismatic personalities (Katz, 1971).

In 1968, however, these considerations were overcome when Israel found itself in charge of two million Palestinians in Gaza and the West Bank, following the Six Day War. The politicians decided that this population should not be exposed only to broadcasts from the neighboring Arab countries. Thus, Israeli television started with the idea of telling our version of the conflict to the other side, that is, out of seeing it as an instrument of political propaganda.

Unlike most Western countries, in which viewers have had an ever-increasing choice of channels, Israel has had twenty-five years of only one, BBC-like, television channel, publicly owned and managed. Broadcasting hours were more limited by the fact that the one channel was divided between Educational Television, broadcasting until late afternoon, and Public Broadcasting in the evening. A second channel was founded only in 1991, again following the British example. This channel was also public, but was financed by advertising rather than by the license fee that financed the first channel. Broadcasting on the Second channel is divided among three companies, each of which broadcasts two days a week (taking turns on weekends), and a news company, financed by all three.

The long-standing monopoly of Public Broadcasting has been undermined also by various technological changes, offering segmented audiences easy alternatives to national television. Israelis bought video recorders in large numbers, giving rise to video libraries. Satellite broadcasts from Europe and the US are received by roof "dishes," and pirate cable channels speeded the legalization of cable television.

The second channel, originally defined as no less public than the first, has brushed aside this definition, and behaves like a commercial channel in every way. Aiming for the lowest common denominator, in order to maximize advertising profits, it has started a ratings war, in which the First channel, restricted by its commitment to public service, as well as by inferior financing, is bound to be the loser.

THE ROLE OF TELEVISION NEWS

Until the establishment of a second commercial television channel, television news in Israel consisted of only one major news program in prime time plus several short bulletins of hard news. This monopolistic situation may have been unique, serving as the sole focus for prime-time viewing of news, and providing a common agenda for public debate.

Independent of the salience of the conflict, the centrality of prime-time news can also be credited to the characteristics of Israeli society. Traditionally, Israelis are highly literate. They are highly politically involved, and, as such, avid newspaper readers, radio news listeners, and sophisticated news viewers. This interest in news may also have to do with the Jewish habit of keeping close watch on anything that might be threatening, developed through centuries of living in exile. The diasporic notion that anything that happens anywhere may affect the Jews was adopted by Israelis. Moreover, Israel's isolation from its neighbors, the distrust of any information generated by Arab radio and television channels, and the language barrier have added even more to the dependence on Israeli radio and television for news.

News producers, for their part, understood their role in terms of providing the daily agenda for public discussion. Thus, the evening news was, and still is, devoted mostly to political items rather than to melodramas of human interest, addressing itself to viewers in the role of citizen, not consumer. The 30–45-minute broadcast allows enough time for party representatives and for professional commentators to elaborate the main issues, following the more open European format rather than the closed format in the US tradition of television news, in which items are neatly packaged as coherent narratives, introduced and rounded up by the anchor person (Hallin and Mancini, 1984).

As the only television channel, Israel Television was closely scrutinized and regularly attacked by politicians on all sides. Keeping to its professional standards was a way to withstand pressures and to survive in relative independence. One side effect of the focus on news production was that locally produced entertainment shows remained poor, and local drama was virtually non-existent. This in turn made news even more central, as the best drama in town.

Thus, the centrality of news arose from the Israeli reality of living as a garrison state, constantly on the alert for the next outbreak of conflict. Israelis have internalized the idea that the most important function of the medium of television is to supply information rather than to entertain (Katz and Gurevitch, 1976). Thus, contrary to the US where national television news was never popular, everybody in Israel (about 70 percent nightly) watched the news, two-thirds in the company of spouse and children. Many reported that they talked about it afterwards,[1] and most viewers also believed in the credibility of what they saw.

Within months of the introduction of a Second channel, the Public channel moved its news program from 9pm to 8pm in an effort to compete with the choice of 8pm by the Second channel, whereupon viewership of the news on both channels together dropped to less than half of what the viewership of the one channel had been. The ethnographic study described in this volume – conducted during the period just prior to the multiplication of channels – is a nostalgic reminder of an unusual era, now past.

THE INTIFADA AND BROADCASTING

The intifada began in 1987, following a seemingly trivial incident. It was a car accident in which an Israeli lorry driver ran over and killed three Palestinians in Gaza that started a series of riots and violent demonstrations, spreading from the Gaza strip to the West Bank. It took Israelis a long time to realize that a new phase of the occupation had begun. Yitzhak Rabin, then Minister of Defense, did not hurry to return from a visit to the US. On his return some weeks later, he announced a simple solution – "one has to break their bones." Israel Television, following the government line, reported on incidents of "unrest" and "violations of order." In this case, the closer one was to the events, the harder it was to perceive what was happening. Accustomed to twenty years of sedate, relatively docile, occupation, Israelis were fooled into thinking that this could go on forever, not noticing a new generation had grown up since the Six Day War. Subject to the daily humiliation of military occupation, the young Arabs in the territories saw no hope in sight. Reporting from the occupied territories, the US television channels were much quicker to perceive that something new was happening, as they were not trapped in the Israeli framing. While Israeli television reported on particular incidents, ending with "the army is restoring order," US correspondent Martin Fletcher of ABC gave the history of Israeli occupation, described the sorry state of the Palestinians, and enumerated the reasons for what he correctly perceived as an uprising.

When the riots did not recede, and the IDF soldiers were attacked daily by masses spitting, cursing, throwing stones, blocks, sometimes Molotov cocktails, Israel Television came to. The new reality in the Territories was given a name – the intifada. Interestingly, it adopted the Palestinians' own name, in their own language. Was this a way of accepting the definition of the other side? Probably not. More likely, it was a way of creating a distance between us and the uprising, by giving it a meaning in a language foreign to Israelis. Uprising in Hebrew would have been too threatening.

The government, and the IDF, for their part, tried to control reporting the ugly scenes of armed soldiers facing an unarmed population. The desk of "Reporter for the Territories," successfully (perhaps too successfully) carried out by Rafik Halabi, was abolished in Israel Television's news department even before the intifada began. In the wake of events, when the Territories became a hot spot for reporters, with the usual invasion of foreign journalists, the government vacillated between declaring certain areas "closed military sites" and being branded as repressive and undemocratic, or being branded an aggressor if it did not stop the cameras.

Israel Television was generally less informed than the American networks. This was due in part to lack of resources (or the unwillingness to allocate them), which meant Israeli reporters were slow to get to where the action was. American (and other foreign) reporters solved this problem by equipping local Palestinians with cameras, and making them into auxiliary reporters, which made them even closer to the Palestinians than they would naturally be, as outsiders identifying with the victim. As a result, American viewers probably had a better picture of what went on. Some of the most shocking pictures of Israeli soldiers' brutality shown on Israel Television were taken from the American networks; these stunned Israeli viewers and contributed to public debate. As the intifada continued, at a more or less steady pace, interest in the US and elsewhere waned, and the conflict reverted to being a local story (see chapters 6–8 for analysis of intifada reporting).

Israel Television, of course, could not report the conflict from both sides. Even if it wanted to, it had no access to the other side, except indirectly, via foreign broadcasts. It was also closely monitored by the censor, and when the scene was particularly unpleasant, Israeli viewers made it clear that they thought their television was going too far.

Our interest, it will be remembered, lies in examining the ways in which reporting conflict from "our" side works. Before delving into the specifics, however, it is important to pose the question of what other kinds of conflict does the intifada resemble? How can the study to be reported here generalize to other news of conflict? What other conflicts can be expected to receive similar treatment by the media?

TO WHAT KIND OF CONFLICT DOES THE INTIFADA NEWS STORY GENERALIZE?

The intifada story, of course, best fits the kind of conflict which involves an external enemy or an internal but marginal group, with hardly any legitimacy to begin with. The Palestinian uprising was a borderline case (literally as well as conceptually). Formally incorporated within the "greater Land of Israel," the Palestinians under occupation remained a separate community, seen behind an opaque glass by most Israelis, throughout the period of the occupation. Television named intifada items sometimes as *civil war*, more often as *riots*. The camera, however, showed armed soldiers facing crowds of violent rioters, who were seen but not heard. Hawks were therefore left with the conflicting need to see the uprising both as internal, as it takes place *within* our land, but also as external, as violence serves their ideology of no compromise.

Second, the case of the intifada generalizes to conflicts that constitute a direct challenge to the established means or ends of a society. Thus, it does not apply to legitimate contests such as election campaigns – where adversaries are equally normative and equally matched. Nor does it apply where the adversaries are perceived to be unequal but made equal by television – as was the case in the thoroughly studied fluoridation contest (Crain et al., 1969), where the small minority of opponents was raised to equal status by the media. Here, too, routines of journalism overrule the personal predilections of journalists.

Labor disputes and licensed demonstrations of all kinds come a step closer in that they typically involve unequal contests. Even if the confrontation begins within the rules and for legitimate ends, the weaker side is often tempted to trespass beyond the normative boundaries in order to attract media attention (Wolfsfeld, 1988). The staging of a strike is a publicity-seeking ceremony and rules of coverage may incite strikers to excessive action. These dynamics of coverage have not changed since the Glasgow group analyzed how media attention results in showing the bosses as rational and responsible, speaking from behind their desks, while the striking workers are shown in action, giving the impression of unreasonable troublemakers.

Such displays of disorder approximate (sometimes overlap with) those of social and political protest, especially when they escalate into violent confrontation, partly in response to the requirements of the rules of access to the media. In such situations, as in the case of the intifada, violent protest engenders violent response on the part of the agencies of the law. Industrial protest, like militant protest – against unpopular wars, or against nuclear proliferation, or against military or colonial occupation – evokes differential attributions both on the part of television and on the part of viewers. Together they distance us from the unruly side. They assign inherent or dispositional blame to "them" while excusing "us" situationally. The process of distancing and stigmatization also may apply to certain forms of television treatment of marginal groups whose very existence is sometimes portrayed as threatening core values. This is all the more likely when such groups – the poor, the homeless, the sexual minority – attract the media by provoking an event, or more typically, by being associated with threat, for example, whereby homosexuals are carriers of AIDS, or the homeless are trespassers and squatters. In effect, this is to frame a chronic problem in terms of an acute confrontation between a healthy, peaceful "us" and an unwelcome and threatening "them." Unlike protestors, these groups do not often seek exposure; their presentation may be the result of our own "moral panic." The main point is that they are seen to threaten society – not necessarily by protest, but by existing on its margins – and thus invite viewers to activate the attribution error.

While a number of studies have touched on these themes, most of them are based on content analysis or on interviews with journalists and producers. The present study, however, benefits from the participation of real viewers who come to the media not as tabulae rasae but with their own social psychologies and ideologies. The media commit the attribution error not only because journalists are also viewers but because the conventions of news facilitate such perceptions, for professional or hegemonic reasons or both. Viewers take it from there, having to assimilate what they have seen and heard through the prisms of attribution and of attitudes.

From our analysis of the decoding of intifada news (chapters 7–9), Israeli viewers may be regarded as the ideal viewers of the active audience theory. According to this theory the meaning of media texts emerges out of the negotiation between the content as encoded by the producers and its readings by viewers in various cultural and ideological contexts. The closer the viewers' reading is to the meaning the encoder has intended, the more it is hegemonic (Hall, 1985). Theoreticians of active audiences argue that viewers' framings of media texts are consolidated in conversation within the "interpretive communities" to which viewers belong. Israelis certainly answer to this description. They have a history of political involvement, tend to view television in company, and enthusiastically interact with both the characters on the screen and with friends and family in the living-room. As we shall argue, family viewing of the evening television news in Israel has become a site for the political socialization of children to their parents' outlook.

Before examining the way in which Israelis negotiate with the news, we shall define the rules of encoding which journalists and news producers follow. The next chapter looks at the manner in which journalists negotiate with the military censor. We argue that censorship is based on continual dialogue, showing how Israeli journalists vacillate between commitment to the collective and exercising free speech.

Chapter 4

Internalizing censorship
How journalists reconcile freedom of
expression with national loyalty and
responsibility

Asked to choose the greater danger to a free press – that of censorship by the
military (in the name of political self-interest) or that of censorship by press
owners (in the name of economic self-interest) – senior journalists in Israel
unanimously name the latter.[*] Military censorship, they believe, is more
negotiable, and less opposed to journalistic values, than capitalist censorship. This is not surprising when one remembers the history of the Hebrew
press, which started as a pre-state revolutionary press, committed to self-
censorship in all matters which may harm the Zionist movement and the
incipient state (described in chapter 2). And the commitment did not vanish
with the establishment of the state, as it was commonly accepted that the
nascent Israel was still vulnerable and in need of protection.

THE GROUNDS FOR PRESS CENSORSHIP IN ISRAEL

Founded in 1948, Israel is a parliamentary democracy in the tradition of
Great Britain. With no constitution, and a Bill of Rights pending since 1973,
Israel's common law protects a free and independent press while its statutory
law restricts and controls it. While Israeli government retains draconian
powers not only to suppress the publication of material but to close down
newspapers, Israeli journalists enjoy, culturally and politically, considerable
status and prestige, and this often translates into an appreciation for the
importance of an autonomous press. Attacks by the extreme right for being
"hostile" to "the people" confirm that the press does not automatically
support nationalist positions. Seemingly, then, there is a deep contradiction
in Israel's situation. It is a democracy committed to freedom of the press,
which, at the same time, has a formal military censorship, which intervenes
(only within a very limited area)[1] prior to publication, on its printed and
electronic press (Limor and Nossek, 1995; Negbi, 1995).

Israeli political scientists Horowitz and Lissak (1973) explain this

[*] This chapter is based on interviews conducted with Theodore Glasser for a collaborative study
in progress on Israeli journalists' views of censorship.

anomaly by defining the whole of Israeli society as "a nation at arms." The way Israel manages to preserve its democracy in spite of continuous wars, they argue, is by maintaining permeable boundaries between the military establishment and the civil realm. The fact that everybody takes part in the effort makes it possible to have a democratic government in spite of the salience of the issue of national security in daily life (Limor and Nossek, 1995).

Lahav (1985, pp. 265–8) goes back in history to explain these contradictory elements in terms of the influence of four enduring dichotomies which "coalesce into one fundamental libertarian–authoritarian dialectic." The first is the tension between "enlightened Zionism," which cherishes "the values of the enlightenment," and "pre-emancipation Jewish culture," conditioned by a ghetto mentality and rampant antisemitism, which frowns upon "political and religious dissent." The second dichotomy is between British liberalism, with its disdain for "authoritarian devices of suppression," and British colonialism, with its "elaborate legal system of political suppression, including censorship." The third dichotomy concerns the conflict between Anglo-American liberalism, particularly its emphasis on individual liberty, and Continental liberalism, particularly its emphasis on a strong, central state. And the fourth dichotomy involves the contradictions between the legal formalism of nineteenth-century England, with its attention to the autonomy of law, and a more contemporary "sociological jurisprudence" that recognizes "the connection between law and politics" and understands the former "as a reflection of social mores as well as an instrument for shaping them."

Thus, the grounds for censorship in Israel – i.e. the authoritarian side of the "libertarian–authoritarian dialectic" – need to be understood in terms of "the pre-emancipation Jewish tradition, British colonialism, Continental liberalism, and legal formalism" (ibid., p. 267).

Ironically, as Lahav points out, the Israeli government has formally adopted the repressive rules which were established by the British colonial government against itself, as it were, in order to control the Jewish and Arab press. As described in chapter 2, these were the rules that inadvertently stimulated the formation of the fighting national press, Jewish and Arab, as foci of mobilization. These consist, first of all, of the Press Ordinance of 1933 which requires a license for publishing a newspaper, and prevents closing of a paper if it publishes material which may "endanger public order." Second, the British emergency regulations of 1945 were similarly adopted. These require submission to censorship of any material which may impede public order or the defense of the state. As mentioned in chapter 2, the press editors accepted the fact of censorship with the founding of the State of Israel, as they felt the new state was in need of protection.

However, as Limor and Nossek (1995) point out, the written law on which censorship is based was effectively "frozen" early on, while its place was taken by a voluntary arrangement between the army and the Zionist dailies (including the Broadcasting Authority). By the terms of this agreement, the military censor undertook to disqualify only news, not views, and has given up the right to take criminal or administrative action against offenders; instead, the censor brings what are regarded as offenses before a "tribunal" which consists of representatives of the public, the Editors Committee, and the Chief of Staff.

While the agreement "inoculates" its members against closing down or imprisonment, the principle is criticized by legal experts – notably by Moshe Negbi (1995), a legal journalist and advocate of the freedom of speech. Negbi reminds us that the press editors themselves also relinquish *their own* right to go to court, with the result that the censor's decisions has never stood an objective legal test which would determine if he, in fact, keeps to the limitations of the agreement (to disqualify only information concerning security), or even to the limitations of the law (only what may cause damage to security or public order). A Supreme Court decision, responding to an application by the editor of a local paper who did not belong to the Editors Committee, was needed to insure that.[2] Worse, perhaps, the existence of the Editors Committee creates a discriminatory situation, in which marginal papers, the ones which need most protection, continue to be subject to sanctions. Nevertheless, even Negbi agrees with the journalists that the censorship of publishers is far more undermining to press freedom than that of the military censor, as journalists cannot afford to rebel against their publisher or editor, and no one would ever know that such censorship occurred.

Thus, in terms of censorship, the press is freer than it looks (freer in fact than on paper), although some would still say that it has wittingly become the voice of government. Our position is that the press is socialized enough to the demands of hegemony so as not to need external coercion or cynical calculation. That this, at least, is the *bona fide* approach of sophisticated and critical journalists may be illustrated by the interviews we conducted with a number of top editors and writers, and with the chief censor himself. Almost all agree that the stories which do not get published are mostly the ones that were – or would have been – censored by the journalists themselves.

The internalization of a deep commitment to the Zionist endeavor, and, with it, the acceptance of the need for censorship, especially in anything having to do with "the existential threat," i.e. the conflict, is clearly one of the major means through which hegemony has worked in the Israeli press. Unlike the almost unself-conscious manner in which journalists adopt establishment framings for the conflict – in naturalizing place names, for example ("Judea and Samaria" in place of "the West Bank") – acceptance of censorship is, at least to some extent, a *self-conscious* process. Seen by journalists, it is not only an imposition, but often a choice, that is, their own decision. And, as will be shown in what follows, the relationship between editors and censors may be defined as one of negotiation, in which the two sides are conducting an ongoing conversation.

This chapter focuses on the relationships between the Israeli press and the military censors, within the cultural context in which they evolved. In the case of Israel this means that the formal definition of censorship is inadequate, if the concept evokes an image of coercion by the state, on the one side, and an irate press or one which is coopted, on the other.

The quintessentially Western model of press and censorship posits press and censorship as competing adversaries, with journalists as "inquisitors" and public officials as seeking to present a particular public agenda. In this view, when journalists take the side of government it is tantamount to cooption, cooption being a form of acquiescence that jeopardizes journalists' autonomy and independence. The image of a coopted journalist is the image of a journalist whose judgment has been clouded by undue influence. The journalist has become a collaborator in promulgating the state's agenda.

According to this model, Israeli journalism can only be seen as coopted, plain and simple. Thus, for example, Lederman (1992), a foreign correspondent with twenty-five years' experience in the Middle East, claims that Israeli journalists are coopted by government officials and serve, essentially, as functionaries of the state. Seen from his perspective, Israeli journalists agree to a voluntary, self-policing type of censorship because the alternative, confrontation and ultimately control, is far less appealing. "The preferred choice was cooption" he writes, "because, inevitably, it was easier to buy someone off than to fight with him or her" (ibid., p. 30).

Cooption implies cynical calculation on the part of journalists, who knowingly operate against what they acknowledge to be the true norms of their profession. But this seems a grave over-simplification in the Israeli context. Seen from the journalists' point of view, we will argue that in most cases journalists are moved not by considerations of short-term convenience or fear of control (as they see it, there are ways of getting round the censor), but by a deeply felt responsibility toward the collectivity. Strange as it may seem, Israeli journalists insist that their commitment to a free press and the demands of censorship can be reconciled.

The idea is not to celebrate censorship but to understand how it works in the culture, that is, to look beyond the laws and regulations usually used to define censorship in order to examine the relationship between censorship and freedom of expression in a more socially contextualized view, in which there is a culturally imposed partnership between press and censorship, locked in an ongoing dialogue, based on commonly held assumptions and commitments.

These commitments are implicit in the professional role definitions of both censors and journalists, as in the status that they share as citizens and as members of the interlocking networks of the Israeli elites.

ROUTINES OF NEGOTIATING WITH THE CENSORS

Observing the routine management of difference within a shared hegemonic outlook is what the rest of this chapter is about. It assumes that understanding the role of censorship in Israeli culture is one way of seeing what is taken for granted as out of bounds for public debate, how the boundaries of consensus are negotiated, and in what circumstances hegemony may crack. In order to gain insight into the points of view of the participants in the process, we conducted extensive interviews with editors, senior journalists, and the chief censor.[3] While both sides share a basic understanding that military censorship cannot be altogether discarded, both concede that there are changing cultural definitions of the type of information that is out of bounds for public discussion. These definitions are challenged and change largely with the shifts in framing of the Arab–Israeli conflict.

Reluctant censors

The Chief Military Censor is loathe to exercise authority. From his point of view, he is caught in a double bind. On the one hand, the Israeli government considers it crucial to withhold information which, it believes, is damaging to Israel's security; on the other, it regards as no less crucial the promotion of its image as "the only democracy in the Middle East." The exercise of punitive measures against the press is, of course, bound to boomerang in the ensuing publicity. Moreover, closing down a newspaper following a breach would be like locking the prison doors after the prisoner has escaped, adding image damage to security damage. As a result, the censors have in practice given up the use of formal sanctions against member newspapers of the Editors Committee (and have only once in recent memory closed down a non-member Hebrew paper, for all of two days,[4] bringing it into the fold). This abandoning of formal sanctions has created a two-class system, by which "members of the club" (the Hebrew dailies) are controlled only indirectly via an ongoing dialogue between the censor and the press – managed by fax, phone, and face-to-face interaction.

Ritual debates

Hegemony probably does not sound the same in different countries. Outwardly, routine conversations between an Israeli editor, senior reporter, and a censor may sound like loud, rude, and violent arguments. True, confirms Nahum Barnea, a senior columnist in *Yediot Aharonot* (and former editor of an elite weekly),[5] the two sides often raise their voices and even use abusive language, but from the participants' points of view, on both sides, the interaction is considered civilized. The discrepancy between the rhetoric of the negotiation and the way in which it sounds inheres in *the culture's passionate style of interaction* – what qualifies as a normal Israeli (and Jewish) form of conducting a conversation (Schiffrin, 1984; Katriel, 1991) – and in the ritualistic basis underlying the argument.

An old boys' network

Beyond the dictates of an overriding social consensus, internalization of censorship is reinforced by an even closer understanding between editors and army officers as *members of the social elite*. The often-cited argument that the press cannot be critical of government as the two are part of the same elite circle is intensified in this case by the mutual invasion of the military and the civil realms in Israeli society. This makes the dialogue between journalist and censor part of an ongoing conversation within the Israeli establishment to which both belong. The common background, shared by these elites, constitutes the Israeli version of the old boys' network, in which elite army units play the part of ivy league universities.[6] "It so happens," explains Barnea, "that they [journalists and army officers] served in the same unit in the army; it so happens that they live in the same apartment building in Ramat Aviv, in Tel-Aviv." Yes, "it so happens," but not quite by coincidence, one should add, as dwelling neighborhoods to some extent, and army units to a much greater extent, are organized according to a hierarchy of social prestige. Whether they know each other personally or not, the identical phases of socialization through which they pass – the wars, the rituals, the experiences and responsibilities of growing up in a collectivistic society under siege – mean that journalists and army officers understand and respect each other.

A shared culture

Indeed, underneath the tough bargaining about specific stories, says Barnea, the journalists and the censor understand each other, an understanding which, he insists, is not based on the principle of "I scratch your back, you scratch mine." This deeper understanding originates, rather, in shared membership in *a society based on consensus*, at least when security is at stake. This consensus, however, has undergone various stages. During the 1950s, not only the press but the whole intellectual community voluntarily undertook to share the practical and spiritual burden of nation building, accepting the politicians' authority to define the boundaries both of the social–cultural dialogue and of political action (Keren, 1988). From the 1960s onward, when the state emerged out of this first phase, Israeli society grew more open. Nevertheless, at the beginning of the 1990s, concern about security was still central enough for journalists and censors to communicate as "people who basically understand each other."

This understanding between censors and journalists is not only abstract or ideological but rooted within the most profound realm – that of the safety of their loved ones. As the Chief Military Censor sees it, "the editors have children [sons], just as I do, and my children and their children serve in the same army, for the same security [reasons], for the same state." Thus, the most cherished personal concerns are closely bound up with government interests, bringing about the (now classic) remark of one editor who is quoted as saying "if there was no censor we would have had to invent one."

True, within this shared understanding both the censor and the press see themselves as representing adversarial positions. "We are not enemies," explains Barnea, "[but] *each plays a different role in the game.*" The censors' role is regarded as legitimate, even crucial, and the Chief Military Censor is personally respected as a professional, "like a doctor who knows what is causing damage." It is almost as if the journalists are relieved of the burden of responsibility for deciding where the lines of free speech should be drawn.

Thus, internalizing hegemony means that editors and journalists believe that what they have in common with the censors exceeds their confrontational roles, and assumes that their role constitutes only one (perhaps not even the most important) aspect of their shared membership in a society (Goffman, 1974). Thus, even when editors conduct an all-out fight against censorship in a particular case, risking retaliation, they still do not question the *institution* of censorship.

Throughout many years of living together – seventeen years of the present Chief Military Censor – a *modus vivendi* has developed between the editors and the chief censor, and, with it, a vested interest in continuing the relationship. Thus, perhaps ironically, the journalists themselves had a say in the deliberations of the Minister of Defense over nominating a new censor. As it happens, the journalists' lobby contributed largely toward the decision to keep the present censor from being replaced.

It should come as no surprise, therefore, that most of the military and political correspondents oppose the abolition of the Emergency Rules under which the censor operates (originating, as recounted above, in British Mandatory Law) in favor of a new Censorship Law which would formalize and rationalize the censorship process. After all, they share the idea that some censorship is necessary, are aware of their own influence over the censor, respect his judgment, and have access to the mechanisms of protection against sanctions in case of transgression. "I cannot remember times when I wasn't fighting the censor," says Shimon Schiffer, the political correspondent of *Yediot*, "but once there is a law it would be devastating for the press ... all our games will be over ... the censor will go to court and journalists will need lawyers to defend themselves in court."

INTERNALIZING CENSORSHIP

In the following pages we will illustrate the workings of this process of negotiation. It will be shown that the outcome, typically, reflects the journalists' *acceptance* of censorship and self-censorship. Sometimes, however, the process results in rejection of censorship and in the journalists' resolve not to allow themselves to practice their own inclination to self-censorship.

In both cases – acceptance of censorship as well as rejection – we shall show that the process has two major cognitive ingredients. One of these is the shared concern over security; on most occasions, of course, this works to reinforce censorship. In certain cases, however, the journalist may decide that the official definition of security must be challenged in the name of "true" security.

The other term in this equation is a concern for public appreciation of journalism; sometimes this reflects the journalists' perception that the public wants to know more than it is being told; more often, it reflects a judgment that the public would rather know less than more!

The constraints working for self-censorship and acceptance of censorship are presented first, subdivided by "security" concerns and concerns over "public" expectations. Then we turn to those constraints that lead to rejection of censorship, in which the journalists resist the censor. This discussion, too, is divided between concerns over "(true) security" and concern over public expectations.

"There is a little censor in each of us," says Michal Sela, the spirited correspondent of *Davar*, the veteran Labor Party paper, known for advocating the Palestinian plight. "If there were no censorship," she says, "things would not be dramatically different." Barnea expresses the same sentiment, arguing that even if there was no censor, the journalists themselves would censor things which they believe to be harmful.

This ideology of self-censorship, in the name of social responsibility (Siebert et al., 1972), is indicative of the constant maneuvering of Israeli journalists between their professional role and their membership in the community, a maneuvering which occurs mostly regarding the various dimensions of the Arab–Israeli conflict. Acceptance of censorship occurs when commitment to the community takes the upper hand, becoming the "closer" and more relevant role (Goffman, 1974), or when journalists give voice to, or give in to, the demands of the public.

Commitment to collective security

Sharing the need to protect the collective means that daily decisions on what stories should be submitted to censorship are made informally, based on journalists' intuitive understanding of where to draw the line. Sela, for example, feels confident enough not to have even seen the list of subjects which have to be checked with the censor. "I know there is such a list," she told us dismissively, "but the practice is different." The reporters themselves make decisions about borderline items instead of sending them to the censor because they "know how the censor works." "I only send to the censor things about which I know there is some technical military information and I am not sure what the judgment will be," says Barnea.

When acting as concerned members of society, editors and journalists are of one mind with the censors concerning the prohibition of public exposure of issues considered crucial to the physical welfare of Israel or to its ideological *raison d'être* (even though the public may not share that view). An obvious example is information about Israel's nuclear capability,[7] or about secret negotiations with neighboring countries, which are still technically at war with Israel, over issues such as water distribution, or the tacit agreements over immigration and rescue operations of Jews living in countries – Soviet Russia, Yemen, Ethiopia, to name a few – which do not want these activities to be known. All these have to do with projects operating behind the scenes aimed at insuring the survival of the state or at carrying out the ideological aims of Zionism. As these may involve clandestine acts in totalitarian countries, negotiations with declared enemy states, or an embarrassment to a powerful friendly state – notably, the USA – the success of each one of these operations, our interviewees explain, may be jeopardized by publicity, certainly by publicity that comes too early.

Consider the story of the existence of undercover Israeli soldiers masked as Palestinians in Gaza, which was a well-kept secret of the intifada for some years. Michal Sela, who was Arab affairs correspondent of the weekly *Koteret Rashit* at the time, recounts the argument she had with her own editor after having come across some of these soldiers in her routine work. Both agreed to publish the story in "low profile," but in this case it was she who insisted on not showing the photographs of the soldiers so as not to endanger them. When Reuters, the American news agency, picked it up, Sela asked them to do the same. Reuters could not resist giving the item maximum publicity and decided against submitting it to censorship. Although it was a matter of great concern to the Israeli army, the news agency did not suffer severe sanctions. Instead, Israel's Chief of Staff initiated major coverage of the unit on television's prestigious weekly newsreel. Once the story was out he made sure to use the opportunity to glorify the unit and, perhaps, to make potential Palestinian terrorists feel less secure in their own territory.

This example illustrates a not unusual itinerary of censoring information. It began with the partial censoring of the semi-protective, ambivalent, Israeli press, to the publication by the non-participant foreign press, weighing the "scoop" against the possible repercussions of sanctions, to (once the news is out) its cooption by the Israeli political and military establishment, attempting to control the story by framing it in the "right" light.

Another example that illustrates the priorities of Israeli journalists when it comes to protecting the security of the state or of its people, as well as the dramatic lack of contact with communities outside the consensus, is the story of the recent immigration of Jews from Yemen. It was a sensitive undercover operation, conducted with the assistance of the US, and involving the cooperation of unfriendly, non-democratic countries. The censor asked the Editors Committee not to publish the story as any publicity could jeopardize the operation. They all willingly cooperated (granting the new immigrants the status of Israeli citizens in advance, in the best Zionist tradition), and the story was indeed kept secret for many months. In this case the silence was not broken because of publication abroad, but because the presence of "new" Jews in the country emerged in small religious Israeli newspapers. The context was in stories reporting a dispute about which educational system the new immigrant children should belong to, that is, who has the right to their souls. As these papers are not interested in national politics but in their own communities, and are considered marginal and sectarian, the censor did not stop these publications. But as the discussion gathered momentum national papers joined in, calling the newcomers immigrants from "a country of plight," in an attempt to disguise their identity. Only when photographs appeared, showing the unmistakably biblical-looking Jews, complete with long black beards and curly sideburns, did *Maariv* apply for and receive permission from the censor to reveal the story, making the other newspapers feel they had been cheated out of a scoop.

While these examples illustrate classic concerns that have characterized the "protectiveness" of Israeli journalism for a long time, recently, the balance seems to be shifting from social responsibility toward greater independence. This may be shown by the words of Yoram Peri, *Davar*'s editor at the time, who told us: "Luckily I did not know anything about the Oslo negotiations at the time," implying that otherwise he would have had to deal with the dilemma of choosing between the demands of the professional role and the role of citizen.

Reacting to public sentiments

In other cases, however, journalists may engage in self-censorship not because they fear the actual implications of publication for national security, but because they fear that the public will interpret it as such. They prefer to act as part of the consensus they attribute to their readers and not to alienate their public. In such cases, the press contributes to tightening the hegemonic binding because the assumption that some information would not fit with the expectations of the public (socialized to a particular view of the world) is self-fulfilling, as it reinforces this expectation.

"We publish," says Barnea, "only what we feel will be justified as socially responsible by our readers. The censor can threaten or carry out short-term sanctions; the sanctions of the public, however, may cause long-term harm to the journalist's image and alienate the readers." According to Barnea, journalists have to be careful "[lest] the public think they broke all the rules in order to publish at any cost."

Obvious contexts in which this consideration may constrain the press are any questioning of IDF measures during a security crisis, or in exposing the ugly face of Israelis "retaliating" against Palestinians following terrorist attacks, and the brutality of soldiers against Palestinian civilians in the occupied territories. Whereas anti-Palestinian street riots are shown and reported, the reluctance of the press to expose failure on the side of the military institution or of individual soldiers is striking.

The great unwillingness to shatter the public's faith in the IDF during a crisis is still well remembered from the period of the Gulf War. In winter 1991, when Iraqi missiles fell over Tel-Aviv, the press cooperated with the IDF in not casting any doubt about its instructions to Israelis to go into the "sealed room," even after it became apparent, following the first "conventional" attacks, that the use of conventional bomb shelters might have been safer. As the weeks went by it became more and more obvious that the Israeli media were determined not to exercise their right to provide vital information which, the journalists sensed, the public would prefer not to know (Katz, 1992). Only when authority figures such as Yitzhak Rabin, then a Knesset Member, admitted in a radio interview that he had been going down to his air-raid shelter, not into a "sealed room," did the press regain public legitimacy for asking the painful questions.

The brutal actions of Israeli soldiers against Palestinians, which became more common in the course of the intifada, are also very sensitive from the public's point of view, as the image of the moral quality of the Israeli soldier (labeled the "purity of arms" in 1948) is central to Zionist ideology. This explains why stories of army brutality against Palestinians are rare, and appear mostly following their publication by foreign television reporters. The items are short, pushed into inside pages, with bland but asymmetrical language reporting events in which Palestinian "boys" (not children) were "*hit* by the fire of Israeli forces," while "Palestinian *terrorists killed* Israeli *children*" (Roeh and Nir, 1990).

A telling glimpse into how public influence on editors works was provided by Amos Shocken, the publisher of *Ha'aretz* and a network of local weeklies, who, in a meeting devoted to the freedom of the press, mentioned the pressure put on the editor of *Kol Hair*, the Jerusalem weekly, by stand-owners in the outdoor market who refused to buy the paper and returned the unopened batches delivered to them. Soon after they expressed their anger, intifada incidents virtually disappeared from the pages of the weekly.[8]

This self-censorship in anything to do with shattering the faith of Israelis in the military is not in operation in the case of hooligans (belonging to Kahane's group of religious right-wing extremists or the like) "avenging" themselves on Arab passers-by following terrorist attacks, or West Bank settlers clashing with soldiers or vandalizing Palestinian property. And sure enough, criticizing "Jews" became a major trigger for a right-wing car-sticker campaign against "hostile media," in the familiar tradition of blaming the messenger. Each of these eruptions brought about right-wing militant derision of the press as a leftist mafia, serving the enemy, concerned only with injustice done to Arabs, not with the suffering of Jews. Incitement against the press took the form of curses, assault, and the vandalizing of cars and cameras in the course of covering the violence.

The anti-press campaign provides proof that, in these cases, reporters did their job, even though it is "us," not "them," who are shown in an unflattering light. It may be argued, though, that the ugly Israelis shown are marginal extremists who do not have public sympathy. Thus, in these cases exposure constitutes no risk for the popularity of the press with the public at large. Nevertheless, one can wonder what are the long-term implications of continual populist incitement against the press, even to the willingness of television crews to risk appearing on the site of a terrorist attack.

All in all, the under-reporting of "deviant" behavior by Israeli soldiers in the intifada is not so much a reflection of direct censorship or of other forms of army control (such as closing off an area to reporters), or of the journalists' own limits of social responsibility, but seems to be the reflection of self-censorship for fear of being condemned by a public, which contravenes a journalist's professional conscience.

Beyond the (supposedly) deviant actions of individual officers and soldiers, the profile of the intifada as a whole in the Israeli press was low, with the implication that the debate over the effects of the occupation on the army and on Israeli society was played down. This also was due to a large extent to the editors' wish not to alienate the public, which demonstrated indifference, bordering on denial, toward the meaning of the continuing occupation for Israeli society (let alone its effects on the Palestinian population) and toward the evidence of the damage to the moral fiber of which the Israeli army is so proud. The groups interested in calling attention to the possibility of moral erosion in the IDF were considered marginal and could safely be ignored by both censors and the editors (Alexander, 1981; Hallin, 1994).

WHEN DO ISRAELI JOURNALISTS BYPASS CENSORSHIP?

Commitment to the collective security

Contrary to appearances, fighting against censorship may be just as much *in the name of* security as in opposition to it. Acting against censorship in this way is also hegemonic, of course, in that it reflects a lag between the rules of a formal institution which represent the residual ideology, and the evolution of the culture's emerging ideology, as perceived by its professional observers, the journalists. It does not reflect a libertarian – "publish and be damned" – theory of the press (Siebert et al., 1972), but an expression of loyalty to the culture's true values.

In bypassing censorship rules, even for the best of reasons, the journalist may invite immediate sanctions against the newspaper and/or against him- or herself personally. The underlying assumption is that the cause is well worth it and would enlist public sympathy, that the sanctions will be purely formal, will blow over, but that the story, and the journalist's glory, will become part of the collective memory. Of course, journalists sense the way in which dominant ideology is heading before the trend ripens, and may misjudge the risks. Thus, blatant violation of censorship may occur for the same reasons as collaboration with the censors.

A dramatic example of such violation, in the name of the security and well-being of the state, as well as its often-proclaimed values, was the attempt to mobilize the Israeli public against the decision to go to war in Lebanon in 1982. Shimon Schiffer, the political correspondent of Public Radio at the time, told us how he tried, at the risk of losing his job, to mobilize public opinion against the impending government decision to go to war in Lebanon. Violating censorship rules on a top security issue is rare, and scandalous, but this is also exactly the kind of issue which may be considered important enough to move a journalist to take personal risks.

A week prior to the war, Schiffer, now a senior political columnist in *Yediot Aharonot*, found out that half the ministers in Menachem Begin's Likud government objected to Defense Minister Sharon's plan to start a war against Lebanon.[9] Horrified by the idea of the government starting a futile and unnecessary war, both as a citizen and a professional whose duty it is to inform public opinion, Schiffer considered it mandatory to report this information. The exposure of the rift within the government, he assumed, would trigger a public debate on the wisdom of the plan and on its far-reaching implications. It was exactly this kind of debate which Prime Minister Begin and Defense Minister Sharon tried to prevent by invoking one of the basic rules of censorship. By this rule, when the cabinet meets as "The Ministerial Committee for Security Affairs" the meeting is automatically closed to public coverage. In the weeks prior to the Lebanon war this privilege was widely exploited, effectively prohibiting press coverage of most of the government's meetings. Schiffer ignored the rule and reported the split of opinion in the government. Public Radio was reprimanded by the censor and Schiffer was called to the Appeals tribunal, after which, he says, he was threatened by his boss, Radio's Director General, and told, "if you have one more incident with the Appeals' Committee I will fire you." Israel's Prosecutor General considered prosecuting, but the Director General of

Public Radio shouldered the responsibility. Schiffer, however, was moved from the political desk to another desk.

From his point of view, Schiffer had managed to make public information he considered crucial but the opportunity to have an effect on the course of events was missed, as the Israeli public failed to pick up the cue. The disillusioned Schiffer draws the conclusion that contrary to appearances, the press has no influence on politics. "All the journalists were opposed to the war," he recounts, "but Begin and Sharon had made up their minds, leading the nation to the first – disastrous – 'war of choice' in its history."

From our point of view, the story shows a far greater alertness on the part of the press compared to the lazy obedience to censorship in the days prior to the Yom Kippur War. In that fatal week, accepting the request of the Defense Minister not to hurt public morale and raise war hysteria, the editors collaborated with the misreadings of official intelligence in ignoring the worrying signs of an impending war. The difference in behavior may show that journalists have learned a lesson or, more likely, that taking an independent stance is made possible when the political elite itself is divided. On a more intuitive level, journalists may have sensed what the public only realized within the following months – socialized as it was to trust its leaders with the most crucial decision in their power, that of when to go to war – that Lebanon was not a "war of necessity," and as such, could not justify sacrificing human life, particularly as the culture was becoming less collectivistic.

Reacting to public expectations

Whereas Schiffer may have misjudged the reluctance of the Israeli public to acknowledge the split in the government over starting a war in Lebanon – as casting doubt on the wisdom of the decision would raise too much anxiety – on other occasions journalists accurately sense that the public will welcome the bypassing of censorship. Knowing that (as mentioned above) the censors themselves operate through consensus, journalists assume that they, too, will eventually succumb to the pressure of public opinion.

Whereas some years ago journalists would not have attacked the army, as this would only turn the public against the "hostile media," as Israeli society has become less collectivistic (Katz and Haas, 1994) the heretofore "untouchable" institutions have become increasingly legitimate subjects of criticism. This may be seen in the growing number of stories that reveal conservatism, negligence, and deviations from accepted norms in venerable institutions – such as the Law Courts and the IDF – which for many years could do no wrong.

Examples of the trend may be found in the detailed reports of soldiers killed due to negligence in training or to "friendly fire." Such stories used to be censored, but, in recent years, they have become central news.

Paradoxically, the more permissive journalistic norms create the impression that things are getting worse while statistical data may show improvement (Kepplinger and Roth, 1979). Thus, while statistically there is a definite decrease in such accidents due to negligence during army training, and, sometimes, in action, public awareness, and, with it, a growing demand for control measures, is constantly growing; and the press, aware of public interest, hurries to give it detailed expression. Particularly active are bereaved parents who sometimes make it their life's mission to "find out exactly what happened" and to demand punishment of those responsible. (In such episodes the army is under suspicion for trying to protect its high commanders and sacrifice the lowest in the hierarchy.)

A recent example which demonstrates this trend is the knowing violation of censorship by *Ha'aretz*, which reported the presence of the IDF's Chief of Staff in a military maneuver in which five soldiers from an elite unit were killed by accident. While the censor was concerned with the damage caused by giving publicity to the highly secret maneuver and its aims, *Ha'aretz*, responding to the growing concern of its readers, was more concerned with the army's possible attempt to cover-up carelessness resulting in the loss of lives. In this context it made sense to insist on knowing about the Chief of Staff's proximity to, and possible involvement in, the accident. This incident resulted in the newspaper's editor dramatically walking out of the Editors Committee, choosing, instead, to face censorship in court. Over the years this affair escalated – with media demands for prosecutions of an increasing number of officers, and with acrimonious attacks on the Chief of Staff in the press and television – in a spiral in which the institutions in charge of norm-enforcing fed on each other.

STRATEGIES OF BYPASSING THE CENSOR

Head-on collisions with the censors, such as Schiffer's censorship offense prior to the Lebanon war, are rare. Such collisions concern major security secrets and occur, as stated above, only in cases when journalists are prepared to pay the price, in the name of "true" security, or when they sense that public sentiment runs so high against censoring certain stories that (long-term) loss of credibility in the eyes of their clients seems worse than the (immediate) retaliation of the censor. The latter case is an indication of the growing gap between the assumptions of formal institutions and the changing values of society.

More common are a number of non-confrontational tactics. These include marginalization of borderline stories, sidetracked to back pages, to local subsidiaries of major papers, or to feature articles; the transference of items from the Arabic press (suffering from much closer scrutiny) to Hebrew papers; the "editing" of supposedly unrelated items next to each other creating a semiotic frame of reference; and publishing following the publication of the censored story by the foreign press (sometimes even passing the story on to overseas colleagues).

Marginalizing

One technique of having your cake and eating it lies in the journalist's risking less but giving up on having a major scoop. This means lowering the profile of a story by marginalizing its publication. This may be done first by sidetracking sensitive news items from major newspapers and from front pages to weekend supplements, to back pages, and to "human interest" stories and features, considered safer, perhaps less under hegemonic scrutiny. A variation of this lies in handing over the story to the local subsidiaries of the major papers which, presumably, attract less attention when publishing problematic items. These local weeklies, the number and bulk of which are constantly on the increase, are run by young people and considered less oriented toward political issues of national importance.

Thus, for example, the story of the kidnapping of Mordechai Vanunu, an Israeli who had given the London *Times* the story of Israel's nuclear reactor, appeared on the local network of weeklies that belongs to the *Ha'aretz* publishing company, following eight months of negotiations with the censor.

Another practice is shifting censored items that were to appear in the Arabic press to Hebrew newspapers. The censor's discriminatory treatment of the Palestinian papers, which arises out of concern with the anti-Israeli effect of certain information on the Palestinian public, means that stories that are considered political in a Hebrew newspaper may be defined as "security" if they appear in an Arabic one. Cooperation between Israeli and Palestinian journalists, says Michal Sela, means that a Hebrew-language journalist may edit and publish articles given to her by Palestinian colleagues. One historical example for a story which made its way to the Hebrew press is the proposal to give up "Gaza first" in a possible peace negotiation with the Palestinians, an innovative idea at the time which started circulating in the Hebrew press, possibly affecting the unexpected political developments which were to come.

Playing a semiotic game

Particularly creative tactics for bypassing censorship were employed early on by *Haolam Hazeh*, the anti-establishment weekly mentioned in chapter 2 (which featured political leftist radicalism and prurient sensations). The following example concerns the reporting of "the affair" – Israel's most notorious security scandal, involving dilettante plans that culminated in the betrayal of an Israeli spy network in Egypt. In 1959, the weekly published two seemingly unrelated items next to each other – one, the story of a decision taken by Ben-Gurion, Israel's Prime Minister at the time, to demote his Defense Minister, the other, a reminder of the capture of the Egyptian Jewish spy ring, which happened five years earlier. While officially the current political crisis was about the rejection of the minister's proposal for reforms, politically sophisticated readers could guess the meaning intended by the editor's juxtaposing of the two stories. The censors were helpless, as they received only the separate stories and had no way of censoring the page-layout!

As the militarily "unfortunate affair" became a political affair, threatening to destroy Israel's ruling party, the press was allowed to discuss the political development without telling the "military" story. This led to the agreed labeling of mysterious characters such as "the senior officer," "the officer on reserve," "the third person," "the man," and, later on, "the secretary." When the whole country was speculating about the players' identities, *Haolam Hazeh* published a crossword puzzle in which the correct answers were the real names of the main characters: "It could be filled correctly only if you already knew the names," explains the editor, Uri Avneri.

Later still, Avneri chose the eve of Pentecost to tell his readers the first part of a fictional story, entitled "The Alexis Affair," by a supposedly unknown Greek writer by the name of Nikos Konstantinos, featuring a Greek spy ring in Turkey, in the context of the battle over Cyprus. The story was studded with elements of "the affair," complete with forged documents, lying witnesses, the transfer of orders through housewives' recipes broadcast on radio, and a one-armed Chief of Staff (the equivalent of the one-eyed Israeli General Moshe Dayan), who may or may not have given orders for overt military actions in Turkey. In answer to the chief censor, who objected to publishing the second half, arguing that an international scandal would harm the efforts to release the Egyptian Jews still in prison, Avneri said that it could never be proved he was not telling an imaginary story, and, anyway, he could not drop the second half which his readers were promised after the holiday. His offer to submit the second half to the censor was rejected on the grounds that such a procedure would only confirm what the real issue was. Finally, the two agreed to the censor's unofficial reading of the story – "in the role of literary critic" as it were – and making informal suggestions about possible modifications.

Making use of the excuse that the story has been published abroad

In some cases journalists allow themselves to bypass censorship orders when a story has already been published in the foreign press (sometimes with the active assistance of an Israeli colleague). In stories which embarrass the Israeli government, the cause for censorship is that publication in the Hebrew press is equivalent to an official acknowledgment that the story is true. According to this logic, as long as a story is not acknowledged publicly and is not published by the Israeli press, other friendly countries are not forced to react (Katz, in Noelle-Neumann, 1985). Journalists' increasing reluctance to play this game is an indication of the normative change in press culture which allows for slowly cleaning up remains from the period in which the press was an arm of the political establishment. Considering that the damage to security has already been done, journalists tend not to cooperate in saving the government political unease. And the censors, sensing that there would be little public support for sanctioning the press in such a case, go through the motions, but ultimately acknowledge defeat.

An example that illustrates the drawing of the line between security and political censorship is the case in which journalist Schiffer learned that a senior Israeli military representative in South Africa had transferred money belonging to Jewish citizens of South Africa (where transferring money out of the country was illegal) to Israel, through his own bank account. The censor rejected the story, arguing that it was sensitive as Israel had never formally admitted to having a military mission in South Africa. *Yediot*'s editor argued that the story had appeared in the foreign press, complete with the Israeli General's photograph. The censor did not relent, on the grounds that acknowledgment of an Israel–South Africa connection in this case might force other countries to retaliate. The editor decided to go ahead and publish the story as a front page headline, without asking the censor, and without appealing to the Committee. An hour after the appearance of the story, a red letter arrived from the censor accusing the paper of acting against the Editors Committee agreement, ending with "awaiting your explanation." The editor explained, and that was the end of the story. "Most editors," Schiffer summarizes, "know exactly what kind of story is worth fighting for, what kind to ignore, and what kind to make a story about the story of the censor's involvement."

THE MANAGEMENT OF HEGEMONY SHIFTS INTO THE HANDS OF THE MEDIA

Recent sociological and technological shifts, as we started to show, mean that censorship cannot function anymore as the regulator of hegemony, shifting the burden onto the much more independent shoulders of the press and electronic media. As we have demonstrated, keeping information away from the Israeli public was problematic from the start. Beyond the basic reluctance of the censor to exercise power, as sanctions against transgressors tend to tarnish Israel's image as a democracy, censoring of information has continually depended more on the journalists' cooperation than on the censors' power. With the dying out of the editors who saw themselves as part of the elite committed to nation building, and were personally committed to the political leadership, the entire situation of journalism is changing – including relations with the censor. In addition, the technological changes noted, and the chinks in collectivism and consensus, have contributed to the new journalism.

Generational change

The emergence of a new generation of journalists implies that the press is more independent of the political establishment. This change in the balance of power is demonstrated in cases such as the public criticism brought about by the then Opposition leader Benjamin Netanyahu's attempt to nominate his man as the editor of the *Jerusalem Post*, in the independent stand taken by the editor of *Ha'aretz* in leaving the Editors Committee, and in the new policy of the Shocken network of local weeklies to bypass the Editors Committee, and appeal to the courts against censorship restrictions. Most of these appeals result in the state's agreement to compromise. This itinerary can be demonstrated by the story of the publication of the kidnapping of Mordechai Vanunu, mentioned above. Eight years after the event, the Shocken weeklies negotiated for eight months with the censor, agreeing to change names, hide the fact that the boat was Israeli, etc., yet ended up going to court, in order to publish the story.

The new limits on the censor's power, however, are not only due to the need to negotiate and find a way of coexisting with an ever-changing press, gradually more occupied with the competition for readers and viewers than with establishment framings. It is also limited by technological restrictions, which make the old procedures of handing in press items and video tapes anachronistic.

Technological constraints

The new communication revolution is characterized by a growing number of foreign television reporters, equipped with instant technologies, representing a growing number of television channels, notably CNN, with the capability of broadcasting live when an event is considered newsworthy. In this instantly transferred, open communication environment censorship is left to lament the damage and reprimand offenders, after the fact. The helplessness of the censor, and the Israeli government, in controlling the new media technologies became apparent during the intifada and the Gulf War.

The first years of the Palestinian uprising shattered the delicate balance between the censor and the foreign press. The intifada transformed the glamorous image of the brave and moral Israeli soldier, sometimes fighting a seemingly lost war against a larger enemy, into that of an aggressive and ruthless occupier, and made salient an image of a repressive army – complete with shields, clubs, and rubber bullets – harassing a civilian population (see chapter 6). When this became apparent, Prime Minister Shamir set up a committee to advise him whether it was possible to control the flow of information from the occupied territories, explaining that television cameras acted to increase the violence of the protestors and to hamper the actions of the IDF in its efforts to keep order.

In spite of government concern, the committee concluded that the pictures could not be censored. Prohibiting access to riot areas would create a bad image for Israel. Moreover, the American networks and news agencies handed out cameras to local Palestinians, whose movements could not be controlled. (Paradoxically, Israeli television news, on what was then one public channel, could show very few pictures of the intifada, as it was restricted to showing only those taken by its own crews. As a result, Americans could see much more of Israeli soldiers' transgressions in the intifada, at least during its first months.)

Ironically, however, what the government was helpless in controlling was achieved by the dynamics of news coverage of foreign affairs. The American networks tired of the crisis, in which identical incidents of soldiers confronting masses of stone-throwing, tire-burning demonstrators with their faces covered, repeated itself ad nauseum. What started as hot news became expected, routine, and the intifada came off the television news screens of the USA and Europe (with a few dramatic exceptions).

The Gulf War is another story. Censorship here was concerned not with Israel's image but with the life of its citizens, subject to Iraqi missile attacks. Showing the exact places in which Iraqi missiles hit could assist the Iraqis in aiming better next time. But even in this case Israelis in their sealed rooms were told on the phone – by their relatives abroad, informed by CNN – where the missiles fell.

Live television

The recent prevalence of unedited broadcasting and the proliferation of talk shows have made for casual, sometimes incidental, censorship violations on live radio and television, further weakening the control of censorship in practice. Thus, in an appearance on an evening television talk show, the Chief of Staff himself reported the death of two soldiers, apparently without awareness of censorship regulations that require prior notice to the victim's families. These regulations are concerned first with preventing a situation in which a family learns about the death of their dear one from the media, and, second, with needlessly alarming all the other families who have relatives in army service. (Thus, announcements of the deaths of soldiers are followed by the sentence "an announcement was given to the families.")

Recently, in October 1994, reporters on live television violated the spirit of this rule while keeping to its technicalities, on a night when the whole nation was watching. It was a Friday evening, during the last stages of the kidnapping of Israeli soldier Nachshon Waxman by *Hamas* terrorists; Israelis were watching the popular weekend news and heard Public

Channel's political commentator, Gadi Sukenik, warning that on censor's orders he had to withhold important news, adding that "this was not a happy evening." By the time Yitzhak Rabin, Israel's Prime Minister, appeared on screen to deliver the news of the killing of the hostage, as well as the commander of the rescuing force, the public more or less knew.

In a word, for Israeli journalists there is no simple dichotomy between "press freedom" and "censorship": they find themselves on both sides. As long as the Arab–Israeli conflict dominates the public agenda, that is, as long as the existential threat is not removed, journalists carry with them the concerns of any press at war, asking – Will this story serve the enemy? Endanger a hostage? Increase long-term risks of nuclear war? Thus, in the case of the Israeli press, the terms of freedom and censorship may be seen as dialectical, not dichotomous, and the tension between the two can be understood as not only inhibiting the publication of certain materials but as empowering journalists in the active negotiation of the limits of public debate. Seen in this context, there are times when, paradoxically, censorship simultaneously violates *and* expands journalists' freedom, when it is seen as operating not only to curb press freedom but as an opportunity for it.

Chapter 5

Constructing success
How framing may be an instrument for pacifying a watchdog press

The internalization of censorship provides only a crude and partial way of looking at the workings of hegemony. True, the need to negotiate with a powerful external agent clarifies the areas of shared concern as well as the red lines which arouse the journalists' resistance and tactics of circumvention. These red lines mark the limits of internalization, and often mark the lag between formal censorship and the changing society.

But journalists' management of military censorship is, by definition, restricted to limited (granted, sometimes the most controversial) aspects of the representation of the conflict, and misses out on the much broader field of daily practices. In the routines of reporting tension, violent incidents, and a range of clashes, involving demonstrators, terrorists, victims, and sometimes armies on both sides, journalists are left to themselves to make decisions. The choices they make – sometimes in dialogue with their editors and colleagues – about where to go, whom to interview, what to focus on, what pictures to take, determine the construction of the conflict on press and television. It is this accumulation of routine coverage, not the occasional intervention of the military censor, which adds up to construct and to transmit hegemonic views of the conflict.

In short, arguments over censorship are narrow in scope and, by definition, relate only to conscious, intentional decisions on what should or should not be reported, leaving out the much less self-conscious ongoing processes of sorting out, prioritizing, and framing.

Put differently, negotiations over censorship, as they emerge from the interviews we conducted, focus on the *what* – what to tell or what not to tell – but tend to ignore the much more tricky terrain of *how* stories are told. Clearly, discussions about censorship are legitimate and need to assume the existence of stable categories of content and of journalistic genres. Distinctions between matters of politics and security, and between the genres of news and views, constitute the basis for negotiation, and must be taken as given.

This chapter argues that hegemony resides not only in what is told to the public versus what is hidden, but in the ways in which a story is told. (If most of intelligence work is done by reading newspapers, it should be assumed that classified information may be flaunted in routine, or trivial, or insignificant stories.) Even if the censor gave journalists a free hand in covering the bombing of the Iraqi nuclear reactor, the journalist would have to decide for him- or herself whether this was a security story or a political one. And if the journalist chooses to delve into the motives of terrorists – to take another example – is this to be reported as fact or as commentary?

We shall argue that genres of reporting, including the genres of reporting fact, have hegemonic overtones, much more subtle than those involved in accepting or resisting censorship. It is obvious by now that any telling involves making choices, adopting perspectives, and constructing narratives. It is less obvious that these choices themselves carry latent messages.

Take, for example, the way in which the Israeli press reported on Yassir Arafat's occasional announcements about his commitment to *jihad* (Islam's call for a holy war on Jerusalem), at the time in which he was conducting negotiations and signing agreements with Israel. Any of these reports may well have put an end to the talks. But press framings played down the threat (keeping it in the inside pages); Arafat was somewhat condescendingly reprimanded, but excused and understood. Belittling Arafat's double-talk constructed him as a less than equal opponent, and, more important, protected the government peace policy.

Ways of telling signal not only whose words should not be taken seriously, but also who is taken for granted as a credible source. Those routinely chosen are thereby given status. The same holds true for the decision to report a military action as a struggle between equals or unequals, or as success or failure.

Our aim, then, is to point out some of the mechanisms of hegemonic reporting in the framing of news of the conflict. In order to do so we move from what journalists tell us about their work to the texts that they produce, positioning ourselves as interpreters of these texts. In this role we open ourselves to the critique that our own interpretation is subject to the same rules that we posit. It is one possible meta-framing, made from *our* point of view, of the journalistic frames. Our advantage may be that we are less dependent on pleasing clients or employers, and we make a conscious effort to position ourselves from the journalists' point of view, and yet necessarily remain outsiders.

We start by reminding ourselves what democracy requires of journalists, and point out why the enactment of this model is particularly problematic (technically and psychologically) in times of war or in a security crisis. We go on to illustrate and elaborate this dilemma by analyzing a case study of press and television coverage of a terrorist attack on the shores of Israel. This case is chosen as it seems fitting as an illustration of how the press acted out of its watchdog role in favor of a hegemonic one. Rather than point to structural weaknesses of the system, it chose to celebrate the successful outcome of an event, not its near-failure. As such it is a missed opportunity. Proceeding from the chronology of the event to the characteristics of its framing, we show (1) how the different elements of coverage add up to a hegemonic representation, (2) how powerful framing can be, and (3) how "reading between the lines" (without having additional sources of information) may produce an alternative reading which turns the story upside down. We then explain how journalists should not be blamed as cynically assisting the political establishment to cover up its failings. Instead, we propose to see them as involved participants who can hardly help not acting as professional observers.

JOURNALISM AND THE PUBLIC'S RIGHT NOT TO KNOW

The expectation that journalists should provide the public with more information than the political institutions are ready to disclose is not easy at the best of times. Ideally, the role of journalism in a democratic society is to serve the citizens' right to know, by contributing an independent voice to public debate, one which is not motivated by the interest of the ruling elites to survive in power (Molotch and Lester, 1974). Having access to information and interpretation which do not depend on government sources is supposed to give citizens a better chance to perform their role in an enlightened manner. Whereas until recently the voice of journalists was supposed to be that of a distanced professional, with privileged access to the truth, journalists are now thought to act more as involved participants speaking for themselves in the public debate (Alexander, 1981; Dewey, 1954; Hallin, 1991; Katz, 1989).[1] Continuous dependence on government as the main source for information (and the need to keep on good terms, that goes with it), on the one hand, and on the wishes of the public, as their clients, on the other hand, makes it difficult for journalists to provide an independent voice.

The recent "participant" model may even be more problematic than the "professional" model, as in endorsing involvement it may posit journalists dangerously closer to hegemony. Involvement, as it were, is difficult to separate from giving expression to prevalent establishment concerns, or to public sentiments, which, in their turn, may be cultivated by the establishment. Involved journalists may inadvertently legitimate – sometimes celebrate – these sentiments.

Voicing opposition is particularly difficult, of course, in times of war or crises of national security. Even the most conservative norms should be dissatisfied with a journalism that speaks only in the voice of establishments. In a security crisis it is often crucial for the public to know not only how its government is functioning but how to take action for survival. Yet the annals are full of examples of how societies might have fared better if journalists had sought out informed opposition – their own or that of other experts – to question an establishment position (e.g. Diamond, 1975; Lipstadt, 1986).

journalistic
involvement
forming the media tool

Thus, during the Gulf War, as mentioned above, Israeli journalists never questioned the army's directives for civilian defense, even though it became clear during SCUD attacks that people were being misdirected to use "sealed rooms" rather than conventional shelters which offered greater protection. The establishment did not change its mind, perhaps because conventional shelters were not equally available to all. The journalists did not change their minds, perhaps because they were deeply committed to serving the national morale and prided themselves on reinforcing national unity (Katz, 1992).

Short of war itself there is also the gray area of everyday government operations in which Israeli journalists are not alone in being torn between collaborating with the government, army, or police "in the interest of security," and their professional conscience. Professionalism requires journalists to question assumptions behind issues such as selling arms to the Contras or investing in the USA's "Star Wars" program, and laying them on the table for public discussion. But, as we have seen time and again in events such as the Vietnam War, the Bay of Pigs invasion, or the Irangate affair, politicians only too easily convince journalists not to debate decisions which were in fact motivated by narrow political interests or by a particular point of view. In allowing the establishment to extend the definition of national crisis to such cases, the press risks positioning itself in the role of government or army spokesperson and misses out on its watchdog role just when a multiplicity of voices is most needed.

To make matters worse, there is evidence to suggest that in such cases the Israeli public is not unique in its inclination to prefer not to know. As Hallin (1985) tells us, the American public too is not at all eager to know what has gone wrong, or might go wrong, on security matters. But if one accepts the definition of journalists' role either as a public serving profession or as contributing to the makings of an active public, journalists' fear of isolation should not take the upper hand. As professionals, journalists are charged with diagnosing social problems, regardless of the "patient's" reticence, because they are permitted to know better what serves the public good in the long run (Katz, 1989). By expressing alternative views of reality, they may combat what in times of high-riding national consensus becomes a natural slide down a spiral of silence.

It should be emphasized that we are not arguing for the existence of an objective reality to be reported "as is" or even for professional neutrality. Rather, we want to propose that professional norms imply that among the different possible versions of the story journalists should prefer the anti-establishment version – i.e. that journalists should read oppositionally (Hall, 1985) – because such a reading, more than others, serves the public's right to know. Opposition, of course, entails restatement of a situation that problematizes the official version.

Terrorists on the Nitzanim beach – sequence of events

A case study of the broadcast and press coverage of a near-miss terrorist attack in Israel is illustrative. Rather than addressing the blatant problem that the attack represented, the press coverage served mainly to increase the aura of government and army. We begin by presenting a chronicle of the events of May 1990 at Nitzanim beach, extracted from what was repeatedly told by the various media. Granted that an unbiased report is not possible even at the hand of researchers, we regard the chronicle as relatively unobtrusive. Following Hayden White (1980), the chronicle is an attempt to impose on events as little as possible of the formal coherence and closure of plot that a historical – and, it may be added, a journalistic – account does by definition. We believe that this summary would enlist high agreement among the various tellers. It will be used here as a hanger for various interpretations (Fish, 1980).

> 30 May, 1990, 06.45: The Jewish holiday of *Shavuot*, a non-work day. A speedboat, with five Palestinian terrorists on board, having run out of petrol, was discovered by Israeli Navy radar, 20 kilometers off the shore, north of Tel-Aviv. By 07.15 they surrendered to a Dabbur navy boat and informed their captors that another boat was on its way to carry out a dramatic raid on a beach in Israel.
>
> 09.30: The second speedboat approaches the Nitzanim beach, south of Tel-Aviv, with a Dabbur unsuccessfully chasing it, and an army reconnaissance plane above it. The boat manages to get to the shore and eleven terrorists disembark and run east toward the sand dunes, 500 meters south of the crowded beach.
>
> 09.35: Two cobra helicopters arrive, and four terrorists are killed by their fire.
>
> Approximately 10.45: A police force arrives and evacuates the beach.
>
> 11.00: Anti-terrorist units of the army and police arrive and overpower the seven remaining terrorists. Police stations are flooded by telephone calls in which worried citizens, exposed to widespread rumors, summon the police to capture (imaginary) terrorists. Public anxiety is exacerbated by police and army road blocks on main junctions around the country.
>
> 15.00: First broadcast report of the army spokesman on national radio announcing the successful termination of the incident.

The key questions from the journalists' point of view

From this moment and for the next few days this was the lead story on television and in the newspapers. According to our understanding of the role of journalism, one might have expected the reporting to focus on the key questions arising out of the event:

1 Given that there was two-and-a-half hours' notice, why did the army not succeed in capturing the terrorists at sea, before they landed on the beach?
2 Should not the beaches have been evacuated immediately, packed as they were with holiday bathers?
3 Where were the reconnaissance planes and the helicopters, which are supposed to be best at identifying and hitting targets at sea, and where were the ground forces to defend the coastline – the popular beaches, at least?
4 Why did the army delay the reporting of the incident for three hours, denying the bathers the right to know that their lives may be at risk?
5 Would an earlier public announcement have reduced the exaggerated rumors and the traffic jams created by holiday travelers who might have stayed home, and made the road blocks more effective if the terrorists had got beyond the beach?

It is surely the role of journalism to raise such issues. Doing so would have pointed to a number of possible failures in the functioning of the security forces, and might have created external pressure on the system to draw the relevant lessons. In a case which ends successfully, it is too easy to avert criticism, even self-criticism.

A "test" case

The Nitzanim case provides an unusual opportunity to "test" the hypothesis that, in a security crisis, journalists prefer to celebrate the establishment (in this case, the army) uncritically, rather than to criticize it. Typically, source control limits access to such critical information and not every journalist can be turned into an "investigative reporter." In the present case, however, the fact that hundreds of people were witnesses to the incident, and thousands were indirectly affected, meant that journalists had independent sources of information which could have provided a basis for critical reporting.

Moreover, in this case the government itself was over-zealous in supplying detailed information. The heroic rhetoric should have aroused suspicion, and the internal contradictions should have been recognized as a cover-up for inefficient action. For the government, the attack provided a good opportunity to restore the image of Israel as a victim of continuous violence and to counter its new image of a repressive power, which has dominated press and television coverage since the beginning of the intifada.

Finally, the incident was unequivocal enough in the sense that the failures of the army were blatant, and there was no need to protect an ongoing operation (as the event was over before it was made public), so that the journalists' reluctance to speak with an independent voice cannot easily be excused. On the contrary, in such a case the relevant crisis is the *next* incident, which some journalistic criticism might help avert.

Journalists did not take a critical stance, however. Instead, without actually lying or even omitting evidence, broadcasters and to a lesser extent the written press framed the event as a heroic victory rather than an operational failure which, by sheer luck, ended well. Journalists did so by leaving official reports unchallenged and by refusing to piece the evidence together to show that an oppositional interpretation was plausible. Instead, the official version was presented as an unproblematized account of the events.

In what follows, we propose to deconstruct the journalistic framing strategies[2] by detailed examination of the involvement over time from a more "open" to a "sealed" frame during the first phase of the television reporting, and by analysis of the use of rhetorical means of framing, such as fitting pictures to texts, and evoking metaphors, allusions, and connotations, that together construct a reality which may be taken for granted.

What's in a frame?

The major framing strategies are as follows: (1) directly quoting the army's announcements, with or without attribution; (2) focusing on the vital statistics of the perpetrators and the political implications of the event, thus distracting attention from failures on "our" side; (3) authenticating the hegemonic framing by introducing naive witnesses without interpreting their statements; (4) applying the myth of continued existential danger to Israel, which is familiar to all Jews, to this incident, in which the performance on both sides was unimpressive; and (5) applying the rhetoric of "miracles-for-Jews," by making the army's ostensible success into a miracle, not just luck, in spite of its failures. The coverage may have contributed to the boosting of public morale but sacrificed the opportunity for exposing faults in the system.

We shall elaborate on these points, one by one. First, however, we must repeat that our object is not to expose a servile press corps that is eagerly and wittingly following its master's voice. Notwithstanding that the different historical evolution of the press in the USA and Israel caused the Israeli press to be more protective of the establishment, we still believe that Israeli journalists share the norms and ethics of other Western democracies. As we have argued in the discussion of the (discerning) acceptance of censorship (in chapter 4), rather than suspect government cooption, we maintain that journalists, like the rest of us, breath a sigh of relief when a happy ending emerges from ominous threats, and cannot easily forego the frame of celebration in favor of a frame of accident or scandal. In the present instance the mood called for a "conquest story" (Dayan and Katz, 1993), which not only bolsters the overall frame and allows the press to share in the glory, but also distracts the attention of writers and readers from the watchdog role. The rhetorical elements in the conquest story frame are bound to push out critical elements.

ANALYSIS OF THE FRAMING STRATEGIES

Prioritizing the army's version of the event, in terms of time and space

Trying out the frame: afternoon

A victory story calls, first of all, for a word from the victor. At five o'clock in the evening, the first television report interrupted normal programs with a festive announcement which repeated the army spokesman's radio announcement made two hours earlier:

> Good evening and a good holiday. The IDF and the police today foiled an invasion attempt of terrorists along the country's shores, from the Gaash region north of Herzlia down to Nitzanim, north of Ashkelon. Four terrorists were killed and twelve terrorists were captured. There are no casualties on our side, neither among the security forces nor among the citizens.

In this first telling, the seeds are sown for the selection and organization of elements of a victory story that, as the evening broadcasts continue, combine into a foolproof plot, complete with a formal coherence and a social–political message:

1 The opening greeting indicates that the army managed to preserve a happy holiday for the country.
2 The verb "foiled" implies an active management of the invasion by the collaborative action of the two security branches, the IDF and the police.
3 "Along the country's shores from ... to ..." gives the impression that a whole series of attacks between the two extreme points of Gaash and Nitzanim were foiled.

Although it could be argued that in this first report the perceived need to reassure the population about its safety was legitimately given the upper hand, the next bulletin could be expected to expose some of the cracks in the official version. The initial framing, however, only takes another step toward formal and ideological closure as the evening proceeds.

Filling the frame: early evening

Appearing next on the screen, in the early evening, is General Shomron, Israel's Chief of Staff, in a press conference initiated by the IDF, where he reports his version of the event in a special interruption of regular programs.

In inviting this type of direct free speech, the reporter and editor relinquish all control over their source (Roeh and Nir, 1991). The incident is thus endowed with an aura of a media event, a celebration around which the nation unites in another victory over its enemies. The actual news event was already over; new technical details were added, serving the purpose of Israelis congratulating themselves on "how we did it." The embarrassing questions of the news reporters that highlighted the weak points in the report were edited out (as discussed later).

Only the night owls who happened to watch television at 1 a.m. had a glimpse of the accident and scandal elements lurking behind the celebration advertised by the army and the Public Broadcasting system (Molotch and Lester, 1974). At that hour the editor allowed some critical questions to remain (directed to the Chief of Staff during his press conference) – such as, Why were the beaches not evacuated when the threat became real? The Chief of Staff, recounting the story as a chronicle delivered in the present tense, makes the following statements:[3]

1 When the system detects a force approaching *we put all systems into action.*
2 *When a navy boat* approaches *the* (terrorist) *boat north of Tel-Aviv, they* (the terrorists) *surrender.*
3 *At the same time*, a navy boat and a reconnaissance plane identify, *at the same time*, a boat south of Tel-Aviv moving fast toward the shore. The naval boat also shoots at it (but) it succeeds, a very fast boat, to land on the shore, with a reconnaissance plane above the terrorists, identifying them, counting them, telling exactly where they are.
4 *In a few minutes* our force arrives, an airborne force, which stops this force on the spot, and does not allow it to move away from the shore. It is already evident at this stage that they cannot proceed.
5 And, *of course, our forces, ground forces, start arriving* in vehicles and in helicopters.
6 *On all the beaches we made it possible* for the citizens of the State of Israel *to continue to enjoy the holiday, to suntan, and swim in the sea*, confident that we are capable of *providing good protection.*

The report of the Chief of Staff glosses over the fact that there was a two-hour gap between the discovery of the first boat and the landing of the second. Note the expressions "we put all systems into action" and acted to overwhelm the two boats "at the same time."

Celebrating the frame – prime time

The key question which should have been raised by the press is What was done during this time? Why was the second boat discovered so late? Why was it not apprehended before it landed? Why was only a reconnaissance plane in the air when it approached the beach? Why were there no ground forces on the spot to meet them? Instead, the main evening news at nine o'clock in effect adopted the Chief of Staff's framing unquestioningly. The "headlines" were as follows:

> Good evening. An attempted mass terrorist attack was foiled today by a combined action of the security forces – the IDF and the police – at sea, in the air and on land. Sixteen terrorists tried to penetrate the shores of the State of Israel by fast boats, armed with various massive weaponry. Four terrorists were killed by the security forces and twelve were caught and taken prisoner. *It was a successful action which prevented a tragedy on the holiday.*

As can be seen, this opening wholeheartedly embraces the Chief of Staff's frame, adding its own praise in conclusion. This opening makes explicit what the initial report only implied: glorification of what has become "the *combined* action of the security forces." This theme gathers momentum by contrasting it with the magnitude of planned destruction ("mass attack") and the operational potential ("various massive weaponry") of the attackers. The opening statement then goes on to promise an extended coverage in the main body of the news, with reports from "the field," filmed by "five of our crews" and concludes with the moral of the story: it is thanks to the security forces that the peaceful holiday did not turn into a national disaster.

Unlike cases such as the Gulf War in which journalists had no easily available way of challenging official army sources, as the targets were mostly out of reach, and the witnesses on the spot were only on the enemy's side, here the nagging questions emerge from comparing General Shomron's own account with information from any of the hundreds of witnesses to the event. It is the editor who has chosen to ignore them, be it for reasons of routine reporting of security events, in which one relies on official sources, or in order to join in the celebration of unity rather than play a critical role. Thus, the Chief of Staff's attempt to overlook the many obvious faults in the management of the response is further smoothed over in the almost festive opening of the main evening news, which provides a television story of immediate reaction, perfect coordination, and total control.

Of course, major significance should be attributed to the opening of the newscast since it functions as the most important element in the hierarchy of the elements which constitute the frame. According to the narrative conventions of the news the opening message encapsulates the details of the plot to follow, and often offers an implicit moral.

The next morning in the newspapers

The next morning, the headlines in the two most popular papers chose the same frame, almost repeating the television headlines: "A mass massacre was foiled," announces *Maariv*, and *Yediot Aharonot* echoes with "The target: A massacre in the heart of Tel-Aviv." Even when there is a hint of criticism, in a few less-certain headlines, the newspapers prefer to quote an army source rather than speak in their own voice, when indicating that the operation may have been "only a partial success," or in stating in a subhead that "In the IDF, investigation will continue today to discover...."[4] Thus, the paper obediently trusts the army with criticizing its own failure.

As we have stated at the outset, a careful reading of the press provides enough material to turn the framing upside down. Thus, in one of the smaller items, headlined by the indisputable fact that the sea cannot be closed off, one can read that "he [General Shomron] could not explain how [in spite of the army's continual preparedness] the terrorist boat managed to land." A critical reframing of the report would certainly have found this more relevant for a headline.

Contextualizing the event by moving the spotlight from the tactical (failure) to the strategic

The latent function of a large number of reports concerned with the attack is to distract attention from the event itself and to reinforce the official framing. Thus, television provides an abundance of detailed information about the vital statistics of the terrorists, the politics of terrorist organizations, equipment, etc., as well as visual demonstrations of "our" strength. These strategic concerns also constitute the main content of the newspaper coverage in the following days. Other background themes included analyses of the political implications the attack may have for talks with the PLO and for relations with the USA, general information on the Palestinian terrorist organizations and their capabilities at sea, and assessments of the extent of Libyan involvement in recent terrorist actions – all demonstrating the continued threat to the state by the terrorist organizations.

Although journalists are often criticized for lack of contextualizing, the broad military and political coverage of the enemy's side serves to frame the event in congratulatory terms, supporting army actions and government policies. The incident becomes an occasion to expose the true face of the PLO which has proved once again that it cannot be a partner for a dialogue with the USA. This theme appears in the next two days in newspaper headlines such as "The US: If the PLO is responsible we will draw conclusions" and "Arafat knew about the attack"; and on television, in reports about condemnations and protests from various sources, such as the Egyptian ambassador, the American State Department, American congressmen, etc., who are all obliged to condemn terrorist acts.

It also serves to show what the Israeli army is up against – "the terrorists have sophisticated means", "the boats in the terrorists' hands are among the most reliable in the world" – thus arguing either that their capture was a complicated affair or, alternatively, explaining why they cannot always be caught.

Background distraction may also be seen in the abundance of visual material in the newspapers. The front page is occupied by photographs and charts which show a massive presence of "our" army in the air, at sea, and on land – fully in charge, having overcome the terrorists. Soldiers on the beach, jeeps, command-cars, radios, helicopters, captured terrorists, bodies of dead terrorists, the deserted boat – all these ignore the fact that when the terrorists landed there was no army present to stop them. A casual insight into what the operation actually looked like emerges from a newspaper story, hidden in the corner of a page entitled "The radio reporter wanted to rest on the Nitzanim beach" – where the reporter proudly tells how his wireless phone was borrowed for communication among the Chief of Staff, the Head of the Command, and their forces in the field.

Authenticating the hegemonic framing by introducing "naive" witnesses, and by ignoring their critical potential

Interviewing witnesses in the field is a way to get to the "real" event. For viewers and readers the story of someone who "has been there" receives higher status in terms of truth-value than those of politicians or journalists who are suspected of having axes to grind. For journalists, interviewing a witness may serve as an elegant and safe way to raise difficult questions concerning the official line. This is not the case here. Although the accounts of the witnesses on the beach expose problems in the army's story, they are recounted in such a way that the problems are ignored and the official version is authenticated, even strengthened.

Authenticating the frame: the rhetoric of eyewitnesses

A good case in point is the story of Deddi Shemer, a member of Kibbutz Nitzanim, and manager of the beach. Shemer describes on television how, when he saw a boat heading toward the beach with a pursuing Dabbur shooting at its tail, he felt that this might be "an unpleasant event." Thereupon, he walked over to the lifeguard and instructed him to evacuate the beach by "announcing quietly to the bathers that there is a suspicion of a terrorist event." According to him there were between 800–1,000 bathers present. "When the fire became more intensive," he continues, "I told Motti, the lifeguard, to evacuate the bathers from the northern beach as well."

Shemer's story exposes a grave army failure, but viewers were not prompted to learn from it that there was no warning of the imminent attack, no army forces on the beach. Shemer had to decide by himself what to do with hundreds of unprotected bathers, in spite of the fact that the army had learned about the danger two and a half hours earlier. The framing of the story does not make this point. Authenticated by attribution to a nonexistent eyewitness, one newspaper carries Shemer's story under a title, "The boat raced towards the beach, a Dabbur at its tail, its machine guns spitting fire." This heading focuses attention on the drama of the chase and on the army as the imminent victor. Shemer's latent criticism appears, in small letters, only half way down the report, which ends with another victory of the military, this time that of the ground forces.

The celebration frame, to which the beach manager himself contributes, both on television and in the press, implies that Shemer operated *as part* of the security forces rather than taking over in their absence. And, true to the frame, when the television reporters return to the beach the next day, in order to show how life returns to normal, Shemer and his team are there to celebrate the army's success with a toast to the victory.

Another eyewitness who could have threatened the celebration is a Kibbutz member, holiday fishing with friends 20 meters from where the terrorists landed. While according to the Chief of Staff the terrorists were neutralized by forces from sea, air, and ground at the moment of landing, this interview shows them unrestrained and free to murder the four fishermen as well as other bathers. But again the reporter prefers to ignore the subversive meaning and goes on to tell the human interest story of the Kibbutznik with a son in the Israeli Naval Commando, who assumes the terrorists are "our" boys and that his son might be among them.

A fisherman eyewitness was chosen to end the central Nitzanim item on the television news. His role was to reinforce the evaluation of the event by the army and television reporters. In his opening words the interviewer repeats the army's evaluation of the action as successful, adding "That was also the conclusion of the fisherman we met on the beach." This evaluation, however, is nowhere to be found in the interviewee's own words. It reminds one of the naive radio reporter-cum-eyewitness who came to the beach on holiday and found himself lending a radio phone to the Chief of Staff. His story, too, contributed to the frame of cooperation rather than opposition. The reporter's excitement at becoming part of the action overcame any professional criticism which would have left him emotionally isolated from the collective victory.

Authenticating the frame: in the eye of a home video camera

The most dramatic oppositional version of the story on television appeared not in words but in the eye of a video camera. It belonged to a bather who, having planned to photograph his children, caught sight of the boat approaching the crowded beach. Instead of employing the film to demonstrate the lack of army presence and the ominous danger to the bathers, Israel Television's military correspondent used the film only to describe the dramatic chase – "The Dabbur follows the boat" – adding (a statement for which there is no evidence in the picture) "It [the Dabbur] closes the gap." He then explained that uncertainty as to the identity of the boat prevented the Dabbur from hitting the attackers directly. In contradiction to the accepted cliché, according to which one picture is worth a thousand words, this shows that, at least when passing by on the television screen, pictures do not own an independent voice and it is the privilege of the words to fixate meaning (Barthes, 1975). The same thing may be said of the power of verbal framing in the case of the home video in the Los Angeles Rodney King affair.

Resorting to the myth of continued existential danger to Israel

In general, the reporting of terrorist attacks in the Israeli media is loaded with connotations of the ever-present danger to the existence of the Jewish state, which still tends to perceive itself as living with the immediate danger of extermination (Nossek, 1994). This is reflected even in the presentation of an event like the attack on Nitzanim as an existential danger to the state. The bombardment of background information on the terrorist organizations (which distracts from the failure on "our" side) also has the function of framing the event as an existential threat by evoking, in the collective memory, the long chain of hostile acts in the history of Israel and of the Jewish people. Constituting the incident as another link in this chain increases dependence on the army and the government and reduces the journalist's degree of freedom in criticizing the establishment.

On television, Prime Minister Shamir thanks "the guardians of Israel who were at their posts *once again, as on many former occasions,* and overpowered the terrorists." Connotation of the existential danger can also be found, for instance, in the press headlines of the morning after which remind Israelis that a "mass massacre" was foiled. The readers are made aware of what might have happened "if ... " by a front-page headline of Muamar Gaddafi, the Lybian leader, declaring: "Gaddafi, responsible for the action: 'Palestine will turn into the graveyard of the Jews.'" The accompanying photograph shows the Lybian's happy smile, with the caption: "And Gaddafi laughs." Detailed quoting of terrorist organization leader Abbu el-Abbass discloses that the attack carried the code name "Jerusalem," was intended to shatter the holiest symbol of the state, and "is part of the policy to continue the military struggle against Israel."

Additional information about the attack includes the threatening discovery that the terrorists acquired chemical and bacteriological weapons – a clear allusion to the Nazi means of "final solution" – and had already tried them on chosen victims. Moreover, under the title "And now also chemical warfare" there is a quote from the terrorists: "We are going to [fight] to the end," making the chemical danger seem imminent. Only a close reading of the item itself shows that it is a story about life in the terrorist camp of Abbu Nidal in Lebanon, which bears no relation to the Nitzanim incident but is incorporated in the general context of the terrorists' determination to inflict total destruction on Israel. Fighting "to the end" turns out to be the standard oath taken by the camp trainees. All these general stories about terrorist routines and designs create the feeling of a stifling ring tightening around Israel's neck.

Turning a miracle for the army into another miracle for the Jews

In reporting the first moves of the terrorists after landing – mainly the fact that they did not attempt to shoot at the bathers on the beach – press reporters make extensive use of the term "miracle." The labeling of near-disasters as miracles draws on a long line of near-disasters in Jewish history from which the Jews were saved (by divine power, of course) miraculously, at the last moment, such as the story of the escape from Egypt and the story of Queen Esther, both of which have been remembered and celebrated ever since. The redemption at Nitzanim refers backwards in the scrutiny it provided to the ongoing celebration of the Shavuot holiday, which might have been turned into mourning.

Describing the happy end as a miracle has critical implications for the functioning of the army. If things were under control, why is a miracle needed? Interestingly, television coverage stays away from this label, but the press accepts the idea that a grave disaster was avoided "only by miracle." But the miracle is not external, it is the army's own action even if, in the words of General Shomron, "luck also has to be assisted."

"Miracles" may also reflect on the poor performance of the terrorists themselves – their running out of fuel, their decision not to attack after having landed (turning eastward toward the sand dunes rather than in the direction of the crowded beach). But such criticism would not be compatible with the victory frame, which demands that the enemy be given equal status.

Through our own "oppositional reading" of a complete corpus of television and press reports we have attempted to demonstrate why the victory frame was preferred to more critical frames and how the choice of frame determines the rhetorical techniques through which an operational failure is constructed as a story of success. We have given attention to what questions were answered in the television and press stories but no less to what was left unanswered, from the point of view of journalistic responsibility.

Our deconstruction of the journalistic story may be considered an exercise in the kind of media literacy that might be taught to readers and viewers in order to make salient the ways in which attention is selectively focused on certain elements in the story once a frame has been determined. Crucial evidence – visual and verbal – for diametrically opposed framings actually exists in the journalists' texts but, as we have demonstrated, the structuring of the final product directs attention elsewhere. We have shown the process through which a frame is fashioned in time and how the degrees of freedom available to journalists are increasingly constricted with each additional reporting: the first public announcement of the incident was still open; the next, decisive, stage was the decision to relinquish the journalistic role and leave the stage to the Chief of Staff who addressed Israelis directly and exclusively in a special interruption of ordinary programs. Here, the definitive version of the story was framed. From the moment the journalists accepted the victory frame, the type of coverage – abstaining from overt criticism, postponing the questions and answers from General Shomron's press conference to 1 a.m., editing eyewitness interviews to brush out army failures, evaluating the army action as "successful," etc. – all followed from that choice.

Our claim is that an oppositional, critical story can be unraveled, especially from the newspaper reports. Newspaper texts are more open to aberrant meanings, be it because of differences in the type of institutional control, in the amount of space, or in the definition of its target audience. Moreover, unlike the disappearing text of television, the written texts permit a second reading, which – as Barthes has discovered for fiction – is free of the desire to know the end of the story and invites reflection on its construction.

To discover such criticism in the press – when the press does not intend it – also takes hard work. First, the only criticism labeled as such is army criticism of itself, which is mostly formulated in positive terms such as "partial success" rather than failure. Second, criticism is hidden in the body of reports which start and end in praise, and the most explicit criticism is to be found in the weekend reviews which have the least news value. Third, when criticism is expressed it is not voiced by the reporters but is delegated to eyewitnesses. Fourth, unlike elements which fall within the frame, critical remarks which do not fit are not elaborated on. Thus, no headline was given to the fact that the first terrorist boat was caught only because it ran out of fuel, and the consequences of this are not followed through. Reading the story in the press one also refocuses some of the ambiguous sentences in the television interview of the Dabbur officer.

What emerges from this analysis is that critical thinking is required for journalists to fulfill their roles as independent voices, and for viewers to fulfill their roles as citizens. What Molotch and Lester (1974) consider types of coverage which fit different events are frames which may all be applied to the *same* event. In our case Nitzanim was reported only from the official angle; it could just as easily have been reported as an accident or even as a scandal if journalists had been more strict in performance of their watchdog role, and better prepared to risk their popularity, their relations with their sources, and their own sense of "what a relief."

Cultural analysis may explain how journalistic reporting of a local terrorist attack evokes the frames used for reporting national security crises. Thus, in Israeli culture, Tuchman's (1978) "what a story" would be typified by stories of successful or unsuccessful enemy attacks against a civilian population, as representations of the existential threat to the collectivity. These stories may be (1) either "spot" or "developing" stories and (2) stories that lead either to victory (overcoming the enemy, minimal casualties; Entebbe, for example) or end in disaster (as in the Yom Kippur War, to name a worst case). In this context the framing of the Nitzanim case may be understood as a cultural expression of national relief as experienced by the journalists in perceiving the event as (1) having ended and (2) with "our" victory. The "happy end" after hours of anxious uncertainty and a fear of having to report a disaster creates a catharsis which overwhelms the professional demand to be distanced and critical.

Last, in terms of democratic theory, the centrality of criticism in the role of journalists may be derived from confronting two contradictory conceptions of the nature of the public. The first, more optimistic one, in the spirit of Dewey (1954), is based on the belief that if the political establishment supplies the public with sufficient information, an intelligent public discussion will ensue. In this view politicians are "experts" whose job is to investigate all the relevant facts; the public is enlightened and willing to judge the implications of the data for the general good. A more pessimistic, less naive concept of the public (and of government) assumes not only that the government's interest is to present only the information that suits itself but that the public is not so keen on knowing the facts. On issues that involve anxiety or moral unease, information is all the more essential to the existence and the character of society. This model puts more responsibility on the press and calls for a detached, professional journalist who, like other professionals, often has to reveal unpleasant information, even to clients who don't want to hear it. At its worst, journalists, in fact, take over public debate.

Chapter 6

Us and them

Israeli and US coverage of the intifada and the Gulf War

If a relatively unthreatening event, such as the failed terrorist attack on the shores of Nitzanim, is the cause of such journalistic euphoria, it is easy to assume that an actual war would evoke a much stronger sense of protective identification and commitment to one's own society. On the other hand, it could be argued that the sheer length of time, and with it the bulk of incidents, heroes, villains, and victims, and a certain "getting used to," may lead to the construction of a less simplistic picture of reality, with shades other than black and white. A third possibility to be considered is whether the kind of participation in society and its fate is culturally specific to Israeli journalists, or whether it is also to be found in other Western societies with more sophisticated or professionally socialized press cultures.

This chapter, then, examines the workings of hegemony in the framing of war. It does so by analyzing the portrayal of two recent Middle Eastern conflicts – the Gulf War and the intifada – on the television screens of "our" side of the conflict. The two wars are suitable for examination because both are limited wars, and both may be examined from the point of view of a democratic press. Clearly, when one's society is fighting for survival, distinguishing between the journalistic role and the citizen role becomes exceedingly difficult. The coverage of "our" war therefore should reflect this strain, especially in wars that threaten a society's very existence. Lesser wars, however, are equally "ours." Wars – such as Vietnam, Lebanon, the intifada, and the Gulf – where lives (but not societies) were at stake are probably more suitable cases for examining the constraints at work on journalistic practices.

In spite of the barrage of various "small" local wars which have occupied the screens of global television news during the last years, the Gulf War and the intifada remain distinct in public memory. The Gulf War was proof that the US had not lost its capacity to plunge into massive military involvement in a far-off country, and a symbol of the two contradictory lessons learned by the US in World War II and in Vietnam. The intifada is not forgotten because it triggered the active phase of the Israeli–Palestinian peace process, as well as the organized terrorism which is attempting to destroy it. The two wars continue to occupy media scholars as well. Americans are asking how could the political and military establishment exercise total control over the normally independent American journalists, leading them by the nose, as it were (Gerbner, 1992; Hallin and Gitlin, 1993). Israelis, to a lesser extent, are starting to wonder about the reasons for the sparse reporting on the intifada in the Israeli press and television.

In what follows, we broaden the scope of our inquiry to look at the constraints of hegemony in the framing of conflict. Specifically, we show how war is framed differently when it is "ours" compared to how it is framed when it is somebody else's. Continuing our analysis of journalistic texts (as was done in chapter 5) we expand in two directions: this chapter moves from the detailed micro-analysis of the journalistic framing of one particular "closed" event, told from "our" point of view, to the cumulative macro-means of the framing of a continuous war; and from focusing only on Israeli journalism to the comparative analysis of press coverage in two societies.

The intifada is "our" war for Israeli television and "their" war for US television. The Gulf War was "our" war for US television, and "their" war for Israeli television (notwithstanding Israel's role as a recipient of some of the violence unleashed by that war).

The argument for hegemonic coverage is made by analyzing the parallel framing mechanisms which operate in the coverage of our war, in the representation of the other side versus our own side, also pointing to the striking difference in the *salience* of the coverage of the two wars on the respective "home" television screens (in spite of the parallel, relatively marginal, place they occupied in both countries).

THE WARS: COMPARABLE OR NOT?

Though at first sight the intifada and the Gulf War could not appear to be more different, in some respects these two conflicts are clearly comparable. First, and most obviously, they took place in the same geographical region. Also, in both cases the balance of power was heavily weighted to one side from the start. Moreover, it was possible in both cases that the weaker side could "win," as in Vietnam, but only if the more powerful side were reluctant to make use of its full military potential, for whatever reasons.

Of course, on the other hand, in almost every other respect these are very different wars. While the Gulf War was short and clearly bounded in time, the intifada was a prolonged conflict, which fizzled out, but whose end is uncertain to this day. The Gulf crisis had a clear beginning, middle, and end, and thus a clear linear chronology; the intifada has less clearly defined beginnings and consisted of a sequence of repetitive but semi-random incidents lacking in visible progression. Because of its linearity, the story of the Gulf War could be told as a classical narrative that begins with a disruption, continues with a hero who appears on the scene in order to restore the balance, and ends with a "new world order." The story of the intifada lacks these narrative elements.

Moreover, whereas the Gulf War was perhaps the first true high-tech war in history, the intifada is as low-tech a war as could be in our time. The first was fought with computers and smart bombs and only standby soldiers; the second has been waged with stones and knives on one side, and clubs and rifles on the other. In the Gulf War armies confronted armies; in the intifada an army confronted a sometimes-organized civilian uprising. The different character of the intifada is illustrated by the fact that the label "war" was used by both sides only intermittently (Schiff and Yaari, 1990).

Comparison of the two events, therefore, hinges not on their intrinsic similarity but rather on the analytic usefulness of the exercise. As suggested above, it offers a provocative case study for the comparative analysis of journalistic performance in the coverage of military conflicts, ours versus theirs.

THE COVERAGE: COMPARABLE OR NOT?

For Israeli television, the intifada was "our" war, even if the label "war" is debated not only by the contestants but also within each side. Among Israelis, the hawks rejected the label on ideological grounds because of their insistence that the territories are (and should remain) under Israeli jurisdiction, and, accordingly, that any conflict with the Palestinians is an internal revolt; yet hawks found the war label useful as a justification for military action. Israeli doves accepted the label ideologically because they regarded the intifada as a conflict between two nations; but operationally they found the confrontation between army and civilians disconcerting. The army itself vacillated between the two positions. While the debate continues after the intifada has officially ended, the daily skirmishes between uniformed Israeli army units and Palestinian crowds that characterized the intifada appeared visually as armed confrontations and not simply as public disorders.

American television covered the intifada as an observer of "their" war. In spite of the generally friendly relationship between the United States and Israel, and the partisan American Jewish constituency hungry for news of the conflict, the intifada on American television took its place alongside a number of seething conflicts in other parts of the world.

The Gulf War, on the other hand, was "our" war for the American media, but not quite "theirs" for the Israelis. Israeli television could not remain outside the conflict as an observer the way US television did for the intifada, because the war implicated Israel, both directly and indirectly. Nevertheless, Israeli television kept its distance not only because of the ambiguity of Israel's involvement but out of necessity, because it was dependent – as was the rest of the world – on American media coverage. Of course, Israeli television covered the damage done by Iraqi Scud missiles in the Tel-Aviv area, as well as the debate on whether Israel should acquiesce in the non-combatant role defined for it by the Gulf War allies. Visually, however, Israelis saw their (the American) war in the CNN version (i.e. as "our" war), supplemented by Hebrew translation and commentary.

Our analysis was initially conceptualized as a two-by-two comparison, in which we compare American and Israeli coverage of the intifada as theirs and ours, as well as coverage in both countries of the Gulf War as ours and theirs. However, because of the dependency of Israeli television on CNN's coverage of the Gulf War, we cannot claim that Israeli coverage of the Gulf was either ours or theirs; rather, it contained elements of both.

The data for analyzing the coverage of the intifada consist of a representative sample of the intifada news items broadcast on what was at the time Israel's only television channel and on samples of the coverage by two American networks (ABC and NBC) in the first two years of the intifada. The items cover six two-week periods between December 1987 and December 1989.

Analysis of the coverage of the Gulf War was based on all items from American television (mostly CNN) that were broadcast during the extended nightly news broadcasts on Israeli television. The coverage of the intifada was formally coded; coding categories were initially developed through pre-testing a small subsample. Two coders applied the formal instrument. All episodes of violence in the occupied territories were first sorted into whether they were *studio announcements* only or filmed items. The anchors' announcements, or introductions to filmed items, were coded for the type of *contextualization* provided (broad/event specific), for the terms used for *identification* of victims and aggressors (names, demographics, roles), and for a mention of the cumulative *death toll*. The *logo* for each filmed item (three frames used on Israeli television and three on American television) was coded, as well as time and locus, and type of incident. In the filmed items, *accounts* given of the incident – identity of spokespersons, attribution of cause, possible outcomes, evaluations – were coded. *Spokespersons* were coded as interviewed in the field or in the studio, and categorized as soldiers or officers (on the Israeli side), intifada activists and leaders (on the Palestinian side), witnesses, victims, and politicians (on both sides). "Technical" military terms used to describe army activity were also coded. The Gulf War coverage, more massive and less tightly structured, was systematically scanned for comparisons with intifada coverage.

The difference in the screen-space that the two wars occupied in the media agenda, both in the United States and Israel, is of course the first element of framing that is encountered in the study. As mentioned above, the Gulf War dominated the media agenda in both countries while the intifada did not dominate the news agenda even in Israel. This contributes to the validity of the comparative exercise. If one asks why our war received maximum coverage in one case and lesser coverage in the other, when neither constituted a mortal threat to the society, the answer may be, as will be shown later, that television coverage reflected establishment attitudes in both countries. In the United States this meant allowing the stories of Operation Desert Shield and then Desert Storm to dominate the news, while in Israel it meant playing down the intifada. Journalists' assessment of the different dramatic potential of the two stories may also provide a partial explanation. But the presidential construction of the Gulf War on media, as a highly dramatic story, as well as the establishment down-playing of the story potential of the intifada, are in themselves a major element of the hegemonic framing.

FRAMING MECHANISMS

The constraints that our wars place on broadcast journalism are reflected in a series of framing mechanisms that highlight the overall process. We call these framing mechanisms *excising*, *sanitizing*, *equalizing*, *personalizing*, *demonizing*, and *contextualizing*.

Excising

The Gulf War has become a classic example of how a conflict can be portrayed without showing the other side. In the months preceding the war, television viewers saw stories about refugees streaming from Iraq and Kuwait, Europeans held hostage by Iraq, and food shortages in Baghdad. But when the battle started, the other side faded away, except for Saddam Hussein as its evil symbol. The enemy was excised. Only burning oil wells and oil-soaked birds represented the enemy's actions, with some very rare exceptions, the most dramatic of which was the story of the bombed shelter/command post and, later, during the land war, the surrender of Iraqi soldiers.

It is true, of course, that in most wars access to the other side is usually difficult or denied altogether. But, as was noticed by a number of media scholars (Hallin and Gitlin, 1993) in this war it seems that there was little interest in showing the other side. Rather, as will be argued below, an effort was made to sanitize the war by minimizing its human cost, not only to our side but to theirs. Indeed, the exception illustrates this conclusion. The work of Peter Arnet, the sole American broadcasting presence in Iraq during the war, was greeted with a government and public outcry when he showed even a glimpse of the kind of consequences (that might have been expected) of the bombing of the bunker/shelter. Weren't our broadcasters performing a service for the enemy?

Israeli coverage of the intifada shows a similar tendency to ignore or obscure the other side. Coverage of the action on Israeli television focused on Israeli soldiers. In some of the stories the camera followed army units on patrol or on search operations to locate intifada activists.

On some occasions, soldiers were shown walking through ghost towns, with the local population watching them from behind shuttered windows. These items were unlikely to involve confrontations; indeed, they were sometimes inspired by the army, to show that it was operating by the rules. Television cameras were often banned if skirmishes got out of hand. When Palestinians were in the picture, they were seen from a distance, as a rioting mob. Such crowd scenes were sometimes juxtaposed with the "quiet after the storm" of deserted streets, strewn with stones and still-smoldering tires. Like the burning Iraqi oil wells, these were evidence of the absent enemy. Almost invariably, interviews were conducted only with Israeli soldiers and officers, whereas Palestinian spokespersons and participants gradually disappeared from the Israeli screen as the intifada continued.

In contrast, American television coverage of the intifada showed both sides. But there was a clear tendency to foreground the Palestinians, rather than the Israelis. American television did not excise either side, but the effort to present a "balanced" coverage, as well as the need to tell a human story with which viewers may identify, resulted in greater attention being paid to the weaker side. After a skirmish, the reporter went home with the Palestinians, not the Israelis. The cumulative toll of Palestinian deaths and injuries was a characteristic opening line in many American items on the intifada. By comparison, the Iraqi death toll remained untold.

Sanitizing

Coverage of the two wars tended to avoid showing blood, theirs as well as ours. Coverage of the Gulf War is famous for sanitizing the technology of destruction, as if it were a computer game, devoid of human consequences (Katz, 1992). Damage to military installations was graphically described, even if the count of successful hits varied wildly from one day to the next (and the overall count was drastically lowered after the war was over). But victims remained unmentioned. On the few occasions when they were shown – as in the destruction of the Baghdad bomb shelter – one was reminded that war kills people and that neither the administration nor the viewers wanted to know this. While the powers that be, as well as many members of the public, faulted CNN for being on the scene, others began to ask whether they were viewing the tip of the iceberg of destruction that was willfully concealed. It will be recalled that the US President's wish to enter the war had to overcome the collective memory of the trauma of Vietnam. Everybody – administration, viewers, and newspeople – seemed to feel more comfortable with a press conference about survival bombings than with blood and bodies, or even "sanitized" body counts.

Israeli television's coverage of the intifada also minimized the portrayal of human damage to the Palestinians. The cumulative death toll was only occasionally reported, and visuals of Palestinian deaths and injuries were only rarely shown. Of course, television cameras were rarely on the spot at the right moment, and the Palestinians themselves made haste to bury their dead, but the fact remains that American television showed much more destruction and many more victims in its coverage of the intifada. American coverage, as we have said, constantly provided a cumulative account of the toll of victims. Israeli coverage not only avoided cumulative numbers but also apparently understated the daily toll by limiting the headline count to the casualties confirmed by official army sources, only later acknowledging the possibility of additional victims as reported by Palestinian sources.

The Israeli understating – typically limited to studio announcing – of the almost daily Palestinian casualties contrasted with the very different reporting that characterized stories concerning our (Israeli) casualties who, at the time of the intifada, were, by comparison, very few. A considerable amount of air time and attention was given to these cases, in terms of the placement of the stories, in detailing the incidents, in the search for sources, and in the attempt to provide a thick description relating to all possible aspects of the event, including attention to the fact that the Israeli victims were more likely to be civilians than soldiers.

The ratio of victims on our side to victims on their side was probably quite similar in the two wars. It is also not surprising to note that the American coverage of the Gulf War was similar to the Israeli pattern of sanitizing the blood on their side and paying considerable attention to the losses on our side. While it is probably true under circumstances of very low casualties on our side, one might speculate that if American casualties were higher there could have been pressure to sanitize the human losses on both sides, in order to contain adverse public reaction. This might also be true of the Israeli case, were the Israeli casualties higher. One remembers Lebanon as well as Vietnam.

Equalizing

Keeping the enemy out of sight, and even minimizing the enemy losses, does not mean that the enemy is thereby trivialized. The opposite is true: had Israeli viewers been exposed to the close-ups of the Palestinian boys without their threatening head-dress, or had American viewers witnessed in close-up the faces of the Iraqi soldiers in hiding, we might have been struck by the power inequality between us and them. The absence of such close-up portrayals works to mystify and attribute greater threatening power to the other side, with the result of equalizing the protagonists' military threat and legitimizing the mobilization of forces by the "superpower" (United States, Israel) to overcome the opponent. This process of equalizing serves the media in their quest for balance (in that both sides are equally "empowered") and for a good story. The drama of contest – if such a frame is chosen – obviously requires matched sides.⟩

In the Gulf War, as Katz (1992) has noted, the process was evident in the effort of the US administration – adopted wholeheartedly by American television – to frame the war in terms of World War II, complete with Hitler, Munich, allies, etc., thus rendering Saddam Hussein and the Iraqi army far more formidable than even the (failed) intelligence services could have predicted. Iraq's arsenal of atomic, biological, and chemical weapons was also much touted (and still is) even after the country's pitiful military performance was over.[1] The latent function of building up the enemy, of course, is to contribute to make the victory all the more glorious.

In the intifada, too, there is no doubt who is the stronger party, especially when one side (at least during the first years of the intifada) was fighting a war of civil resistance. Equalizing in this case was manifested in the use – by army commanders as well as by reporters – of the language of military operations. Visually, Israeli television tended to portray small groups of fully equipped soldiers in confrontation with huge, impassioned crowds, armed with rocks "that can kill" (indeed they did).

Equalizing goes on, too, when Israel points out that its soldiers must obey restraining rules that, in effect, handicapped them and prevented them from exerting their potential superiority, even while Palestinians did not play by the rules. This "Gulliver" image also served to remind us of Vietnam, and even of the Gulf War, where it was obvious to all that the use of nuclear weapons by the United States was unthinkable. American television refused to equalize in the case of the intifada, suggesting that an obvious framing of the combatant sides in "their" war is empathizing with the weaker side. Rather than choose the frame of contest, or even the Gulliver frame, American television preferred the David–Goliath frame, that is, of a victim in distress rising against a powerful oppressor. Use of this metaphor is ironic, of course, in that it reverses the traditional image, which by now seems remote, of the State of Israel as David overcoming the Arab Goliath (Elizur and Katz, 1990).

Personalizing

Apart from excising the other side so that it is symbolized but not seen, there is another more subtle form of framing that characterizes coverage of our wars. This might be called *personalizing*, in that the humanity of the two sides is asymmetrically portrayed. Even intra-society conflicts encounter this bias as, for example, when unpopular protest groups, such as urban rioters, strikers, anti-Vietnam demonstrators, or Israeli settlers who oppose the IDF's retreat from the West Bank, are shown from "within the bounds of official discourse" (Hallin, 1986, p. 12; Iyengar, 1991; Wolfsfeld, in press) or as disrupting public order (Glasgow University Media Group, 1976). The more protest groups are deprived of voice by television, the more they resort to violence to call attention to themselves. But voiceless violence only works against them. Hallin (1986) attributes this to a populism that takes account of the consensual rallying to establishment in crisis, expressed particularly in issues of national security.

The intifada evoked populist feelings of this kind among Israelis *vis-à-vis* the Palestinian violence. Feeding these sentiments, unwittingly perhaps, Israeli television tended to excise not only Palestinian rioters but also the minority of Jewish Israelis who protested on behalf of a different way of handling the Palestinian problem. When the Palestinian side of the intifada was portrayed, there was a strong thrust towards depersonalization. While both sides may have been seen in action, Israel television showed only "our" side with regard to spokespersons – high-ranking army officers, professional in appearance, slow-speaking (connoting, perhaps, solidity of character and authority of role), in neat uniform – who offered their (what seemed like) well-considered version of what had happened, either from the field or from the studio.

The human suffering of both sides is also treated very differently. Israeli intifada victims had names and ages. They were shown in the hospital and in the cemetery. The manner of their death or injury was reported in detail, with eyewitnesses, families, neighbors, officials, and doctors supplying human and professional angles to the tragedy. For example, on August 3, 1989, Israeli television carried a report concerning the death of an Israeli child, killed inadvertently by Israeli soldiers on intifada patrol. The report consisted of six separate stories detailing the circumstances of the incident. The first was a construction of the event by the television reporter, complete with the position of the car in which the child was traveling with his father, the road block, and the army patrol; in the second, the Commander-in-Chief in "Judea and Samaria" further elaborated on the military angle; the third story presented an eyewitness view of the incident; the fourth featured the family's neighbors in the West Bank settlement, who told about the daily hazards of commuting in the occupied territories; in the fifth, the head of the local council defended the behavior of the dead child's father (who opened fire on the army patrol, mistaking it for a Palestinian ambush); the sixth story covered the child's funeral. The entire report lasted eight and a half minutes.

Immediately following these stories came a 15-second announcement of the death of two Palestinians and the injury of one, the first death being that of an eight-year-old child from the village of Shatti, killed "under circumstances as yet unclarified"; the second was "another death reported by Arab sources" of a 23-year-old man killed during a demonstration and a seven-year-old child who suffered a head injury. No names were given. As a matter of reporting routine, Palestinian victims, during the intifada, were announced by the studio presenter. Sometimes their names and ages were reported, and at other times they remained nameless "boys" (*nearim*) or "young men" (*tzeirim*) from a certain town or village. The manner of their death often remained ambiguous; they were usually "hit by fire" of unspecified (Israeli army) origin (Roeh and Nir, 1990). When the information was attributed to a Palestinian (not an Israeli) source, the fact of the death itself was routinely reported as unconfirmed, and the story typically concluded with the ritual ending, "The IDF are investigating the circumstances of the incident." The results of these investigations were almost never reported on television.

It is interesting to note that at the early stages of the intifada, television coverage was more balanced, that depersonalization of the Palestinians emerged only as part of the routinization of intifada news when the violence had not yet been defined as an uprising or a "war," that Palestinian faces and voices did appear on Israeli television. Typically, these were not political leaders but bystanders or third parties, such as storekeepers who were victimized by the changing circumstances. In its early weeks, then, before the frame of "us and them" had become dominant, Palestinians were allowed to have a face within the frame of "innocent victims." In an early incident, for example, an Arab headmaster was permitted to deny the police version that "his boys" were involved. Although the television story was based on the police version, the headmaster's story implied that there could be other versions, and that a respectable section of the population was implicated against its will. In another early item, on the Gaza strip, a Palestinian was shown complaining about the indifference of Israeli television to Palestinian suffering, citing television's gross understatement of the incident in which four Palestinians died as a result of an accident involving an Israeli truck. He blamed the Israeli media for asymmetrical coverage of Jewish and Palestinian victims, and argued – perhaps prophetically – that Israeli public opinion was therefore indifferent to the suffering of Palestinians.

Coverage of the intifada war by American television tended to personalize the Palestinians. Following a violent incident, American television correspondents would show the human consequences on the Palestinian side. Personalization took the form of hospitalized victims, bereaved families, village graveyards, groups of relatives and friends inspecting the ruins of their demolished houses, and the like. American television correspondents sought out "village notables" and eyewitnesses for comment. They also looked for intifada activists in an effort to present the conflict from their own point of view. Among these young Palestinians, speaking for themselves, there was an eleven-year-old child, shown throwing rocks, who says on camera, "We are not afraid to die, we are very strong. Schulz [former US Secretary of State] will never help us, he helps the Israelis." When it was further reported that this child's friend was killed "shortly after his declaration," the fear for the boy we (the viewers) had just met became urgent. The item concluded with a picture of the village dignitaries and others coming to express their condolences to the family of the now familiar dead boy.

On the other hand, American television treatment of the Gulf War follows the "our" war principle: it personalizes only our side. While the Iraqis were nowhere in sight, Americans were everywhere: soldiers in tearful farewell scenes; personnel in the desert of Saudi Arabia; families conducting split-screen conversations between desert and home; pilots expressing emotion before and after their mission. Our side was not only the central presence; it was *the only* side personalized and, therefore, given a human face.

Another aspect of the process of personalization can be seen in the treatment of the American versus the Iraqi leadership. The US President, the Secretary of Defense, the Chairman of the Joint Chiefs of Staff and, of course, General Schwartzkopf, appeared regularly to inform, explain, and reassure. The personalization of the war through General Schwartzkopf made it almost appear as if it was his war, and certainly turned him into the war's most dominant television personality. The only human presence on the other side was Saddam Hussein. But his was a demonic presence.

Demonizing

Coverage of the Gulf War was pervaded by the language of good and evil (Alexander, 1981). On the whole, American television adopted the President's rhetoric of a just war, fought on moral grounds, in which Saddam Hussein was cast in the role of a present-day Hitler, constituting a threat to the whole of the free world. This was more than the familiar "good guy" standing up to the outlaw; it was a crusade against evil, to which an outraged President had rallied the support of traditional allies and potential victims. Debate over American motives and over the wisdom of the President's determination to declare war resumed after the war, with added new doubts about the over-compliance of the media (Zelizer, 1991). But on the whole, the predominant emphasis was on the demonic machinations of the Iraqi leader and the horrible weapons and elite units he was holding in reserve for some mythical showdown. The other side of this American equation, of course, is the moral triumph credited to ourselves and our leaders – excepting the inglorious failure to support the Kurdish uprising – that was expressed in postwar parades and celebrations of heroes.

Caught in the lenses of Israeli television cameras, the Palestinian fighters were demonized, too. Unlike Saddam Hussein, they were demonized without being personalized; indeed, as already noted, depersonalization facilitates demonization. Instead of young boys we saw shadowy figures with covered faces, whose attempts to hide their identities from the Israeli soldiers contributed to their demonization. They appeared in disorganized, hysterical crowds, brandishing flags, shouting abuse, hurling rocks, lighting fires, writing on walls; this is all we knew about them. In reporting the clashes, Israeli television referred to the Palestinian fighters as "face covered," "lawbreakers," and "Molotov cocktail throwers."

Adopting the perspective of the underdog in their war, American television did to Israeli soldiers what Israeli television did to the Palestinians. For American viewers, the soldiers were threatening figures, heavily armed with clubs and guns, their faces hidden under steel helmets; like the Palestinians on Israeli television, they acquired the identity of the roles assigned to them in the television conflict. Thus, in one report of ABC correspondent Dean Reynold, the demonic Israeli stays on the dark side of an item informing Americans that some Palestinians arrested in a skirmish were "rounded up, roughed up, and in this case spat upon." On another occasion, commenting on the visual of a Palestinian boy being dragged by the scruff of his neck, Reynolds says that "this is the daily symbol of the victor among the vanquished," for the benefit of any viewers who needed verbal explication.

Contextualizing

Our evidence suggests that more context is provided for "their" wars than for "our" wars. This is less paradoxical than it sounds if one takes account of the reasonable expectation that viewers of our wars are familiar with conflicts and are supplying their own contexts (Gamson, 1992; Gamson and Modigliani, 1989). Certainly after the fighting begins, concern about the overall context virtually disappears, as everybody is occupied with the details of daily violence; close-ups do not leave room for the larger questions. Their wars, on the other hand, make no intuitive sense without the provision of context (which is why third-party reportage is so vulnerable to criticism by the opposing sides).

There is a further reason, however, for the minimizing of context in our wars. At least in the case of the intifada, Israeli television preferred to present the conflict episodically, as if each fresh outbreak were a surprise or an accident, and the worst might well have been over. This may be seen as one of the ways reporting serves the hegemonic need for preserving the sense that the government has not lost control (Edelman, 1988). As long as the frame of a series of disconnected incidents, with victims mostly on the other side, can be maintained, the intifada does not have to be perceived as threatening, and does not demand any outstanding action.

Presenting the fighting itself in almost ritualistic terms is another aspect of context avoidance, as if group dynamics were an explanation in itself, or as if conflict is something that may be understood as a game.

American television, by contrast, presented the intifada as the culmination of years of frustration under the occupation, as the continuation of centuries of violent struggles between Arabs and Jews, and as a continuously accumulating and escalating conflict whose end is nowhere in sight. Even though they were briefer than Israeli news items, American items were striving to contextualize the events by connecting incidents that were ostensibly separated in space and time, for example, by locating the incidents on a map.

Most of the context of the American coverage of our war in the Gulf was provided in advance, during the debate over whether to take action and how to mobilize the support of others. As the conflict escalated, American television moved from the geopolitical context toward the immediacy of a frame of a military confrontation. Even the occupation of Kuwait and Saddam Hussein's human rights violations receded as the dynamics of the conflict – the ultimatums, the mobilization, the logistics, the diplomacy, the preparations for the land war, etc. – took center stage.

While contextualization deals with the extent to which action comes wrapped in historic and political frames, it remains to be noted that the content of the framing – even when there is ostensibly little of it – varies in the different contexts of our and their wars. During the first months of the intifada, the logo used by Israeli television in its intifada stories labeled outbreaks of violence as "law and order" violations. Later, the logo changed to delineating the problem zone, "Judea and Samaria," inadvertently, perhaps, stating that "it is ours," and, at the same time, squashing any doubts the items may evoke about this. Calling it by the geographical region also avoids the specific terms of uprising or violence.

At the outset incidents were treated mainly as accidents. As time went on a broader context was occasionally provided, relating the incident to issues of economic and demographic frustrations. Israeli television avoided the preferred context of the American coverage, namely, the Palestinian struggle for national liberation. The logos in American television denoting this ideological frame were variations on the theme of a *kaffia*-clad Palestinian opposing the Israeli flag. While American coverage showed sympathy, and certainly understanding, for the Palestinians' need to call attention to their plight, Israeli television journalists did not display similar attitudes, perhaps for fear of being accused both by their government and their audience of wittingly allowing themselves to be used by the insurrection.

American framing of the Gulf War suggests that our wars can either be minimized as police actions or inflated as a mortal threat. The Gulf War, like the intifada, offered both possibilities. In the American case, the media choice replicated that of the political leadership in maximizing the Iraqi threat, just as Israeli television followed its country's leadership in minimizing theirs. Coverage of their war is free from such constraints.

It is not surprising, therefore, to discover that journalists' treatment of their own country's wars is different from the way they handle other people's wars. The "surprise," if any, lies, rather, in observing how reluctant journalists are to acknowledge this dilemma, not only by conceding the multiple and diverse pressures under which they operate, but also by acknowledging their instinctive loyalty to their own side over the attachment to the ideology of their profession. This emerged publicly when, in the aftermath of the war, American journalists indulged in a series of public introspection and "soul searching" exercises, the brunt of which were complaints about the control and manipulation of the media by the military authorities, concluding that because of these constraints the media "lost the war." In hindsight these read more like attempts to shift responsibility to the "other side" (the military) rather than honest acknowledgment of the role they played during the conflict. Similar outcries, albeit couched somewhat differently, were often voiced by Israeli journalists when they complained about the difficulties under which they labored in covering the intifada. Perhaps a more honest response would be to acknowledge that the luxury of the detachment offered by the ideology of "objectivity," "neutrality," and "balance" – even if it had not been discredited by a growing number of journalists and scholars as operating in the service of hegemony – is reserved for reporting other people's troubles, not one's own.

Chapter 7

Dominant readings and doomed resistance

A case study of one family's attempts to decode oppositionally

Having shown that media framings of the conflict construct an "us and them," in which the other side is depersonalized, dehumanized, sometimes demonized, does it not follow that television viewers would see the conflict through the same frame? The obvious answer is that if the viewers' view of the conflict is mediated by television they should see the conflict through an even more tightly sealed frame than do the journalists. As most viewers see the conflict only on their living-room screen they are indeed captives of the powerful, redundant, pictures constructed for them, and do not have a chance to face the more open and ambiguous reality which journalists and camerapersons face in the field.

Of course, this description of captive audiences is slightly over-dramatized, if one keeps in mind that media frames are ones which, to a great extent, circulate in the culture, and as such *reflect* peoples' perceptions as much as affect them. As mentioned in the previous chapters, journalists are very much part of their community, and "us and them" representations of the conflict are not only dictated by technical and institutional practices, but also by what the journalists assume to be acceptable to their audience.

Moreover, people's understandings of the conflict, let alone the kind of possible solutions they envisage, vary considerably. This of course depends partly on the extent of the availability of alternative channels for viewing; some viewers also read newspapers, others may have first-hand experience in the field, as participants, observers, sometimes victims; still others are, or have been, acquainted with people from the other camp (in other contexts). But even first-hand experience is no guarantee against carrying contradictory views, and there are differences in the framing of the conflict among people who see it only on their small screens.

The next three chapters are devoted to our attempt to understand the relationship between framings of the conflict by media and viewers, focusing on the ways in which viewers' frames are constrained by hegemonic media frames, on the variety of attempts to decode oppositionally, and on the reasons why these attempts are often doomed to failure.

Stated differently, we examine the decoding of the Arab–Israeli conflict in order to study the central question in the study of communication, that of the relationship between texts and audiences, a question which, in itself, is part of the larger issue of media effects, and how to study them. Recent developments in the field of media scholarship – with its new focus on cultural studies and social identity – modify the notion of powerful ("hypodermic") effects, and, with it, the idea that these effects may be measured by straightforward quantitative analysis of media content or of audience survey data. Where we stand now (since sometime in the early 1980s) is to acknowledge that there are no direct, linear effects, as both producers and receivers are part of the same culture, and mutually echo one another (Carey, 1989), that viewers' interpretations are made in and constrained by the social context in which they live, and that both media discourse and people's discourse should be studied in terms of how reality is constructed, what is constituted as self-evident, and which power structures are served thereby.

Our focus moves then to observing how hegemonic elements in the culture circulate in the process of negotiation between television texts and viewers in particular settings. To begin with, we analyze the reception of television news within one family, in order to identify some of the mechanisms through which journalistic framings of the conflict are recycled, debated, amended, sometimes ideologically restructured, through the processes of reception.

Specifically, this chapter presents a case study in which members of one family, viewing the evening news on Israel Television, interact among themselves and with the news. Inasmuch as journalistic texts were analyzed within the specific historical, cultural, and professional context of their production, decodings are also analyzed as texts, expressed within their social and familial context. In line with critical emphases (Hall, 1985; Liebes and Katz, 1993; Morley, 1980), the contextual understanding of both encoding and decoding is essential for going beyond the individualistic, historical study of reception.

We will show how conversation within a family while viewing the evening news provides insights into how hegemonic processes work – where potential opposition emerges, and how it is weighed, debated, and often squashed. Particularly insightful is the sometimes contradictory interface between viewers' life worlds and personal experience on the one hand, and the picture of the conflict on screen on the other. In the competition between various pictures of the reality of the conflict, the accepted way is to prioritize the news, giving it the status of the definitive picture of what the world looks like. This of course is quite different from the way *journalists* define the reality of news, which is more in the direction of "flagging" worrying signs of deviant trends. On the viewers' side this acceptance of news as reality makes for the naturalization of conflict. And yet family members, so we shall see, conduct heated arguments, activate various mechanisms of interpretation, and are generally much more active than gratificationists, let alone hegemonic theorists, would have credited. What is new in our understanding of the role of readers?

THE CONTEXT OF FAMILY VIEWING

Observation of news viewing within the family offers insights into the process of decoding as it is reflected in the interaction between parents and their children. Moreover, it allows for intercepting the processes of socialization *to* different styles of decoding and *via* different types of decoding. Considering the "laboratory" conditions that existed in Israel (until 1995), the situation of news viewing in the family living-room could serve as a focal point for observing the way family members decode the news so that it served their different, sometimes contradictory, outlooks. In an ethnographic study conducted for this purpose, within families of Israeli Arabs and Jews (see chapters 8 and 9), most of the Jewish families were found to be ideologically homogeneous, while others were in disagreement. The latter family-type offers clues to the ways television is drawn into the argument, particularly where ideologically divided parents make use of television in the socialization process.

Our case study presents one such divided family, where the parents disagree ideologically over the conflict. It is a family in which the younger generation has moved ideologically to the right of their parents (particularly the mother), a trend which was found to be dominant in Israeli society. The analysis shows how the hawkish family-father has no problem in decoding the news referentially, in a way that is compatible with his hard-line views, whereas the more dovish mother fails in her attempt to enlist television in her cause. We illustrate how the advocates of compromise need considerable sophistication in order to interpret the news in ways which are acceptable to them.

The case study also clarifies how the decoding of news in Israel, probably everywhere, cannot be separated from attitudes towards censorship and the credibility of television news. In other words, we argue that viewers' "meta-frame" – that is, what viewers think television *should* show, as compared with what it *is* showing – is related to viewers' decoding styles, as are different ideologies. We analyze both the substantive arguments and the tactics used throughout the discussion.

Analysis of the discussion shows that decoding television news is a hegemonic process in that "news" is mostly defined as reflecting the normal, only rarely as reflecting the deviant; in that common understanding is that news *should* represent the normal (even if it is thought not to do so); in that this definition serves only one of the two ideological outlooks, namely, the hawkish ideology; and in that, nevertheless, hawks criticize television representation of the conflict (and accordingly demand more censorship) more than do the doves, as their expectations from the reporting are clearer and more unequivocal than those of the doves.

The Dekels: a family profile

The Dekels (a fictitious name) are one of a subsample of families drawn from a survey of closed interviews with a representative sample of 400 Jewish families (parent and adolescent-child couples) in Jerusalem,[1] in which we studied patterns of news viewing (including family interaction about the news), attitudes toward the news media, and political outlooks.

A subsample of 52 of those families was observed while viewing the news, commenting on it, and responding as a group to several open-ended questions we addressed to them.[2] One of these families was the Dekel family, whom we visited at home, to join in their viewing of the evening news, and to record the subsequent family discussion, which we facilitated by occasional probing and by keeping the conversation to the news when it wandered off. Our aim was to simulate, albeit more intensively (Anderson and Meyer, 1988; Liebes and Katz, 1993), everyday conversations related to the news, of the sort that might transpire often.

The Dekels are second-generation Israelis of Syrian origin. Mr Dekel is a carpenter and Mrs Dekel is an elementary schoolteacher. They have two children – Amnon, who was at the time serving in the Israeli army, and 14-year-old Yaffa.

The Dekel family may represent what the survey showed to be a dominant pattern in Israeli society. According to this pattern, although "ideological reproduction" (of parents producing their political outlooks in their children) exists, hawkish parents stand a better chance of socializing children with a similar outlook to their own.[3] Accordingly, in the Dekel family, while Mrs Dekel is ready to compromise with the Palestinians, her daughters are not.

In terms of attitudes toward the news, Mr and Mrs Dekel belong to the group we called "deniers" – that is, people who believe the news is credible but nonetheless support censorship (Liebes and Ribak, 1991). The deniers – those who believe in the news but would prefer not to see it – are people who would rather see a positive image of "us" on the screen than worry about the check public exposure may exercise on the absolute power of the political institutions. Deniers believe that "on stage" it is important to present harmony – preferably "good news" – while the actual management of the affairs of the state goes on anyway, as it should, "behind the scenes."[4]

The Dekels: a family conversation

On the evening of our visit, at the time of the intifada, the conflict dominated the news agenda, as on most evenings. There was, however, no direct Palestinian–Israeli confrontation to be seen on the screen. Instead, the news resounded with the internal ramifications of the conflict in two contrasting trials of political extremists: one reported the conviction of an Israeli settler in the occupied territories for the murder of a Palestinian; the other concerned the continuation of a court case against a Jewish leftist newspaper team, accused of affiliation with a Palestinian terrorist organization. An item covering a ceremonial visit of the Knesset Committee for Internal Affairs to the Dome of the Rock, in the Arab part of Jerusalem, also implying a disruptive potential, represents the more consensual expression of attitudes toward the conflict in Israeli society.

PALESTINIANS ON TELEVISION NEWS ARE NOT REPRESENTATIVE: AN ATTEMPT TO READ OPPOSITIONALLY

The absence from the screen of violent incidents between Israeli soldiers or settlers and Palestinian uprisers was immediately remarked upon, at the end of the broadcast, by the greatly relieved mother: "That's already a good sign ... good news. ... " That Mrs Dekel feels she has to comment first on what was *absent* in the broadcast indicates that she measures what she sees in the light of a pre-existing scheme of expectations (Graber, 1984), provided no doubt by the daily menu of intifada news. Labeling the missing item as "good news" is also an expression of the mother's basic trust in the newsmakers, that is, she does not suspect them of omitting newsworthy incidents – editing out items potentially harmful for public morale, for example. Thus, in noting the absence of intifada clashes, Mrs Dekel seems to assume, the way most of us would, that if it was not on television it certainly did not happen. In other words, this would mean she is relating to the news as "real" (or "referential") rather than as "constructed" (Liebes and Katz, 1993).[5]

However, a little later in the conversation, after the first spontaneous expression of relief had been made, Mrs Dekel brings up two more possible reasons for the omission of the intifada, in what may be regarded as a less "naive," more sophisticated reading.[6] Her two remarks, which we classify as *constructional*, point to possible generic and institutional constraints in the construction of reality. The first recalls journalistic norms according to which once violent incidents have become routine (and provided the level of violence does not escalate they are no longer newsworthy). "They [journalists]," says Mrs Dekel, "got used to the situation ... they are not reporting much any more. ... " Her second explanation brings up the possibility of intervention of the political establishment in the workings of reporters: "Maybe it's because it is now forbidden to take photographs, that they banned journalists from there; perhaps that's the reason."

This remark poses two problems for our analytic model. First, why classify this second explanation as *constructional* and not as *ideological*? Our answer is that it implies external constraints imposed upon journalists by the power elites, and does not refer to an (inadvertent or advertent) ideological framing of the journalists themselves. Another possibility would be to split the *ideological* mode into manipulation by journalists, or manipulation by politicians (although the two are sometimes not easy to separate). Labeling political control as constructional also means that "constructional" is by no means a neutral category; in fact it may be considered an oppositional decoding *par excellence* if it is, indeed, meant as a criticism.

The second problem for the classification is the apparent contradiction between the immediate *real* "sigh-of-relief" remark (about "no intifada today") and the subsequent *constructional* ones. Are we faced with a naive or a sophisticated viewer? The answer is that our typology of readings relates to modes (or meta-frames), not to people. It is not at all unusual for referential and critical readings to be voiced by the same people. Different types of readings may be employed in the context of different "interpretative paradigms" (Wetherell and Potter, 1989) or "accounts" (Gilbert and Mulkay, 1984). The status of Jerusalem, for example, may change places dramatically when different identities come into play. In the context of "our historical right," when the identity of Jew and Israeli is activated, it is the most cherished dream, whereas in the context of daily life, when the identity of mother is activated, it is argued to be a dangerous alienating place. Various readings are seen, in this view, as strategic tools in the struggle to score points in the discussion, and not necessarily to express a consistent attitude.

Substantively, the two *constructional* reasons offered by Mrs Dekel for the lack of intifada stories resemble similar conclusions reached by media scholars (cf. Nir and Roeh, 1993; Roeh and Nir, 1990) and by political analysts in the press, and though they might have been triggered by the presence of an observer (Dahlgren, 1985), the potential was still there. Nevertheless, it should not be ignored that while media scholars would be damningly critical of both routinizing violence and censoring it, Mrs Dekel, judging from everything she says, did not think that an evening with no intifada was a bad idea either way. As a compromiser who believes that news represents reality she found it difficult to argue her case if that was what reality looks like.

Unlike her mother, teenage Yaffa is quite happy at this point to take television at face value, that is as *real*. "It [the intifada] may have calmed down," she suggests. But Mr Dekel discards the daily variations as insignificant, though still assuming a fit between the lack of coverage and the parameters of reality: "Not every marginal incident can be broadcast on the news. Does every little thing, like if they threw a stone, have to be put in the beginning of the newscast? Not everything can be reported."

Note how Mr Dekel adopts the anonymous, depersonalized "they," established (as we have seen) by television's framing, to identify the stone throwers. This vagueness of the generalized "they" is used not only to plead ignorance, or to deny contact (Van Dijk, 1987), but to deny the specificity of blame and to incriminate a collectivity.

The different readings revealed in the discourse of mother, daughter, and father about the missing intifada may also be examined in light of their different political outlooks and their attitudes to authority. Mr Dekel, who expresses his belief that what is shown should be strictly controlled, is not disturbed by *not* seeing what he believes *does* exist; Yaffa prefers to stick to a naive reading, which assumes the transparency of the news; Mrs Dekel emerges as the family's ambivalent viewer. She is relieved at not seeing the intifada which she finds emotionally stressful and ideologically problematic but, on second thought, she struggles against her own tendency to deny reality by doubting the truth of her own first reaction.

Continuing to commute between her original trust in journalists and her unease with what she sees, she is critical when considering intifada coverage on other evenings. Television, she protests, distorts reality by exaggerating Arab violence:

> It's not exactly like they are telling it; they [most viewers] think it's [like that] all the time.... Once when they were placing explosives in Jerusalem, people from Tel-Aviv and Natanya were saying "In Jerusalem? It's war there!"... So I don't know, but my feeling is that it's not so serious. They are just sensationalizing [inflating matters too much].

Interestingly, Mrs Dekel is worried about the influence of television news *on others*; whereas she can defend herself against television, she worries about the "third person effect" (Davison, 1983) that television may have. The argument of protecting other, more vulnerable, viewers is often employed by advocates of censorship, who have full confidence in their own resilience.

Thus, Mrs Dekel would not be affected, as she knows, from her own experience, that most Arabs are law-abiding, peaceful, and hardworking. Unfortunately, this silent majority never appears on television. Her point, as it appears in the family discussion, is to convince others (notably her daughter) that not all Arabs are as "bad" as they seem to be on television. Mrs Dekel, as it were, is trying to do no less than to fight against the "us and them" representation of the conflict.

> I think not all of them are terrorists or stone throwers, and not all of them burn tyres, and altogether they are human beings, people who want to live.... And they feel very uncomfortable. They work, these people, this family, and there are other families I know who work. They are feeling very uncomfortable in this situation. They have to get out and go to work, despite all the threats, and their children haven't been to school until now, and they want to live. And I believe them. I believe all those who say that

they would like to live with us. If there are some hotheads, it doesn't mean that they are all like that.

As is evident in this statement, Mrs Dekel is attempting the impossible. She is fighting television's stereotypes by juxtaposing them with another source of knowledge – her own personal encounters. Contrasting one's own experience with what is seen on the screen is one tactic employed by doves in their attempt to modify the black-and-white presentation of conflict.

As they seek compromise, doves have to assume that if in our camp some are good and some bad, the same must hold true for the other side. Mobilizing evidence from one's own experience as an illustration for this idea is a less analytic, more intuitive, way to make that point. It could be argued that this is trying to beat television at its own game (of personalizing processes and situations).

Mrs Dekel seems to attempt these tactics in spite of her own feeling that she is fighting a losing battle. This feeling of futility is evident in her confession, made soon after, that she had reached the point where she prefers to avoid television news altogether. The prospect of seeing only violent – "bad" – Arabs disturbed her so much that for some days she "hasn't actually sat and viewed *Mabat*" [television's evening news]. This last confession indicates that in spite of the professed concern about "third persons" Mrs Dekel feels vulnerable herself, perhaps about the possible dwindling of her resolve to fight television's stereotypes.

Mrs Dekel seems to agonize about the competition between the two types of "case studies," namely, television's framing of the intifada, and her own. The question she wonders about is which of the stories (her own or the news') can be made to look more representative of the conflict. She is discouraged because she believes that television has a better chance to win that one (in the eyes of others).

Another question which could be asked (but which Mrs Dekel does not entertain), is whether some criteria other than representativeness should be applied. Such criteria could be, for example, how relevant is the story to the conflict, or does the case serve as an indication, or warning signal, for future developments. Taking such a position would both save her own anti-us-and-them frame, and preserve the credibility of the news.

As it is, Mrs Dekel herself knows better but is aware that her husband and daughter are staunch believers, comfortable in arguing that television's framing of the other side *is* representative, that is, that the Arabs *are* violent. Perceiving the news as *real*, she fears, leads them to perceive the conflict as hopelessly insoluble, and as more extreme than it really is. This perception, in turn, she senses, would cause an escalation in the real-life conflict. Being an ideological dove motivates Mrs Dekel to wish that television would show the other in a variety of roles, not only in the role of enemy. But the acceptance that this is unrealistic – that is, that everyday roles of the enemy do not make news – brings her to support censorship. The second-best thing to showing the real, multidimensional, picture is to show less hostility.

TELEVISION'S FRAMING IS REAL: HEGEMONIC READINGS

Mrs Dekel's fears are justified as far as her daughter, Yaffa, is concerned. Yaffa believes that what she sees on television is all that is needed to know about reality. Her confidence that television represents the dominant reality is expressed in objective, social-scientific terms. When her mother reminds her of some Arab students they both know as "nice people," Yaffa exclaims that these students are an exception, not the rule. Mr Dekel, for his part, supports his daughter's hegemonic reading of television's representation of us and them.

> *Mother*   I've had Arab students, so I know...
> *Daughter*   OK, but that's an Arab? Ten percent are like that.
> *Interviewer*   And the rest?
> *D*   The rest – let them leave...
> *M*   Meanwhile every place I took you – I took her once to a friend, an Arab as well, in Jaffa, who studied with me...
> *D*   OK, I said ten percent!
> *Father*   She [daughter] hasn't lived with them, but what she said she gets from television. Isn't it enough that this is what people see on television?
> *D*   No!
> *F*   What, "no?"
> *D*   It's enough to see on television that they are killing our soldiers.

The discussion here centers on the extent to which television's representation of "them" is correct, and on the related question of the need – and the legitimacy – of alternative channels for knowing about the other side. Yaffa, concerned with representativeness, enlists numbers to make her argument about the television's view of Palestinians watertight. She avoids the stereotyped form of "they're OK but...," characterizing "apparent concessions" (Van Dijk, 1987), and escalates straight on to the next logical step, in claiming that *only* the minority (of Arabs) is "OK." Thus, television is given legitimacy, as if the rioters portrayed each day constitute the majority. Mr Dekel accepts this definition of the relationship between television and social reality, more precisely, he does not care about it. For him, no matter what has in fact happened, reality resides in the consensual framing of what is seen on the screen within "our" community. Adopting the notion that reality has moved into the television screen he asks, "Isn't it enough that this is what people see on television?" If this is where reality resides, other forms of witnessing or channels of knowledge become irrelevant.

Implicitly, the debate about the legitimacy or validity of alternative channels is a debate about two contrasting political outlooks. If the Arabs on the screen indeed represent 90 percent of the Arab population, there are grounds for Yaffa's demand that "they leave."[7] Since Palestinians on the screen are shown mostly in their role in the intifada, seeing them means that "they are killing our soldiers." Yaffa's adoption of television's reporting of the intifada as an all-engulfing view of "them" is particularly problematic as the Palestinian community includes Israeli Arabs (17 percent of the Israeli population), as well as the Palestinians in the occupied territories. Moreover, Jews and Arabs live on the same narrow piece of land, which, in effect, cannot be divided. Listening to Yaffa's reading of the news makes it apparent why her mother, who believes in compromise, thinks that television closes the option of relating to the other side as human.

It now becomes apparent that while Mr Dekel (see below) approves of censorship because he does not wish to expose moral deviance (or even moral norms?) in *"our" camp* to ourselves, or to the outside world, Mrs Dekel wishes that television would not focus on the "bad" images of *the other side*. She reasons that we can tolerate bad images of ourselves as we know all the good things about our own camp as well. We appear on television in roles which are not related to the conflict, and we are also familiar to ourselves off the screen.

"They," on the other hand, are generally not known to us off the screen, appear on the news only in adversarial roles, complementary to ours, and their other roles are absent. What we *know* to be the exception to the rule on our side may easily be conceived as *the rule* of the others, known to us only from the screen.

The argument about the authority of television's view of the Palestinians continues with Yaffa emphatically discarding her own and her mother's first-hand knowledge in favor of the reality she sees on screen, demonstrating how reality has moved into television:

Int   So you don't think like your mother?

D   No, no.

M   And Hani's parents?

D   Hani is something else.

M   Because you know them! You've got to know them!

Int   Hani?

M   This student whom we visited on the holidays and they came to see us here. And suddenly she said [recalling her daughter's reaction at the time] "Oh, mother, they are terribly nice, they don't look like Arabs at all."

D   No, it's enough to hear about them on television.

It is evident that Yaffa refuses to be confused by any evidence which might modify the image of the other on television. The news clearly reinforces, perhaps nourishes, her perception of the conflict. Mrs Dekel is eager to point out that television news leaves a lot outside its frame. There is a complex and complicated reality out there, where most of them are ordinary, not violent, and some of us *are* violent.

Having failed to convince her daughter that not all of them are bad, Mrs Dekel tries a new tactic. She moves to the parallel claim that not all of us are good, adding that group violence should be framed in an ideological context. Basic evidence is brought from violence she herself had suffered in encounters with ultra-orthodox Jews in Jerusalem:

> As I was saying, no Arab ever threw a stone at me, but some Jews did. On a *Shabbat* I got hit by a stone, on my car, and they threw a garbage bin at me, and they almost jumped at us; she's [Yaffa] my witness; here, just next to the house. I believe more in the Arabs than in the religious Jews, I am not afraid of them. I don't know, this is my opinion. In the morning I sit in the kitchen and I hear under this window, "shabbes!" and "pritzes!" ["shabat!" "whoring!"]; here, under this window lies the problematic Yam Suf street, and they [the orthodox] want to close it [to traffic on Saturdays]. If I got into my car I don't know what they would do to me. They would come in their tens and hundreds, and would anybody pay attention? So they arrest them and in the evening they let them go. On *Lag Ba'omer* [a holiday when bonfires are lit]...[a friend] told me that she went to see a bonfire in the center of town, not in Mea She'arim but closer to the center of town, and she said that the religious started a bonfire there, and burned the Israeli flag.

Beginning her argument with a demonstration from an incident she had experienced, in order to prove that Jews as individuals can also be violent, she then points to the ideological motivation. It is a violence directed against the State of Israel, to the existence of which these extremist-orthodox object. Their violence, she implies, is directly analogous to the Palestinian violence. Both should be seen in a political context, which is missing from the portrayal of the conflict on television news.

MAKING THE ARGUMENT OF PLURALISTIC IGNORANCE

At this point in the heated discussion Mr Dekel brings up the disreputable character of Rabbi Kahane, whose party was disqualified from elections by Israel's Supreme Court on grounds of anti-Arab racism.

The couple has a fierce argument about what Kahane represents. Mr Dekel starts off with what appears as a concern with normative self-presentation, which wears off when he comments on the rumor that a "left-wing professor" had proposed mounting a military attack on Jewish settlers in the West Bank. Mr Dekel counter-attacks the leftist intellectual with allegations usually directed towards Kahane:

Why isn't he [the professor] a racist? Why not him? He is against the settlers. And doesn't he even call himself a refined soul, a man of peace? What sort of a thing is this? They're allowed to say anything. If Kahane would say something like that, then he is a racist; let's get things straight around here: I don't support him and I don't say I am for him, but people say...

Mr Dekel here disclaims his own position ("I don't support"), having just presented Kahane as a victim of the leftist bias of intellectuals. He is then translating, or projecting, his views onto other people, "who say...."

The continuation of this dialogue offers an example of our contention that "genuine" attitudes, expressed under provocation, often hide behind tactical moves. It also shows the frailty of basic democratic norms, and how easily they may be shattered.

> *M* Don't you remember... that he escaped from the States? That he was a criminal there?
> *F* Right, I agree with you. I am not for him.
> *M* And you're inciting your son to be for him. Kahanist!
> *D* [laughs]
> *F* What do you mean, I incite him?
> *M* Kahane. A piece of madman. A criminal.
> *F* You know that there are many things that your leaders also agree with him about, but they can't allow themselves to adopt his opinions. And don't tell me! There are many people who are ready to adopt his opinions and they can't be implemented. So what, so I am for him.

The deep ideological rift between husband and wife, which is revealed here, explains what Mrs Dekel is worried about. Her fear is that television's us-and-them framing of the conflict could increase hatred, which would legitimate moving in the direction of extremist, "transferist" parties, like Kahane's. And she is seeing the beginnings in her own family.

Mr Dekel has now moved into attack, relabeling Kahane not as deviant but as a brave advocate of shared, but not yet declared, beliefs. In a cunning argument, practically an elaboration of the argument of pluralistic ignorance, Mr Dekel claims that most people hold two kinds of values – publicly proclaimed ones, employed for acceptable self-presentation, and unadmitted ones, employed for action. This allows him to admit that he is a supporter of Kahane.

Ironically, according to his dualist attitude to the democratic system (Liebes and Ribak, 1991), censorship of Kahane's undemocratic ideas is essential. Television, in this view, functions as the external facade of the society, and therefore should present the rules of the democratic game, while, at the same time, actions necessary for the operations of the state can proceed discreetly, according to another set of rules. Understandably, Mr

Dekel is certainly not concerned with the "true" representation of reality but only with showing what's best for us. Thus, there is no contradiction between his objection to Kahane's appearing on television, and admitting to sharing his views. While Kahane is by no means deviant, the norm which he advocates should not be shown by definition because it is unacceptable to others – namely, to decision-makers in the West, who are crucial to Israel's security (and who might also not object to the *doing* but only to the *showing* of actions such as transfer). Thus, television is demoted by Mr Dekel to a public-relations facade.

Mrs Dekel also argues for censoring Kahane but her reasons are very different. He should not be shown *because* he is deviant. She carries the same concern that she had about showing us and them in the intifada. She assumes that just as showing only intifada Arabs makes them all bad, letting Kahane, who is one of us, have the stage makes acceptable to us what should remain deviant. Moreover, the ground for legitimizing transfer has been prepared by the televised image of the "bad" other.

Thus, both Mr and Mrs Dekel have a theory of the "third person" effects of television, which makes them want some kind of censorship. Mr Dekel believes television, by publicizing possibly damaging information, can influence public opinion elsewhere in the West against us. Mrs Dekel, who believes in more powerful effects, thinks that exposure of our "dark side" may loosen the inhibitions of those of us who are yet restrained by the perceived legitimacy of their beliefs.

Decoding the news referentially is comfortable enough for Mr Dekel as far as the conflict between us and them is concerned. As a hawk he can capitalize on seeing almost only bad Arabs on the news. For Mrs Dekel the opposite is true. While more educated viewers with dovish positions oppose censorship (Liebes et al., 1991), Mrs Dekel favors it because she knows what the news would show, and has a problem with what she considers its unrepresentativeness. She worries then about viewers like her daughter who do not have other channels to learn about the other side, or who believe television more than their own experience.

A less simplistic understanding of the news would provide Mrs Dekel with a way of explaining television's "bias," as an alternative solution to censorship. Two types of explanations could be given for the particular character of the framing of conflict on television. One would relate to the intifada as protest movement within the society, the other would see it as war.

In the first case, Palestinian violence on the screen would characterize social and political protest rather than represent the large numbers of the inhabitants of the West Bank. Intifada rioters *should* then be regarded as the exception to the norm and the normal, which is their function on the news. In such a case, the Palestinians of personal experience would indeed be better representatives of social reality. Television is then relieved of the burden of having to be representative, and personal experience would count more in the discussion.

If, however, the intifada is regarded as civil war, as it was sometimes labeled on television, the rules of the us-and-them portrayal start operating to obliterate the humanity of the other side. Either way, the key to oppositional readings is understanding the rules of television's construction of conflict.

Likewise, television's presentation of Kahane may have been less threatening to Mrs Dekel had she entertained the possibility that the presentation of Kahane as deviant may boomerang against him, in functioning as a warning against his extreme rhetoric, and eventually mobilize the consensus against him. But this could of course not be guaranteed. Not only did her husband and daughter believe that showing Kahane would grant him legitimacy, legislators and political scientists are divided about this issue. And contrary to Lazarsfeld and Merton (1948), Alexander (1981) argues that publicizing deviance may work both ways.

Chapter 8

Socializing to dominant reading
How hawks and doves cope with conflict news and why the hawks find it easier

The struggle against the hegemony of television news by one brave mother, the heroine of chapter 7, was directed not only against the reality on screen but also its reception by her husband and her daughter in the living-room. The conversation of this one divided family reveals in some detail the everyday processes of viewers' negotiating with television news. With the insights gained from this micro-view we now enlarge our scope to explore how television's framing of the conflict is reflected and incorporated in the articulation of the two major ideological perspectives by 52 additional families.

In what follows, we shall show how television's us-and-them presentation of the intifada years (before the Oslo agreement was achieved) gave more comfort to hardline hawkish positions and made it harder for those who sought compromise. This was all the more significant prior to the communication explosion of the 1990s, when television news in Israel was positioned in the role of tribal campfire and could be regarded as the site for political socialization in the family. This centrality of news meant that television's hegemonic construction of the conflict privileged parents with hawkish ideologies in socializing their children to their ideological perspectives. Thus, television may have contributed to the advantage hawkish parents enjoyed in reproducing their political outlooks in their children, a finding which emerged from our survey of parent–children pairs. Insofar as most families watched the evening news regularly, television may have had a part in the move of the younger generation in Israel toward the political right.

Thus, the purpose of this chapter is to demonstrate how within the everyday routines of Western journalism, the framing of conflict in which "we" are involved favors non-compromising readings, and makes it easier for hardliners to speak up and argue their positions. We do this by first reiterating the conventions of news framings in general, and of the framing of conflict in particular, pointing out their likely bearing on viewers' framing of the intifada. We then turn to an examination of the actual discussions of the news within families, in order to point to the links between journalistic framings and people's perception of the intifada. In addition to arguing that conflict news involving them and us unwittingly reinforces hawkishness, we shall also argue that television news best serves those doves who understand how television news operates. We begin, therefore, with a more systematic review of the characteristics of television news (and Israel's news in particular), bearing in mind that we are interested in the different ways in which such news enters the family debate on all sides.

THE FRAMING OF CONFLICT BY TELEVISION NEWS

On the whole, there is considerable agreement among media researchers – sociologists, political scientists, and media scholars – about the attributes of television news, even if there is disagreement over the relative weight which *ought* to be assigned to commercial, organizational, and professional routines and practices and over whether these practices should be defined as hegemonic. (See, for example, Bennett, 1983; Edelman, 1988; Gans, 1980; Gitlin, 1980; Hall, 1985; Murdock, 1973; Paletz and Entman, 1981.)

Researchers agree, first of all, that Western journalism is a social warning system, exposing the exception rather than the rule, the *deviant* rather than the normal, disorder rather than order, dissonance rather than harmony. Functionalists argue that publicizing deviance works to reaffirm the norm, that calling attention to a breach deters other deviants and demands the attention of those in charge of the norm (Lazarsfeld and Merton, 1948). Publicizing the deviant, however, entails the risk of questioning the very validity of the norm that has been violated. Sometimes, that is, exposing deviance may boomerang, conferring status on the violation itself (Alexander, 1981; Gouldner, 1975; Katz, 1981; Molotch and Lester, 1974).[1] (Recall Mrs Dekel's fierce opposition to showing Rabbi Kahane on the news.)

Deviance is one of the forms of conflict, and *conflict*, often violent, is the major preoccupation of television news. It seems that not much has changed since Gans' (1980) classic study, showing that news consists of (1) crimes, scandals, and investigation, (2) conflicts within the government, and (3) violent protest, in that order.

The representation of conflict, most scholars agree, tends to *simplify* real-life issues and to stereotype participants. Thus, a complex, tortuous process of conflict, including a number of different actors, is framed, typically, as a disconnected series of discrete and violent eruptions, preferably between two opponents. Critical theorists argue that conflicts are often shown as more soluble than they are in order to demonstrate the need for strong government to handle threats to the social order. In this view, the inflation of acute crises diverts attention from the chronic maladies that underlie them (Cohen, Adoni, and Drori, 1983; Cohen, Adoni, and Bantz, 1991.) But this is probably less true the longer the conflict persists. In the case of a chronic conflict in which the government cannot prevent disorder and terrorist acts (such as in Israel or in Northern Ireland), television may downplay each incident in the series and thus risk a loss of credibility among viewers, or it may inflate their seriousness in a manner that justifies punitive retaliation, or it may vacillate between the two.

The third characteristic of television news is its focus on *events* rather than on processes or context. This is the result of the institutional structure that determines the "rhythm" of television news. The nightly show consists of events that occur between one newscast and the next (Galtung and Ruge, 1970), especially those that lend themselves to individual packaging as items. This parade of problems may well conceal the likelihood that some underlying cause connects them. Hallin (1985) would explain this tendency in terms of the bias of news toward strategic rather than value issues, which is his way of explaining journalists' preference in asking whether a particular strategy would succeed over asking what long-term aims or ideologies it serves. Strategy plus decontextualization, then, push toward the unexpected and deviant. Interpretation of the unexpected would make it more expected, and thereby reduce its psychological appeal. Explanation, says Edelman (1988), is scholarship, not news.

A bias for events means a bias for *action*, especially on television. Thus, a fourth characteristic of news is the preference for action. Television favors action, but not necessarily the people who act. The journalists' rule is that weaker groups have to act in order to gain access, while for establishments, talk counts as action. This inequality means that in clashes between "in" and "out" groups, the less favored side may be shown acting, voiced-over by the reporter, while the stronger side is invited to argue its own case (Glasgow University Media Group, 1976). By the same token, the more violent the action, the greater chance of a deviant group to make it past the television gatekeeper. Gitlin (1980) goes so far as to claim that journalists lose their sensitivity to the voices and life worlds of working-class and minority people.

Constructing social reality as a series of simple, dramatic episodes is also the reason for the *personification* of the social and political institutions and trends that are involved. Personalities, rather than social forces, are responsible for conflict. In conflicts that are not associated with known public figures, such as in the coverage of protest, the journalists themselves have the power to create leaders who personify one or both sides and to introduce them to the public. Once chosen, such characters – say, a demonstrator or a police officer – may be personalized to various degrees: by showing the character in action, by giving him or her a voice, by closing-up on his or her face, or by showing him or her in roles other than those the character plays in the news story. Personalization (as we have argued in the context of the presentation of us and them in war) gives support to the side that is personalized. If both sides are personalized the conflict may be deintensified. The same is true of confrontations between establishment and deviant groups and follows from the asymmetry of presenting elites as talking versus dissidents as rioting.

Finally, the *rhetoric* of news programs, as in other television drama, also provides entertainment. Even on public television, in retelling events journalists are telling stories (Epstein, 1973; Manoff, 1986). This implies that the more dramatic the plotline, the more intense the conflict, and the more visual, the better its chance of making the news. More than that, producers make sure that the personae in the news, themselves familiar with journalistic practices, act in accordance with expectations. And, as has often been noted in the case of violent or freaky behavior of deviant groups wishing to call attention to themselves, the greater the dependence on the journalist, the more likely the actor is to conform to his or her role in the journalists' script (Wolfsfeld, 1988; Wolfsfeld, in press). Thus, marginalized groups construct "real life" to express the self-fulfilling practices of journalists.

THE FRAMING OF PROTEST BY TELEVISION NEWS

The preferred frame for the intifada on Israeli television (see chapter 6) was that of violent protest (although it was sometimes framed as an all-out rebellion or civil war). Coverage followed the form of, say, urban riots in the US in the 1960s, even if American blacks can be said to have employed illegitimate means in the name of legitimate ends, such as equality within society, while the Palestinian rioters may be said to be employing illegitimate means, and, from the Israeli perspective, in the name of illegitimate ends. (The means consist of various forms of disruption and violence as elaborated below.)

As in the US riots, or the Catholic protest in Northern Ireland, or the protests of Jewish settlers against the Oslo agreements with the PLO some years later, cameras focus on the violence of the demonstrators from over the shoulders of the security forces. The news is the violence of the demonstrators while the soldiers – although highly visible – are seen to be carrying out their jobs. In describing the coverage of urban violence in the 1950s, Gans (1980) notes that police violence was largely ignored, and the routine police brutality in the ghetto – a major clue to the eruptions – did not qualify for inclusion in the news. Schiff and Yaari (1990) make much the same point about the daily humiliations suffered by the Palestinians under the Israeli occupation. Israel Television news made little room for the long-term effect of government policy in the territories (although some attention was given to the subject in other less popular political programs). Policy takes a long time to be formulated and evaluated and defies the simplifications of television news. Talk defers to action, and process defers to specific incidents.

As noted above, however, the inequality of the two sides leads to a disparity between the display of violent action on the two sides. When the cameras arrive, they exacerbate, sometimes even provoke, the violence of the protestors whose aim is to call attention to their plight. The cameras, and all kinds of journalists, have the opposite effect on the soldiers, who are aware that the filming of over-reaction on their part may lead to military and public censure, and even court-martial.[2] Beyond the site of confrontation, the event continues in the statements of police and army commanders and politicians, thus tipping the balance even more against demonstrators' *action* – rocks, molotov cocktails, and road blocks – versus reason and restraint on "our" side.

Nevertheless, within the context of clashes, the demonstrators are presented as stronger than they are, reflecting the role of adversary granted them by the army, willy-nilly. The face of the enemy, however, is hidden symbolically, because our television news is not on their side, assisted by the Palestinians' own face-covering for self-protection. This constructs a masked, threatening, demonic other. We know them only as the masked enemy, and see them not as people, but as role-players in the conflict. Only occasionally, when we are shown the mothers of stone throwers, or a Palestinian intellectual, do we get a glimpse of them as people.

On our side, however, the violence results in human suffering. Ordinary people are seen to be victimized: babies in hospitals, grieving families, bodies being buried, and funerals are shown extensively. The same human tragedies on the other side are chased from the screen not only because it is ours but because Israeli television reporters would not be welcome by families of Palestinian victims. Thus, the constraints of television presentation of the conflict combine with the cognitive processes through which viewers understand other people, to humanize our side and dehumanize the other side.

HOW THE NEWS REINFORCES THE ATTRIBUTION ERROR OF VIEWERS

The us-and-them rhetoric of televised conflict makes it easy for viewers to commit what social psychologists describe as the fundamental attribution error. The main claim of attribution theory, in its classic version, is that people tend to attribute their own failures to external (situational) causes, and the failures of others to internal (dispositional) causes (Moscovici, 1984; Nisbett and Ross, 1980).

In his critique of the theory, Richard Eiser (1983) suggests that it should incorporate Schenk and Abelson's (1977) "schemata" model, according to which we explain other people's behavior in the same way in which we understand the plot of a dramatic play. In both, our knowledge of the rules and roles we associate with a certain social context applies to understanding and predicting behavior. If this idea is valid for perception of others in real life, it should be all the more valid for an understanding of real characters who are "mediated" (Livingstone, 1990). In the "drama" of the news on screen, we meet characters *only* in those roles that are relevant for the genre.

In the case of the intifada, Israeli television's presentation constrains viewers to attribute situational reasons to the soldiers' behavior, and dispositional reasons to protestors' (Iyengar, 1991).[3] Soldiers perform their role in an institutional context; Palestinians are individually responsible (Wetherell and Potter, 1989). The process whereby television reinforced the fundamental attribution error during the intifada worked in the following way (see Table 1). Compared to our side, (1) Arabs were shown almost only in their role within the script of the conflict, the most newsworthy context from the point of view of journalistic function and dramatic attributes. (2) In this script, well recognized by viewers, Arabs appeared as "terrorists," represented stereotypically as the stone-throwing youth, his face covered with a *kaffia*, so as not to be identifiable. Choosing to be "faceless" in order to protect himself, also made him threatening, inhuman, almost a demonic figure. Viewers could not see him as the young person he is. (3) For most Israelis, and even more so for children, television is the only source of acquaintance with Arabs, whose image on television merges with that of "terrorists." (4) The "terrorist" script portrays arbitrary violence, causing suffering to innocent victims (Fiske and Hartley, 1978). Hardly shown is the human suffering on the Arab side and the situational or ideological context within which rioting might make sense.[4] Thus, in terms of the attribution error, television contributed to the perception of terrorism as intrinsic to Arabs and helped viewers to think of Arabs as "bad."

Of course, in the context of clashes between stone throwers and the army, Israeli soldiers are seen as no less violent but "we" are much less likely to be perceived as inherently bad. After all, (1) "we" know ourselves not only through television – every Israeli man is a soldier himself, or the parent or

Table 1 Us-and-them framings on television and in viewers' experience

	The conflict					
	In television's presentation			In viewers' experience		
	Intifada combatants	Intifada victims	Other TV role	Off-screen reality	Collective symbolic reality	Attributive frame
Us	"Good"/ "bad" soldiers	"Good" family member, citizen	Political and professional elites	Familiar	"Good"	External
Them	"Bad" terrorists	Not shown	Not shown	Unfamiliar	"Bad"	Internal

son of a soldier – and we know the external context that "justifies" our behavior; (2) moreover, television helps by showing "us" not only in the role of "soldiers" but also in the private role of family members, who are victims of the violence; and (3) the ceremonies that accompany those personal tragedies are used to lend meaning to sacrifice in terms of the national ideology.

This asymmetrical picture is not so different from viewers' own perceptions. Reinforced by what is shown on television, Israelis are familiar with their own side, of course. Many are also aware, from personal experience, of the moral dissonance experienced by Israeli soldiers and the human tragedies that result from this unease. They have no personal experience with the parallel context on the other side, however. The resulting framing of the reality of the conflict is therefore, similarly to its framing on screen, dichotomized into the "we" who are pressured by external circumstances into acting immorally, and "they" who must be inherently bad, because that's the way they are.

HOW THE CONFLICT AND ITS REPRESENTATION ON TELEVISION ARE DISCUSSED WITHIN JEWISH FAMILIES IN ISRAEL

This nightly rhetoric on Israel Television's monopolistic news program was differently decoded by Israeli hawks and doves. It is easy to understand our argument that the hawks are better "served" than the doves. The hawks mistake the rhetoric for reality. The doves, for their part, find television news disturbing in its black-and-white biases, unless they happen to know the code by which "their" reality can be inferred from the journalistic practice.

Television rhetoric plays into the hands of hawks

Israeli hawks see the conflict as insoluble, "apocalyptic" rather than "serial" (Back and Gergen, 1963), in short, as a no-compromise, zero-sum-game reflected in the relentlessness of the nightly news. Images that make "us" good and "them" bad provide an acceptable script for these Israelis and help to formulate the discourse for news initiates.

The family discussions provide rich evidence to show that hawks describe reality in television terms: television incidents showing "bad" Arabs are used as proof of what the Arabs are "really" like. Nevertheless, television is attacked for not tilting the balance even more in this direction to provide the situational justification for why we are sometimes forced to behave badly.

Paradoxically, as if ungrateful for "proving" them right, hawks complain that television distorts reality, that journalists are doves, sometimes traitors, who support the Arab side. This paradox is expressed, for example, in an exchange between father and daughter in the Ben-Ya'akov family.[5] Aharon

Ben-Ya'akov and his wife, in their forties, are moderate hawks, of Eastern European origin. Ruth, their 15-year-old, Israeli-born daughter,[6] is an extreme hawk. The family's oldest son, who studies medicine, was not home. Like other adolescents in the study, the daughter Ruth associates herself "officially" with the *Techia* Party, which (before its failure to enter the Knesset in the 1992 elections) regarded the occupied territories as an integral part of Israel and called for massive settlement of the West Bank. Informally, Ruth supports a much more extreme position, believing in "transfer" as a desirable solution to the conflict. Whereas both father and daughter believe that television is not "objective," Ruth claims that her understanding of the conflict is based on what she sees on television. "If this is the case," argues her father sarcastically, "you should be an extreme dove!"

The hawks' hostility to television news can be understood in terms of an expectation of what the news *should* show, which is different to the journalists' definition. Television, they believe, should show the "normal" aspect of reality and not give undue attention to deviance and conflict (Liebes and Ribak, 1991).

In addition to belief in "good" news *per se*, concern is expressed over the show of violence to the world. It is an instrumental view of television, already encountered in the case of Mrs Dekel (in chapter 7), expressing anxiety about the effect of television on others (Davison, 1983). This is ironic in view of the hawks' own reaction to "bad" Arabs on television. They seem to lack awareness that violence on television affects public opinion in the direction of imposing tougher control (Murdock, 1988).

Thus, there is a paradox in the hawks' hostility to television. In spite of the fact that it plays into their hands, Mr Ben-Ya'akov's belief that television is "leftist" is typical, although he can get evidence to the contrary from his own daughter! The daughter is an extreme hawk, worrying even the moderately hawkish father, yet she professes to receive her knowledge from television. The discussion between father and daughter in the Ben-Yaa'kov family indicates some of the processes that contribute to the move to the political right and to the role of television in this move.

Television is the source

F [explaining to interviewer] We try not to enter into confrontations.
D One doesn't come out alive.
F Because Ruth is very extreme in her opinions and I am rather unsuccessful to impose upon her my more balanced type of thinking. [To daughter] Where do you think [your opinions] came from? What do they grow out of?
D From television, from media, and from everything that is happening.

Indeed, Ruth's refusal to acknowledge the relevance of anything that interferes with her most simplistic black-and-white picture of reality seems to reflect the imprinting of television. Whereas the father is concerned about justifying the justice inherent in "our" case in terms of the historical rights of the Jews to the land of Israel and the contemporary suffering of the Jews, the daughter does not need any "proof."

The generation gap is well illustrated when father and daughter discuss what is for her "the murder" of PLO operation's commander Abu Jihad, referred to in the news, which took place in Tunisia a few weeks prior to the discussion. "I would call it the 'execution,' " corrects her father, assuming (as was widely believed) that it was an Israeli Mossad action, and intent on making sure that nobody confuse the image of "our" justice with that of terrorists. Ruth does not see why one should bother. She takes it for granted that we are good and does not think it needs proving. Her favorite way to solve or, rather, to dismiss the Palestinian problem is "let them get lost" ("*sheyauffu*"). Her wish for the Arabs to "vanish" (similar to that of Mrs Dekel's daughter Yaffa), which she expresses time and again during the conversation, is brutal but vague. It is vague because of the preference not to know how this vanishing will occur; it is brutal because it expresses an attitude of dehumanization of Arabs, deeply entrenched, enough to make such a wish legitimate in thought and in conversation.

Resolving the conflict by the disappearance of the rival can be understood as part of Ruth's impatience with the ambivalence and ambiguity she senses in her father: "You are contradicting yourself. Either they are poor or they are terrorists who should be squashed," she scolds him. But this weariness with the complexity of the situation (Benyamini, 1982) is reinforced by television's simplistic view of reality, which shows that "they" are, indeed, brutal and inhuman enough to justify "vanishing."

Ruth is a faithful representative of the majority of adolescents in other families who (1) regard the Arabs as inhuman, (2) admit that they receive their information from television, (3) claim that television shows "90 percent" or "almost all" of what the Arabs are like, and (4) declare they do not want to know any data from other sources that may confuse this picture.

The doves' attempt to amend television's picture

If hawks complain that television's picture is not sufficiently black and white but admit to depending on television for their perception of the conflict, doves (Mrs Dekel being one) express unease with this dichotomized representation and try to transform it into a more balanced picture. In discussions with children and others, dovish parents fail to make their point, however. They are stymied by the consensus against anchoring "evil" terrorist acts in any ideological context that would shift the argument away from disconnected acts of brutality in the direction of a dispute between two political claims. More, although they know intuitively that there is something wrong with the reality on television, they are not aware of the journalistic criteria and generic constraints which make up television's code. Not having critical tools at their disposal, their objections to the simplistic framing seem subjective and unfounded. The only chance doves have to persuade their children – sometimes their siblings or parents – of their position is when they can point to the fundamental attribution error and show how television reinforces the viewer's distorted perception.

However doomed to failure, doves sometimes try to balance the picture, by drawing on their own experience, in the manner tried by Mrs Dekel, giving personal evidence to show that "they" are not all "bad" and that we are not all "good." In terms of the prevalent image of Arabs their effort is to change the equation of Arabs and terrorists and to expand the image of Arabs as human beings, in order to counteract the tendency to depersonalize them.

The following exchange is taken from the discussion of the Horwitch family. Sally Horwitch, in her late thirties, an immigrant from the United States, is the mother of two teenage daughters and a younger son. In discussion with her oldest daughter Sharon, the mother tries to change her daughter's image of Arabs as terrorists by calling on her personal experience:

"Arabs have children and worry about them"
M   We know Arabs who are married and have children, and they worry a lot about their children, and love them.
D   I did not say "all the Arabs"; I said "some of them."
M   What happens is that the young ones are making a lot of noise, the ones who throw stones and suddenly they [soldiers] come and blow up everybody's houses. It's terrible.

Although she seems to be successful here, later in the discussion it becomes evident that her two daughters reject the idea of Arabs as parents who love their children: "In that case why are they ready to kill their daughters?" they ask, referring to widespread ideas about the morals of fundamentalism.

An argument (somewhat similar to the one Mrs Dekel was having with her daughter) about how representative of Arabs as a group is television's image of "bad" Arabs, takes place in the Levi family. This is a politically atypical family. Both parents, in their forties, are hawks, their son Ron (fifteen) following suit. Older daughter Maya (seventeen), however, is an intelligent combative dove who feels responsibility for the soul of her little four-year-old sister. Drawing on the family's acquaintance with Ahmad who had worked for them, Maya tries to fight the "terrorist" image and receives the same response Mrs Dekel got from her daughter: 99 percent of them want to kill us. It is clear that television's picture wins over personal experience.

"What about Ahmad?"
D   Why do you admit Ahmad into the house then?
M   Who?
D   You.
M   He doesn't come in order to... he doesn't want to kill.
D   Ah, so he doesn't want to kill...
M   What, him?!...
S   90 percent of them...
M   99 percent of the Arabs hate the Jews.

In addition to balancing the image of faceless Arabs with known ones, doves use the tactics of balancing the image of "good" Jews with "bad" violent ones. Maya, the older daughter in the Levi home – the only dove in her family – tries to show that there are terrorists among "us" as well!

"Terrorists should be punished"
D   It doesn't matter if it is a Jew or an Arab. When he [a Jewish extremist who hurled a missile into an Arab bus in Jerusalem] is throwing explosives on a bus – then he is wrong. He is wrong because he kills someone who is innocent. If a person comes and shoots a missile on a bus he can't be right.

Another tactic doves use to rearrange the distribution between "good" and "bad" is to raise the possibility of an exchange of roles, asking family members – What would you feel and do if you were in their place? Thus, in discussing the blowing up of houses of Palestinian terrorists, Sally Horwitch, swept into a heated argument with her daughter, demands to know:

"What would a Jew do in his place?"
M   It always makes me terribly angry because they say that for an Arab his house is more important than anything else. I would like to see them coming to a Jew and blowing up his house. What would he do? Would he not erupt? Would he not scream? What is this?

Maya, the Levi daughter, also senses that by changing places in fantasy, the motivations ascribed to the other side may become less deterministic and more situational. Thus, when – as in all families – the discussion inevitably turns to possible solutions to the conflict, she demands of her younger brother Ron to imagine how he would have felt if he were a Palestinian terrorist whose friend was killed by the Israelis:

"Changing roles"
D   What if you were in their place... and they killed your friend? Would you be afraid or would you hate them even more and say, "I will not give them anything. I will revenge myself?"
S   I don't know, I haven't experienced it.
D   Think! Think!

In this exchange, Maya, in her relentless attempts to win her brother over, is trying to create understanding, maybe empathy, by changing places psychologically, thereby creating a subjunctive mood. She then tries an even more daring tactic by anchoring terrorist acts in their ideological context. What television news shows, she continues, are arbitrary acts of violence that sound dangerously similar to our own pre-independence activists against the British. This kind of analogy between "our" freedom fight and "their" terrorism is rare in these discussions. The daughter's remark outraged the family: her idea that television might make them look like us threatens Israeli viewers.

"What about the Jewish Underground?"
D   If you were to found a [new] state, you would do exactly the same thing.
M   How can you compare [us] to them?
F   You must understand one thing. The *Etsel* and the *Lechi* [the Jewish extremist Undergrounds] who were attempting to speed up the end of the British mandate over Palestine did not go to murder: not women nor children. They fought an empire. They didn't throw stones at children or at...women and children.
[Uproar. Everybody speaks at the same time and the tape is impossible to transcribe.]

It is noteworthy that although Maya talks only subjunctively and does not refer explicitly to historical analogies ("If you were to found a state...") the father reacts defensively as if she had explicitly attacked the Jewish Underground. It is crucial for him to keep Arab terrorism "pure," i.e. uncontaminated by an ideological context which might endow it with some legitimacy. This discussion illustrates that the hawkish position depends on maintaining the fundamental difference between "us" as "good" and "just" and them as "bad" and "inhuman." Any challenge to this division of the world creates dissonance.

Accusing her mother of socializing her children to a black-and-white view of the conflict, Maya thus refuses to frame the problem in terms of "good" versus "bad." In fact, she puts her finger on the attributional error that is inherent in this formulation:

Pointing to the attribution error
D   [to her mother]   You are saying to Chen [the young sister]: "Bad Arabs." Where else would she know it from? She will grow up, see the situation, and decide for herself.
M   It's not my fault that she sees the situation.
D   But that's what you tell her.
M   That's what I say because that's what I think.
D   But here you are wrong! That's how you educate your children! I too,

when I was in sixth or seventh grade, I used to say "Kill the Arabs" because that's how I was educated at home; that's what you said to me: "Bad Arabs." That's what I knew.

M   And now you think they are good?

D   I don't think they are good, but I understand the problem, and think that it should be solved.

In the last statement, 17-year-old Maya redefines the conflict *situationally*, displacing the dispositional frame according to which the attributes of the other in conflict are intrinsic and therefore unchangeable.

The family discussions indicate that most viewers adopt a simplistic and dichotomized picture of the conflict. Television "proves" to the hawks that their apocalyptic view of conflict as a zero-sum-game is correct. Doves have a much harder time in intercepting television's message and, while they do not change their own outlook, are bothered by the possibility that television contributes to their children's move to the right. This concern makes for an ambivalence about viewing and for searching for ways to amend this image. Unable to understand the generic constraints on the way journalists report on conflict, dovish parents remain at the ineffectual level of arguing against the unrepresentativeness of television without being able to give good reasons for this intuition. The occasional awareness of journalistic practices and generic constraints – i.e. the acquisition of tools for critical viewing – may have helped some doves to "keep" their children, ideologically speaking. That such media literacy depends on higher education is supported by data according to which, during the intifada years, the only chance doves had to reproduce ideologically similar children was when they were highly educated.

Chapter 9

Reading upside down and inside out
How Israeli Arabs maneuver between the "easy" dominant and oppositional readings

So far, the viewers' readings we have analyzed were all within the Zionist Jewish consensus. Even if viewers unhappily saw television as supporting the other side – hawks and doves for their separate reasons – they shared a basic trust in the credibility of Israeli television news, and on justice being, on the whole, on "our" side.

This chapter and the next look at more radical readings that emerge from having alternative channels of viewing the conflict, or from being outside the consensus to begin with. A particularly interesting group of viewers, in these terms, are Israeli Arab citizens, some 18 percent of the population. Whereas Israeli television news is presented mostly by and for the Jewish majority it is also the main source for viewing the conflict for the far less visible community of Israeli Arabs. While generally regarding themselves as loyal Israelis, Arabs naturally empathize with the Palestinian cause, and are aware of the likelihood of being identified with the Palestinians by Israeli Jews (individually and as a community) whenever the conflict erupts. This chapter examines the ways in which these viewers – from the position of being both insiders and outsiders in Israeli society – make sense of the presentation of the conflict on Israeli television.

While research on viewers' critical abilities tends to focus on consistent positions (such as "hegemonic" or "oppositional"), the case of Israeli Arabs' readings of the conflict may serve to observe interpretations which are not necessarily consistent, and require creative and ad hoc solutions in approaching a difficult text. These readings may fall under the relatively flexible category which Hall (1985) defines as "negotiated."

The problem with "oppositional" readings, as we see them, is that they may be as uncritical as are readings that accept the "preferred" or hegemonic message as given. By totally rejecting the preferred meaning as blatant manipulation, oppositional viewers produce an almost automatic "negative" framing that amounts to a mirror image of the hegemonic text. Negotiated decodings, on the other hand, accept parts of the text while rejecting others, and their position in relation to the text is far more complex and sophisticated. These readings are therefore more demanding for viewers and more challenging for those who study them.

Before looking at how Israeli Arabs read the news of the conflict on Israeli television, let us first introduce the Arab Israeli community and briefly examine its relationship with the Jewish majority.

THE SETTING

Relations between the Jewish majority and the Arab minority in Israel have always been uneasy. Despite their intentions and declarations to the contrary, Arab citizens of the state were generally suspected of harboring divided loyalties and were regarded as potential enemies; indeed, in the early years of the state the Arab minority was treated as if under military occupation. The 1967 war added to this nervous coexistence when the Palestinians from Gaza and the West Bank came under Israeli rule. Twenty years of a relatively calm occupation, largely unnoticed by many Israeli Jews, came to an abrupt end in December 1987, when the Palestinians from the occupied territories began a series of violent demonstrations, blocking roads, burning tires, and attacking Israeli soldiers and civilians with stones and molotov cocktails.

Since the beginning of the Palestinian uprising, Arab citizens of Israel – constituting nearly one-fifth of its population – found themselves divided, and their relationships with both sides became more problematic than ever. Citizens of Israel since its founding in 1948 and with a lot at stake, they had an interest in demonstrating their loyalty to the state; being Arab, however, they sympathized with their Palestinian brothers and were consequently less differentiated from them in the eyes of Israeli Jews (Van Leer Institute, 1987).[1]

The danger that Israeli Arabs might become victims of the presentation of the Palestinian as other on Israeli television during the intifada years was exacerbated by the low level of unmediated interpersonal contact between them and the Jewish community, particularly among the young. Arabs live mostly in their own villages and towns, they study in their own school system, and they do not serve in the army, Israel's most powerful means of social integration. Until the peace process gained momentum, Israeli Arabs were practically non-existent in the Israeli media. When they did occasionally appear on television, it was usually in the context of protests against the unjust distribution of the state's resources.[2] After the outbreak of the intifada there were also a few incidents where stones or molotov cocktails were thrown at Jewish cars from Arab settlements within Israel. Marginalized to begin with, the portrayal of the state's Arab citizens in the news during the intifada served only to emphasize their vulnerability: their divided and uncertain loyalties positioned them as "the other" in the eyes of both Israeli Jews and Palestinians from the occupied territories.

It may come as a surprise, then, that *Mabat*, the evening news program on Israeli television, was viewed regularly by a majority not only of Israeli Jews, but also by a majority of Israeli Arabs. Moreover, Arabs, even more than Jews, regarded the news in Hebrew as highly credible. This preference of the Arab viewers reflected the lack of other trustworthy sources. The main alternatives were the news in Arabic on Israeli television (typically dismissed as propaganda) and news programs from neighboring Arab countries, taken to be the mouthpieces of their rulers.

ISRAELI ARABS' VIEW OF THE CONFLICT

Our observations of how Israeli Arabs viewed the conflict during the intifada are based on our family survey – constructed of a representative sample of 200 Arab families in Nazareth, parallel with the 400 Jewish families, all with adolescent children,[3] and on a discussion initiated with a subsample of these families, following the viewing of the evening news.[4] As in the case of the Jews, our purpose was to gain insight into the dynamics of continuity and change in the Arab communities in Israel, and to understand the role of television news in the socialization process.

A word of caution is required before reporting on some dominant patterns in the discourse. Although Jews and Arabs were interviewed by Jewish and Arab interviewers, respectively, using identical survey questions and discussion guidelines in the two languages (Arab transcripts were then translated by the observers into Hebrew), the similarity ends there. The Arabs were far less forthcoming than the Jews. While stylistic differences between Arab and Jewish transcripts may be attributed either to translation problems or, more likely, to cultural and linguistic differences, Arabs' unwillingness to open up, and their implicit and explicit suspicions, are probably not only the result of their relative inexperience of being interviewed or their puzzlement over the research situation. Rather, it is far more likely that this reserved manner was an expression of general mistrust and insecurity, suggestive and significant in itself and yet introducing an imbalance into the study.

The survey data showed the parents' generation to be relatively more moderate concerning the Arab–Israeli conflict in both the Jewish and the Arab communities. Since our study was designed to understand the expression of such intergenerational differences, we attempted to understand how moderate parents, both Jews and Arabs, "lost" their children to more nationalistic positions (see Liebes, Katz, and Ribak, 1991; Liebes and Ribak, 1992).

As we pointed out, prior to the introduction of a commercial channel and cable television in 1993, television news was the main shared source of information, not only in setting the national agenda but in providing the occasion to discuss and consider it as well. Indeed, the survey showed that just as in the Jewish community, Israeli Arab families also gathered not only to watch the news but also to talk about it afterwards. As will be remembered, we considered the conversation that developed as an opportunity for parents and children to map political relations and argue their views, and as the forum for family members to articulate and try out their opinions. News viewing in Jewish and Arab living-rooms was regarded as a site for the negotiation of political and national identity, both within each community and in relation to the other.

ISRAELI ARABS' VIEW OF THE INTIFADA

The difference in the interview situation in the Israeli Jewish and Arab communities means that Israeli Jews, nationalist adolescents in particular, were uninhibited in the expression of their views. Arabs were less secure and perhaps more suspicious. In their reserved comments, they seemed occasionally to use the focus groups' conversation for sending messages to the Israeli Jewish elite. Some Arabs expressed actual anxiety when asked to talk about the intifada, despite the fact that the interviewer was Arab, that conversations were conducted in Arabic, and that the study was sponsored by American funds.

This tension was manifested, for example, in the reluctance of the Khalaila family to have the discussion recorded, finally agreeing on condition that the audiotape be returned to them later.[5] In another family, in response to the interviewer's request that he explain the news from the West Bank as if he were orienting an uninformed visitor from abroad, Mr Najim replied: "It's sometimes hard to explain. [The visitor] may be an agent, or someone from the security forces. Why ask me? There are newspapers. He can read and understand himself." As we will note later, this tension is also expressed in the preference of Arabs to discuss the intifada circumlocutionally, by analogy to more distant but similarly structured conflicts that are depicted in the news.

Roughly, we identify three types of reading of the intifada news:

1 Dominant reading by Jewish nationalists, who accept the preferred meaning of the text as a whole.
2 Oppositional readings by Arab nationalists, who accept the text as a unified, coherent message, which they invert and read upside down.
3 Negotiated readings of Jewish and Arab moderates, who try to amend what is felt to be a biased picture.

These differences in reading are evident not only between families but, significantly, within them as well. We were particularly interested in those families that demonstrated the intergenerational trend in Israeli society (shown in the survey), that is, the intergenerational move from moderate to more extreme positions. In such families, parents tried to negotiate the text while their children either accepted it unchallenged or rejected it altogether.

In the previous chapter, we showed how television representation of the conflict contributed to the process of growing extremism in both communities, while making the news text incompatible with the world view of moderates. We assumed that the dynamics of this process would be revealed in the situation of the family news viewing.

We found that extremists in both the Jewish and the Arab camps accept the televised portrayal of reality at face value. Let us distinguish these black-and-white interpretations from other, more skeptical decodings. As we have demonstrated in analyzing the difficulties of Jewish doves, moderates in the two communities struggle with the enigma of how television samples from reality, and with its simplified representation of "us" and "them."

Beyond the failure of moderates in both communities to correct (and complicate) the televised picture due to their lack of sophistication in understanding the genre of television news and the rules which govern coverage of violent demonstrations such as the intifada (pointed out in chapters 7 and 8), Israeli Arabs have to confront their own symbolic annihilation in the text, a virtual absence that threatens to render them indistinguishable from the Palestinians in the occupied West Bank and Gaza in the eyes of Israeli viewers (and indistinguishable from the Jews in the eyes of West Bank Palestinians). To Israelis, they are seen as both vulnerable and threatening (Iyengar, 1991; Power, 1990).

The concern of moderates within the Jewish camp over the asymmetrical presentation of the conflict which, they sensed, reinforced the tendency to commit an error in attribution, is closer to home among moderate Arabs. As a minority in a situation of conflict, they felt that the black-and-white picture of the Israeli–Palestinian conflict, coupled with their own relative absence from the news, contributes to the blurring of the distinction between their own identity, and that of the Palestinians from the territories, in the eyes of the Jews. They were also concerned that the absence of visible charismatic leadership might drive their children to gradual identification with the Palestinians in the uprising; having little to lose and facing the choice between accepting Israeli occupation and following Palestinian freedom fighters, the real options open to adolescent Arabs in Israel were severely limited indeed.

Moderates were therefore faced with the most difficult task of interpreting the news in accordance with their world views. But, as our analysis shows, all three types of reading are not sophisticated in their understanding of their source of information, in that decodings are not based on awareness of the institutional and generic characteristics of the news text. The simpler idea that ideological hegemony and manipulation may intrude in the text is more frequent.[6]

DOMINANT AND OPPOSITIONAL READINGS

Both dominant and oppositional readers tend to be comfortable with the news. As elaborated in chapter 8, nationalist readings by Jews have no need to doubt or challenge the accuracy and representativeness of the televised picture of the conflict. The notion of representativeness allows Jewish adolescents to claim that the Arabs are dangerous and should be thrown out of the country, often mentioning that they get their views "from television news."

For nationalists within the Arab community, the televised depiction of the conflict, taken at face value, only confirmed pre-existing notions about the hegemonic construction of the uprising by ruling Jewish elites. Such readings did not seek to correct or amend the given text; instead, it was simply read upside down. Replacing "us" of the text with "them," it was possible to discard as irrelevant internal political disputes between Jews of the left and right, recounted at great detail in the news: "They are all the same, Shamir [then Prime Minister] and Peres [then Opposition leader] are indistinguishable," one Arab youth remarked scathingly, believing that Jews in general hate Arabs. Similarly, viewing a conference of right-wing ex-generals, Mrs Nejma observed cynically that while these generals advocate security-and-peace, left-wing ex-generals advocate peace-and-security: "Left, right, left, right, bloodshed and war prevail," she concluded.

By transforming the Palestinian "them" of the news into "us," nationalistic readings by Israeli Arabs supply the missing Palestinian ideological frame. Going against the grain of a text which depicted the events of the intifada as arbitrary incidents of irrational violence and terrorism, Arab families consistently framed it in terms of "revolution" or "uprising," reminding us of the irony that the Israeli media nonetheless preferred the Arabic term – intifada – the meaning of which was not known to Israeli Jewish audiences. These readers saw heroism and just cause where the Jews (and Israel Television) saw disobedience and immorality.

NEGOTIATED READINGS

Dominant and oppositional readings consist in simply placing a positive or negative frame around the television news. Negotiated readings, on the other hand, involve incorporation into the text of stories learned elsewhere, from either personal or collective experience. Situating themselves in the middle ground and resisting extreme solutions, Arab and Jewish moderates demonstrated a shared concern in rejecting simplistic decodings, and an attempt to negotiate the meaning of the text.

One tactic used by Israeli Arabs is reminiscent of that of Jewish moderates trying to counteract the attribution error, by pointing out that "we" are not all good. Thus, like Mrs Dekel (chapter 7), who recounted her experience with Jewish fundamentalist groups to prove that they are worse than any Arabs she had known, Mr Najib, an Arab father, when discussing tensions between police and fundamentalist Islamic groups in Egypt, says, "These fundamentalists are the most dangerous; their own interests come first." His daughter exclaims: "But they are Muslims!" and the mother adds, "Every Muslim is good." But Mr Najib insists:

> These Muslims are merchants. Like the religious in Israel. These religious Muslims are against Islam, against Arabs, and against the Communist Party and the left in general. Another example is the religious Muslims in Israel. Take for instance the newspaper *A-Siat* that they publish: what they spread around is poison.

Another daughter asks: "Are you not exaggerating, father?" to which he responds:

> These Muslims want us to work and give money to their leading sheikhs. They are dangerous, believe me...in today's Israel, the fundamentalist religious Muslims influence the youth and they are the most dangerous. I support the Jews and not these Muslims – the good Jews, not the extremists, of course.

Another tactic for balancing the sides is concerned with the equal distribution not of morals but of consequences. Used mostly by Arabs, this argument insists that the conflict cannot be regarded as a zero-sum-game: both sides would inevitably suffer, regardless of who eventually gains more points. This lesson is drawn no less from other conflicts portrayed in the news. Thus, when discussing the then eight-year-old Iran–Iraq War, the daughter of the Muhammad family asks whether Khomeini intended to employ chemical weapons. Her father answers that it is hard to predict, but, he continues, "Children, war is always destructive. There is no loser, no winner. In war, everybody loses". The intent of both these tactics, then, is to substitute the given frame of "them and us" with an alternative frame of "inevitable similarity of fate."

These two quotations demonstrate yet another tactic, already referred to, that of distancing the evidence. By diverting the conversation to some other, analogous situation, it is possible to illustrate what takes place next door without having to actually go into what is, by virtue of its proximity, complicated and messy. Arabs in Israel clearly felt uncomfortable talking about the intifada, as this forced them to explicitly take sides. This resistance is striking in the case of the Najib family, who chose to avoid discussing the four intifada items that opened the broadcast and focused only on the following, fifth item concerning fundamentalism in Egypt. These other countries were not interesting in themselves as much as they provided effective analogies to the immediate concern. Thus, in the Badrana family, the father relates to an item about Burma with: "This country has a problem, they have demonstrations there. People want democracy, not a dictatorial regime." The son, Sami, picks this up and responds by saying, "Many nations seek democracy," allowing his father to conclude: "People there are throwing stones; they want freedom." Mr Badrana's final note draws attention to the use of the stone, the symbol of the intifada, in Burma as well as the occupied territories, a rhetorical move which explicates that country's allegorical function in the discourse.

South Korea is another case in point, discussed in one family with the prediction that "the people will win," following the observation that "the students are strong and the people support them." South Korean students are used here as functional equivalents of the Palestinian uprisers – both are young, powerful, and popular. The Kurds also receive sympathy in Arab families: "I think the Kurds deserve a state,"[7] and, in relation to Afghanistan, "No people can rule another people."

Humanizing and personalizing the uprising Palestinians is another tactic employed by Arab moderates, similar to their Jewish counterparts. But while Jews introduce personal contacts, even friendships, with Arabs, in order to drive home in an emotionally powerful way the idea that "there are real people on the other side," the invocation of actual interpersonal contact with Jews in the conversation of Arab families was infrequent.

Israeli Arabs, perhaps for fear of further distancing themselves from the Palestinians, prefer to humanize the other side not by focusing on concrete examples but by labeling the other side in universalistic terms. Family roles in particular are made use of in order to stress common human attributes instead of segregating, nationalistic ones. Typical statements in the discussions take the form of "We know Arabs who are married, who have children, who care about their children and love them," or again, "One Arab mother may send her son to throw stones while another Arab mother, like me, cares about her child; I refuse to make generalizations." These attempts are more fully developed when formalized and the principle behind them articulated, as in, "All in all, they are human beings," and "It is possible to accept somebody as a person, not as an Arab and not a Jew."

This form of humanizing characterizes the discourse of Arabs, allowing them to legitimately sympathize with Palestinian uprisers in their own living-room. Universalistic definitions are also used in order to send an educational message to the Jewish public: "For me there is no difference between a Jewish and an Arab child"; "These students are not study-ing...these are poor [unhappy] children; their mothers are also poor"; "There is no difference between a Jewish and an Arab mother." And, "The tears are the same tears; the suffering is the same suffering. It's a tragedy for a mother to lose her child: a Jewish mother or an Arab mother." Or, referring to an item about the deportation of Palestinians from Israel: "What will happen to the children of the deported?...It won't be easy for them."

A major difference between Jewish and Arab moderates was found in the invocation of historical frames. Even accounts of moderate Jews remained within the ideological consensus of Israeli sovereignty, which did not provide the intifada with any historical or political legitimacy, thus divorcing it from the national aspirations of the Palestinians.[8] For their part, Arabs framed the intifada within the national, ideological context of a humiliated people who, having nothing to lose, arise to demand their national rights.

Jewish moderates, then, did not go further than expressing empathy with victims of both sides while seeing "our" soldiers as enforcing law and order and the Palestinian uprisers as acting in an arbitrary and irresponsible way.

These narrations of Israeli Jews trace the origins of the intifada in one of two ways. Seemingly contradictory but substantively congruent, Jews either explained the intifada by referring to its formal onset only or, skipping over some 3,000 years, they discussed it in terms of biblical rights and conquests. Examples of the extreme decontextualization of the first kind attribute the intifada to a chance accident, as in, "In the beginning somebody just threw a stone," or "It all began when terrorists invaded a military compound in the north and saw that we were not so strong." Primordial framing, used mostly in nationalistic accounts, declared, for example, that "We conquered this land and it is our country; and if it isn't enough that we let them sit here, they come and complain [uprise]!" This serves to portray the intifada as a transient event within Jewish history, and to dismiss its significance since "We have exclusive and eternal right to the land."

By contrast, Israeli Arabs provided a historical context, sometimes told in chronological sequence, to the Palestinian ordeal. They described how the Palestinians were passed from Egyptian and Jordanian to Israeli hands, and how their national aspirations for self-determination had been continuously frustrated. Israel as well as the Arab countries had disappointed them and, "having gotten into a state of desperation, they were forced to turn to [rely on] the stone." Arabs repeatedly used words like "desperation," "suffering," "lost honor," and "helplessness" in their accounts, thereby attributing situational motivation to the uprising, that is, the Palestinians had practically no other choice but to act in this way.

MODERATION FAILS

Tracing these tactics of moderation in family conversations shows that they were easily countered by more simplistic readings of the television news text. In the Arab families as well as in the Jewish families, television's portrayal of the conflict would seem to have contributed to the failure of moderate parents to have like-minded children. Children in particular were not inclined to accept attempts to point out that there is good and bad in both camps, nor were they concerned with the suffering of the other side.

Jewish adolescents often complained that television was too forgiving to

Arabs. Even these "bad Arabs," one argued "are presented in too positive a light," and "are not as poor [miserable] as they appear on television." Arab adolescents, for their part, rejected any criticism directed at the uprisers and discarded differences and disagreements in Jewish politics as negligible.

The survey offered additional evidence for the dichotomized world view of these adolescents by showing, as mentioned earlier, that both Jewish and Arab adolescents disclosed hatred towards the other side more than did their parents. Interestingly, Arab adolescents believed that they were hated by Jews even more than the latter allow themselves to admit: 94 percent of Arab adolescents at that time believed that Jews hate Arabs, as compared to 29 percent of Jewish adults and 44 percent of Jewish adolescents who admitted to such hatred on their part. Further, we saw that the evidence offered by Jewish parents for the presence of good people on the other side was considered by their children to be an exception to the rule. Among Arab parents, there were no such cases of personal proof; and the survey indicates that the need to have personal contacts with the Jewish majority was acknowledged by both parents and adolescents – 91 percent and 87 percent, respectively, supported organized encounters between Jewish and Arab youths, as compared to only 57 percent and 64 percent, respectively, among Jews.

THE STRUGGLE OF ISRAELI ARABS TO CONSTRUCT THEIR OWN INVISIBLE IDENTITY

While Jewish and Arab moderates shared a number of mitigating tactics, their different circumstances were apparent in their discourses, both in what they said and, significantly, in what they left unsaid. Jewish moderates considered themselves to be within a mainstream consensus, discussing an ambiguous "they" who are sometimes Palestinians from the occupied territories but often Arabs in general. Arabs in Israel, on the other hand, relate to two separate "thems" – Israeli Jews, on whom they depend, and uprising Palestinians, with whom they sympathize.

Vis-à-vis television, Israeli Arabs made an effort to render visible the invisible self, their own distinguishable identity which is absent from the news text. The identity of the Arab citizens of Israel, as it emerged from their conversation, was constructed by contrasting it with those they are not. Their children strove, and were being pushed, to be "somebodies," and to define a space of their own between the two warring camps.

It should be noted, moreover, that there is evidence in the discourse of Jewish families to support the feeling among Arabs in Israel that the intifada precipitated the blurring of their own identity with that of the Palestinians in the territories. Drawing a distinction between the two Arab groups was rare even in the conversation of Jewish moderates. The label most commonly used by Jews was the general "Arabs." It is "the Arabs" who are bad, who hate us, who throw stones at our soldiers, who want to kill us. Even attempts to balance this picture, such as "We have Arab friends, too," "An Arab never hit me with a stone – a Jew did," or "There are good Arabs and bad Arabs," inadvertently lumped Arabs from Israel and the territories into one category.

In the Jewish families, the missing historical or political contextualization of the intifada from the repertoire of both television news and of Jewish moderates, left no alternative framing for them or their children to fall back on. In the absence of situational attributions to explain the actions of uprisers, adolescents in such families had little reason to challenge the televised representation of the conflict. For while adults may find like-minded people among their friends, it was far less likely that adolescents will find moderates in their peer group; nor are the schools able or willing to fight against attempts to depoliticize them.

The attribution error inherent in the news was thus acceptable for both Jewish and Arab nationalists. For Jews, the "normal" representation of the conflict – corresponding to the attribution error – agreed with and strengthened an ideological world view that regards this picture as real. Exceptional events – when, for example, Israeli soldiers are shown breaking limbs of arrested Palestinians instead of enforcing law and order – were explained in terms of the ideological manipulation of the leftist mafia that controls the press.

The error in the text suited Arab nationalists as well. They, however, interpreted the "normal" as ideological, and attributed the manipulation not to journalists but to government officials. Exceptions – i.e. bad Jews, good Arabs – are seen as rare glimpses of the real, exposed by accident when political and military elites temporarily lose control.

For moderate Arabs (as for moderate Jews), whose expectations of reality were less consistent (or less prescribed), the attribution error in the news constituted a problem, as the text did not present the more ambivalent and complicated reality they knew and expected to see. Assuming that the news is real – i.e. representative – and interpreting not the normal nor the exceptional as necessarily manipulative, they sensed that the depiction of the conflict is incomplete, that it is somehow biased, but they fail to articulate why.

Chapter 10

Lying low – silent witnesses from the field

How Israeli soldiers reconcile the "enemy" with the images they brought with them

During the years of the uprising, Israeli soldiers often found themselves in the role of policemen repressing a civilian population rather than fighters against an armed enemy. These soldiers – some of them older civilians, doing their duty as army reservists; many, young soldiers on their three-year compulsory army service – came to the land of intifada carrying (in various degrees) the stereotypes of the other side as violent, dehumanized, sometimes even demonized. Even as observers of everyday life in the Arab towns and villages the Israeli soldier cannot be thought to have an unmediated view of the other. Their view is heavily mediated, of course, by the prior internalization of "them" through the outlook of parents, peers, schools, and the image of Palestinians on television news, as filtered by their surrounding social networks. In the field, these soldiers' views are also mediated by the role they are playing, which means seeing the Palestinians while in uniform and behind the helmets of a conquering army. Nevertheless, at least some of them struggled with the dilemma of fitting the Palestinians they encountered – children, adolescents, and families – with the images of the other side they had internalized.

We interviewed a number of such soldiers to access an alternative form of seeing the other side, "after the fact" of television, as it were. As in the case of viewing the conflict on television, it is the soldiers with dovish ideologies who interest us most, as a potential source for oppositional readings. This chapter focuses on these soldiers' framing of the conflict, confirming once again how difficult it is to maintain an anti-hegemonic position. The fight against television frames, the framing of powerful institutions, and one's own stereotypes is very difficult.

THE INTERVIEW SITUATION

Sixteen loosely structured, in-depth interviews, were conducted with thirty soldiers – during their army service, and as young reservists. About ten interviews were conducted in groups of friends who had spent at least some army time together; the other soldiers were interviewed individually.[1]

The interview situation was an unusual one, and it is important to keep in mind that its functions for the interviewees may have had a bearing on what they told us. After all, it was an opportunity to portray a difficult situation in elaborate detail, inasmuch as the interviewers were perceived not only as outsiders but also as motivated by concern over the heavy moral and political issues which the soldiers confronted.

Indeed, the discussions indicated that the interview situation was used as a "griping" or even a "purging" ritual (Katriel, 1985), in which painful and problematic aspects of the intifada could be exorcised. In the group interviews the cathartic function of the interview was increased by the presence of intimate, long-time friends.[2]

Another aspect of the discussions related to the perception of the researchers as civilian representatives of pre-intifada norms, by whom the soldiers felt they may be severely judged. In this sense the researchers may have been regarded as both empathetic and judgmental, that is, as symbolic substitutes for parents, with whom – it was widely held – the soldiers experienced a communication block. This silence at home about the service in the territories may have been caused by a son's feeling that his parents cannot possibly understand the way he experiences the intifada. Dovish parents especially may have been perceived as not comprehending their son's behavior. They may have indeed been disappointed in him, and perhaps even judged him harshly for taking part in morally objectionable patterns of behavior. A painful, reflexive awareness of the parents' reluctance to hear seemed to lie behind a son's reluctance to "talk about it" at home reported by many of those participating in the interviews.

A graver interpretation for such silence is that the soldier may have perceived, possibly subconsciously, that his parents felt guilty or helpless about not being able to change the situation for him.[3] Transferring the role of parent to empathetic outsiders made the judgment and the guilt less personal. Rather than talking familiarly about themselves from within a primary and ongoing relationship, they could present the "case" of themselves to a professional, through modes of confession, self-justification, and generalization.

THE INTERVIEWS: HOW SOLDIERS SAW THE INTIFADA FIRST-HAND

How do these first-hand observers re-see and rethink what they have already seen on television? The interviews fall into two major types. There are soldiers who, confronting the real-life ugliness of desperate protest and hate, align what they see with what they were prepared to see; what they perceive reinforces what they had in mind. However, there is another type of soldier – albeit a much smaller group – who experienced moral anguish, and talked to us about it.[4]

We now turn to consider these two types of framing in the soldiers' own words – the one that accepts the hegemonic framing and the other that struggled to maintain their oppositional voice precisely where it served them least well. The first shirks the problem by seeing only the masked enemy of television. The others, more open to seeing what's there, bear witness to an alternative, more complex, reality – but make problems for themselves thereby.

Not surprisingly, the images of real-life constructed by the soldiers relate to their political ideologies, which, as we have shown previously, are also the images they discern on the television screen.

Interviewees with hawkish outlooks, as we will show, saw the intifada in the field as the realization, or concretization, of the problem. For these soldiers the reality in the field only proved that their own, and television's, framing was right. The hegemonic framing they had brought with them entailed defining the situation of the intifada as "terrorism," or as "war," now offering first-hand evidence to substantiate these definitions. Their discourse took the form of pointing to the dangers to which they were subjected, to the hatred they encountered, and to the problematics of fighting with one hand tied behind one's back.

Interviewees with dovish outlooks, on the other hand, may be divided into two kinds. One group were the ideologically weaker soldiers, presumably afraid that coming into contact with the intifada would un-dove them. Reluctant to test their ideologies in the harsh light of confrontation with the uprisers, perhaps apprehensive of a process of habituation to the brutality of serving as riot police to repress a civil uprising, these soldiers chose *not to see* for themselves. The attempts to escape, so as not to look, took such forms as trying to get into military units in which there was little danger of being sent to the intifada, or staying behind when one's unit was, after all, sent to "the territories." While acting as officers in the field, this group made a conscious attempt to concentrate on the tasks of looking after their own soldiers, preferring to close their eyes to the broader picture.

The second, more ideologically confident group of soldiers, consisting mainly of junior officers with some control over their immediate environment, adopted a more active strategy. Looking at the Palestinians, as well as at their own performance in the often brutal or humiliating confrontation, they tried to fit their ways of acting and reacting to their way of defining the situation. This meant "negotiating" with their commanders and soldiers over the proper course of action, interpreting orders "minimalistically," arguing with superiors over specific orders, and organizing the immediate area over which they had control to fit with their own framing of the situation.

Whereas the first group of soldiers would probably keep to their views but would be less willing to stand up or argue their positions, this second group may be seen as the "hard core" believers, ready to fight for their views even when it meant clashing with the consensual climate around them. Thus, these soldiers may have provided a buffer against a spiraling silence which would have further marginalized their oppositional view (Noelle-Neumann, 1985).

Hegemonic seeing

Soldiers who internalized the hegemonic outlook on the conflict had an easier time. All they needed to do was to prove (to themselves and to others) that the intifada does indeed fit into the us and them frame. Calling it "a state of war," and its repression as military duty, made it simple to prevail over any individual doubts. Being at war was a way of defining a situation that made it possible to admit that one was getting used to brutality. Formulating the threat as acute (which, indeed, sometimes it was) made repression turn into combat. Such a view of the intifada made it possible to reconcile it with army policy. The following quotation demonstrates how an intifada "veteran" uses the frame of war to reduce dissonance.

In war you do what has to be done
Soldiers talk, soldiers express different opinions. There are soldiers who have expressed opposition. . . . Look, in the Six Days War – there were those who said we had to go to war, and those who said that we shouldn't. . . . But when they said "Go," everybody went to war, everybody did what had to be done. That's why we have an army, that's why soldiers are soldiers. And we are soldiers.

Similarly, it was possible to frame the army's repressive measures as necessary not so much for their own sake but as measures to protect the lives of soldiers. What to an outsider may look like corruption is understood as necessary caution once the extent of the danger is understood.

It happens to everyone
They [the newly arrived soldiers] understood it gradually. . . . After we were there for a month already. . . they realized it wasn't just brutality, without reason. . . . After being there for some time, bombarded with curses and stones. . . . In the beginning, they thought that . . . the soldiers really became. . . corrupt. Then they say, it happens to everyone.

Brutality, then, is the price the army pays for insuring the safety of its soldiers. Moral principles get in the way. And the promise that "it happens to everyone" may be directed at friends who are less ready to frame the situation as war.

Again, it is the junior officers who shoulder the brunt of responsibility. The more concrete the threat to their soldiers, the fewer scruples they have:

It's the intifada, not the orders
It's not that I didn't feel uncomfortable with the orders. I felt uneasy with
the situation. When 8,000 people confront you and throw stones at you,
your soldiers are hit in the head and you are helpless. There is nothing
you can do. You can't shoot them. You can't do anything.... The order
not to shoot is right. However, you feel uneasy with the situation.

A further reinforcement of the hegemonic view of the intifada occurs when
the soldier reverses roles and perceives himself as a *victim* confronting the
aggression of violent protestors, threatened by faceless, demonic Palestinians. Although he still opposes the idea of unwarranted repression, he now
perceives the army actions not as arbitrary brutality but as self-defense,
seeing himself and his friends as another link in the tradition of Israelis and
Jews faced with generations-long Arab hostility. These perceptions reflect
the "siege mentality" which has a stranglehold on Israeli society and about
which much has been written (for instance, Bar-Tal, 1990).

Amnon,[5] interviewed towards the end of his military service, was under
such pressure during the period he spent in the territories that he was sent
afterwards to a course for sports instructors as "compensation" (as a prize –
"*Tchupar*"). This is how Amnon expressed what it means to be scared when
one arrives in Gaza for the first time:

Suddenly you feel scared
You see all sorts of things...strange things...a toothless old woman
screams...she curses at me.... You see their hatred...the fact that they
are throwing stones at you...suddenly, you feel scared.

Beyond the immediate fear comes the understanding that for "them," the
Palestinians, an Israeli is someone to be hated absolutely, violently, and
unforgivingly. Israeli soldiers are hated collectively:

She hates me personally
I didn't understand why they hate me. I spoke to one [Palestinian] girl. I
told her I don't hate her personally...she said she hates us...personally.
She doesn't make any distinctions. She sees us all as Nazis.

Amnon's realization of being a victim of absolute hatred was followed by an
understanding that his life was being threatened:

Someone tried to kill me
Someone tried to kill me. He stood above me with a rock and if this rock
had hit me.... He was on the roof and I pointed my gun at him and told
him in Arabic that I would...shoot him. He said: "Shoot me, I don't
care." He aimed and threw the rock at me...I jumped to one
side...escaping the stone.

Preferring not to test one's convictions

Accounts like Amnon's make it clear why doves, especially those who were not absolutely convinced about their views, were greatly tempted to escape their exposure to human confrontation with the uprisers. It is also understandable that parents may support, or even initiate, solutions in which their sons could avoid being in a situation of moral dissonance during their military service.

In the following example Boaz, the youngest of three brothers, describes how (during his last year in school) he made the choice about joining an elite army unit. A major consideration in his choice was the avoidance of intifada service. Boaz points out the role of the family – in this case, his mother – in rousing his awareness of the dissonance that would follow. (This reference demonstrates Benyamini's (1982) finding according to which adolescents in Israel preferred turning to their mothers rather than consulting a friend or a professional in times of hardship).

My mother made me aware of this

And about the current situation.... My mother told me... she supports my going into an elite unit [i.e. a unit defined by a specialized job] – she knows I'm interested in going into a fighting unit – is that... I will serve in a smaller unit. Like my brother, for instance. She thinks that if one goes into the paratroopers or to Golani or to Givati now, he will spend his military service in the territories. Neither she nor I have any doubt about the intifada continuing. It will not end, not tomorrow and not the next day. So she told me that she definitely wouldn't be happy if.... That it is worthwhile thinking of something else.... She has added this considera-tion. My brother is in the army and he was in the territories, about every four weeks, on and off. I don't like the idea of being there for four months, or whatever.... It doesn't seem like a lot of fun. So my mother made me aware of this, I didn't think about it that much. But after she drew my attention to it, I understood that it is very rational, and correct.

Parents' advice to their sons about how to avoid confronting their beliefs may also hint at a reluctance to lose their own beliefs. As we have discovered, parents tend to move right (to more hawkish positions) as if in anticipation of a possible dissonance, when their adolescent children turn eighteen (when they are drafted).

As serving in a unit which was exempt from intifada service became increasingly unrealistic, other ways of staying out (of the territories) entailed maneuvering within the system, which was made easier by some of the soldiers' preference for "intifada work" over other jobs. Thus, for example, when it was the turn of Oren's unit to serve in the territories, he "arranged" with his immediate commander to be sent elsewhere. In this instance, Oren preferred to stay in the camp and give the tanks an overhaul, a job everybody dislikes.

Staying out

The first time I was supposed to be sent down to the territories I had a choice between going down to Gebelia for... a week or so, and staying at the base for a week maintaining the tanks. People were amazed that anybody would volunteer to stay for a week of maintenance because it means working from morning to night.... They couldn't wait to get away from the tanks and they felt they were missing out.... They were waiting to get to the territories. Not everyone would be sent... so they fought over it. It was no problem for me to stay out.

But physical escape was not a viable option for most soldiers. When not looking was impossible, another way to keep one's own framing of the situation intact, while preserving an unproblematic commitment to the IDF, was by associating more closely with one's reference group (Merton, 1957) – "my company," "my battalion," friends, who to some degree shared one's oppositional view, and the moral unease that went with it. With these friends, some of our interviewees told us, it was possible to "do the job" in "the most humane" way.

The following is Uri's story about the way "his" battalion interpreted orders:

Like beating up boys in the neighborhood

In principle, it seems to me that my battalion's behavior was proper, as much as possible. That is, I didn't see... I know there weren't... at least when I was there... any extreme immoral acts. One can argue that on the whole, our being there is immoral. But... I can say that no people were beat up... women or children... apart from... a few... cases... when things got out of control, but this wasn't planned brutality, it was more like beating up boys in the neighborhood...[6]

It should be noted that in the intifada, small units assigned to do policing jobs were spread out over a large area, often with no higher ranking officers on the spot, and this created a broad "gray range" for interpreting orders. Thus, specific standards of behavior could develop within these units (called "gangs" by Martin Van Krefeld (1989).[7] These units often felt that they were on their own, without "backing from above," but also without pushing from above. Finding themselves responsible for a street or neighborhood in a refugee camp, ways of framing the enemy were translated by junior platoon commanders into judgments such as whether or not to enter a house, or how to relate to political conflict in the platoon (Ben, 1991). In this context, the phenomenon of "my army" took on particular relevance.[8]

Naturally, these norms of behavior which developed within the small group could be easily shaken and put into question with the introduction of new commanders. This delicate balance emerged from David's story:

We also gave in
I remember a time when we were careful, we didn't shoot at anything, for a month and a half... until... one day... we were walking with my deputy commander.... I remember... it was a really difficult day.... They surrounded us from all sides, he shot in the air and... hit somebody in the leg... and we realized what idiots we were. For a month and a half, we had been bombarded by stones and curses... running the whole day. Putting out every burning tire by ourselves... he [the commander] comes to the Kasba [Arab marketplace] for only two hours and immediately starts shooting. And then... we ourselves also gave in... a little.

Another way of not looking, or avoiding the dissonance between one's own and the army's framing of the confrontation, was to foreground the self-definition as soldiers, and, better still, as officers, and concentrate on their job, and on their commitment to their own units.[9] Redefining self in terms of army role, committed by rules but more so by loyalties to one's unit, was a way of making salient those values which would support compliance, and playing down other aspects of self that might come in the way.[10] This is how Dan, a platoon commander, puts it:

I have a job to do
The way I see myself in all this, as well as afterwards... is I have a job to do and I have to carry it out. That is... as a person it's disturbing to me, too. It upsets me to beat up a child, it's upsetting to see children throwing [stones]... to shoot rubber bullets at boys. It disturbs me also to see soldiers... shoot with other things.... But on the other hand, this is what we have got to do... I have no choice.

Another officer concerned about the smooth operation of "his" company was threatened by the danger that "radicals" (like himself) might create a stir and obstruct his efforts to get the unit to function harmoniously. The following example shows how David, the company commander, refused to allow the circulation of a petition against serving in the territories, despite his belief in the cause. He justified his decision by reference to his duty to his soldiers.

I could not allow disruptions
I had all sorts of thoughts. There were two girls from my unit who were in the final phase of their army service. They were company sergeants. And before this they had not been acquainted with the intifada. They were in shock.... They got used to it after a while... very quickly... but... they wanted to organize, I remember... a petition... a strike, a petition against serving in the territories, or something. I told them... I could not,

I simply had my platoon. I had so many problems...all sorts of problems: social, disciplinary...[the platoon] started to shape up, and I was beginning to feel pleased. So I told [the two girls], "Anywhere else you can do what you like, but if you cause trouble in the company...I don't know what I'll do to you..." so they didn't have the guts to go on with it.

We read this quote as an example of minimizing the dilemma by emphasizing one's role as soldier. But here, as elsewhere, the texts are open to somewhat different interpretations. Stanley Cohen (personal communication) suggested that the phrase, "This is what we have got to do...I have no choice," should be classified as unquestioning obedience rather than cognitive redefinition of self in terms of role.

Holding on to an oppositional framing

The more ideologically confident interviewees were ready to fight for their views, arguing against friends and superiors.

We did not interview soldiers (the number of whom was negligible) who formally refused to serve in the territories on ideological grounds. The most combative ideological opposition we witnessed was going to the brink of rebellion by arguing with commanders about the legality of army orders aimed at civilian repression, and by contemplating petitions against the army's presence in the territories. The discussion with Gil, Omer, and Yoel is a good illustration:

Contemplating an organized protest
Gil Once, we even considered rebelling....We planned to organize a kind of petition, to collect signatures. We almost did it...but there was an officer, Richard, who had his feet on the ground. He managed to explain to us that we would just get into trouble and that nothing would come of it. First of all, it would be considered inciting a rebellion...
Int What did you want to write in this petition?
Omer That we are actually acting against the values we were brought up on...and the army here... is giving us orders do such things... I don't know... all sorts of extreme things. We wrote a letter...
Int What exactly were you afraid of?
Yoel To get into trouble, to be sent to prison.
Omer We knew that we had only six months left in the army and we were afraid...it was a pity...
Gil But there was something like that in our unit.
Yoel I know that my soldiers prepared a petition stating that they object to what is happening in the territories. They were invited to meet with the senior commander. He told them: "Either you stop it or you go to prison, and that's that." And that's how it ended.

Int   And you did not think that if others joined you, it would be less likely?
Omer   We did not believe there would be enough.

Whereas the examples of soldiers arguing with superiors about "radical" questions of principle – such as the legality of orders and the role of the army in the intifada – were rare, arguments about carrying out specific orders were much more common.

The phenomenon of arguments with commanders can be understood against the background of the loosening of the military hierarchy in the army's actions in the territories (Van Krefeld, 1989). In this situation, the "argumentativeness" of the Jewish-Israeli style of discourse emerged (Schiffrin, 1984). There is a lot of evidence for attempts to negotiate the army's repressive measures against the Palestinians during daily activity in the field.

Personal influence
Gil   There were some officers who were OK, like Yoel's platoon commander, who would simply talk to him. And Yoel would convince him. . . . So whatever Yoel said, he would agree.

Arguing over orders
We argued over the orders. . . . What to do, for instance, with burning tyres in the middle of the road. What should we do? The order was to put them into people's courtyards. That was the company commander's order. He claimed that if we saw a burning tyre next to a house we should throw it into the house, burning. We didn't agree.

There were even cases of soldiers appealing to a higher officer to protest against the behavior of the immediate commander:

Exposing an officer's brutal actions
Yoel   We had a commander who would grab [Arabs] in the street, grab them by the shoulder. He said that Arabs don't feel the pain . . . and they were afraid to react, but the shoulder is a terribly painful spot . . . I talked to the company commander about this officer. . . . But others who did not think like us learned from this officer; they did the same thing, without thinking twice.

Arguing about a specific order could also occur in the actual process of carrying it out, as Alon's story demonstrated:

They didn't bring down the [PLO] flag
There was a curfew and they caught a child. The deputy platoon commander arrived, he grabbed the child and told him: "Climb up on the electrical pole" – it was a high-tension wire – "and take down the [PLO] flag." It was a huge pole, impossible to climb. Impossible. He started and

after a few meters he could not go on. He [the commander] started to hit the child in the legs, and told him: "Go on climbing." He sort of didn't let him get down. We were in shock! The soldiers were enjoying it and Yigal (from my Kibbutz) and I.... Then his father came out of the house – which was prohibited – and he started to cry: "Leave my child alone, I'll take it down." He started climbing. He was quite old, and he couldn't do it. Then he said: "Wait a minute, I'll bring ladders." He tied them together but he still couldn't get to the flag. And he [the deputy platoon commander] started hitting him. Yigal and I started crying. It was really an impossible situation. I started to fight with the commander. We almost started fighting with clubs. The commander said: "They put it there, they can take it down. They can do it. You don't realize how capable they are." I asked: "How will he get it down. It's impossible." ... We were actually fighting in front of the soldiers, and finally he gave in. They did not bring down the flag.

The moral dilemma was obviously most clear in cases of collective punishment, and thus may have led to this type of negotiation. Not only did Alon's commander rescind his order to force Arabs to pull down the PLO symbol, but later this general order was revoked by the Chief of Staff. This activity was probably too problematic, both practically and ideologically.

Attempting to exemplify proper behavior while carrying out orders was another form of acting in accordance with one's reading of the situation, and against the army's repressive measures. Thus, when in a command position, certain of our interviewees reported carrying out searches with minimal harassment of Palestinian families to demonstrate that there is a decent way of carrying out this kind of task.

Orders could also often be interpreted in a broad range of ways. When carrying out repressive measures, the unit commander (junior though he may be) is empowered to interpret the regulations and to implement the army's measures against the intifada. But this kind of tailoring of individual orders to comply within acceptable limits has a price. Trying to preserve anti-repression principles while carrying out orders involves a constant tension.

Thus, there were reports about carrying out orders to smash houses by "smashing only a little", about letting people carry vegetable carts despite the orders of curfew, and about attempts to humanize the routine of searching cars on road blocks. As shown above, this brinkmanship is easier when one is surrounded by a sympathetic reference group. Thus firm oppositional framing was expressed through the carrying out of orders, as demonstrated in the following:

And afterwards we would clear the roads ourselves

My platoon commander was pretty violent . . . I was less violent. . . . Often

I would tell him over the walkie-talkie: "Listen, the whole road is blocked, it's full of road blocks..." "OK, get people [out of their homes] to clear it up...." "Okay, order received." And afterwards we would clear it out ourselves... I found it very hard.

This way of coping is defined by one interviewee as following the orders "one degree less," interpreting the "highest degree" not as the maximum demand, but as the maximum allowed:

How we followed orders
If the order said: "When a person throws stones at you, catch him and beat him up," we would catch him and not beat him.

Or, as in the following example, where Shai prefers not to embarrass the inhabitants while carrying out a house search:

I don't turn the house upside down
All in all, I am decent. If I ask "Who's in this room?" and they tell me "My daughter," I let it go. If it's a room full of mattresses, I don't check and I don't turn the house upside down.... It's as if... I'm embarrassed about coming into your house and turning it upside down like I should be doing.

Two other means were used to preserve and fight for one's oppositional views. One, more passive, was fantasizing the idea of quitting the army, and even the country, once compulsory military service is completed. Such thoughts make it possible to live with the dissonance between the moral legitimacy of fighting an enemy and the reality of harassing a civilian population by restricting it to the relatively short, strictly defined, present.

The other more active way of rationalizing actions which were considered to be against one's conscience, was to regard participation as limited to one's army role and to "counteract" it when off duty as a civilian who opposes the army's role in the territories, or the occupation altogether (Kelman and Baron, 1968). Thus, Gil carried out orders in the field and hurried to a "Peace Now" demonstration on his weekend leave:

Home for the weekend – it kept us going
Gil   When we would get leave and go home... we were lucky that we got to go home a lot... if, for instance, we would not have gotten home so often we would have ended up doing something...
Yoel   We would have been carried away.
Gil   But the fact that we got to go on home leave... we always waited for it. That's what kept us going. We would go home and go straight to all the protest demonstrations. There was a time when... every week there were some demonstrations.

Beyond the various ways of reducing dissonance between the hegemonic view and one's own oppositional framing of the intifada, the soldiers' discourse reveals tendencies to ascribe a value to one's awareness of the unease of the dissonance. This is demonstrated in Yoel's words:

You have to remind yourself that it's not right
I only remembered that it wasn't right. I didn't really believe in it anymore [when serving in the Intifada]. I remember that... I remembered that it isn't right to arrest people... and when a soldier arrests somebody and he [the Palestinian] says: "Leave me alone, I haven't done anything" and the soldier hits him in the face.... The first week it shocked me and I fought all the time with everyone. But after a while... you have to remind yourself that it's not right. Otherwise you don't feel it.

In terms of dissonance theory, which has been regaining popularity in recent years (Zanna and Cooper, 1974; Cooper and Fazio, 1984), our findings suggest that at least in certain cases of loyalty to conflicting values, there is an active effort to maintain an awareness of inconsistency.[11] More than that, we think we also see evidence of a desire to maintain dissonance, almost as if the pain of the dissonance may overcome the drive to rid oneself of it.[12]

DO SOLDIERS' OPPOSITIONAL FRAMES FILTER INTO PUBLIC SPACE?

Whereas the framing of the conflict reported by these soldiers may be a form of oppositional reading, it was articulated only on demand, raising the question of how such readings may find ways of filtering through into the public debate. Even more than in the case of journalists (chapter 2), these soldiers represent the dual role taken by Israelis. In the act of putting on their army uniform Israeli young men slide into the role of a mobilized soldier (Ben-Ari, 1989), one who may know things which he cannot publicly proclaim.

Moreover, the interviews we have conducted indicate that the soldiers who bore witness to an oppositional view of the conflict kept silent about it even – perhaps mostly – in the homes of their own families. How then could this view, this first-hand undercurrent of knowledge, filter into public discussion? Can an argument be made for it influencing the public agenda?

Three options may be offered for consideration. First, that these remain silent voices which may be reported indirectly through the research done by social psychologists, anthropologists, and sociologists (some of whose work was undertaken within the IDF itself, until their conclusions were not favorably looked upon by their employer). This leads to speculation about the question of whether the intifada contributed to the decrease in the motivation of young educated Israelis to volunteer for combat units, and more important, to sign-on as officers, once their compulsory service was completed.

The second option is that private conversations among soldiers in their own camps and living-rooms find a way of seeping through to public awareness, for the very reason that the army is not a segregated professional army but a people's army.

Third, there are the cases of soldiers, mostly officers, who deliberately spoke up, sometimes individually, more often as part of a group, to protest about having to fight against a civilian population. These voices from within the army, and the creeping worry that the occupation may be causing long-term harm to its soldiers and commanders, must have carried particular weight in the decision of politicians such as Prime Minister Yitzhak Rabin, who arose from the army, to move out of the territories ("Gaza first") and to seek some other form of reconciliation with the Palestinians.

Chapter 11

Them as us – Palestinians on Israeli Cinema

How Israeli film-makers fail to transform television framing of the Palestinian

Having argued that Israeli press and television, during the period of the intifada, presented the Arab–Israeli conflict as "us and them," making it difficult for viewers, even for first-hand witnesses, to defend an oppositional view, I will now go a step further to examine the problem inherent in the conscious attempt to *produce* alternative images of the conflict. This chapter examines the self-conscious attempts of certain Israeli film-makers, during the time of the intifada, to position the Palestinian as a hero in Israeli films, and thus to challenge television's image of the Palestinian as "other." In doing so, we will demonstrate that the presentation of the Palestinian as one of us creates its own problems. The next chapter examines the attempt of Israeli television itself, once again in the service of hegemony, to transform the image of the enemy, by looking at the live broadcast of the reconciliation ceremonies generated by the Oslo agreement.

The analysis of the other in films, as in the case of television news, draws on the assumption that meanings of literary, televisual, or cinematic texts are realized in the encounter, or the dialogue, between the ideologies of authors, journalists, and producers, and those of readers who may or may not share memberships in the same cultural community. We therefore examine both the relevant cinematic texts and the manner in which they were received.

In the case of these films, however, we have chosen to examine interpretations given by professional critics rather than to analyze reception by lay persons. Unlike television news, viewed by everybody from their living-room couch, we reasoned that the diffusion and social influence of films depends on the judgment of cultural mediators. While most cultural artifacts pass by us without leaving an impression, some continue to reverberate and are institutionalized in one way or another – in museums, cinematheques, the education system, even as part of "civil religion" (Schudson, 1989). And critics are one kind of gate-keeper who filter cultural artifacts (Griswold, 1987). Critics also constitute an interesting interpretive community. In their capacity of cultural elite they are said to be ahead of their time, revealing incipient trends in social ideas while these are still in their infancy. Moreover, criticism constitutes a text which is accessible and represents an attempt at methodical thinking. If we accept the assumptions underlying Stuart Hall's (1985) analysis, there is a greater chance of compatibility in encoding and decoding between film-makers and critics than between the former and the general public which in any case does not rush to see films such as *Cup Final*.

THE PALESTINIAN IN ISRAELI FILMS

Until the late 1970s the Palestinian in Israeli films was pushed aside into the role of the unseen enemy of the heroic Israeli fighter or into the marginal role of the inferior native. The popular *Burekka* films of that period presented the member of the underprivileged, Sephardi ethnic group as the other within an Israeli society, which was inwardly oriented. "The return of the oppressed" in the 1980s (Shohat, 1989) was a deliberate political attempt to present the enemy as a human being – perhaps as our own alter ego – and to claim that both they and we are closely linked together. Both sides were now seen as victims of the conflict and the message emanating from newscasts – that they are bad dispositionally whereas we are bad situationally and that we are in control of the situation – was misleading and dangerous.

It is in this context that we examine the oppositional representations in films made during the intifada, with the intention of personalizing the figure of the Palestinian, and the critical reactions to these attempts. The dialectical discourse of the critics is demonstrated in the reviews of two films – *Beyond the Walls*, made in 1984, which depicts understanding between Israelis and Palestinians as the only way of defeating the authorities governing the prison in which they find themselves, and *Cup Final*, made in 1991, directed by Eyal Riklis, where empathy is established between a Palestinian terrorist and an Israeli reserve soldier he captures, on the basis of the shared culture of the "global village." In real life they belong to different sides, but as supporters of the same Italian football team they are on the same side. Whereas *Beyond the Walls* was a success with both the critics and the audience, *Cup Final* failed with both, for contradictory reasons.

COMPETING OVER THE IMAGE OF THE "REAL" PALESTINIAN

In choosing to present the Palestinian to the Israeli public, film-makers – and film critics in their wake – are aware of the prevalence in Israeli society of the image of the Palestinian as the masked figure of television news. The basic dialogue of the Palestinian character in Israeli films is, then, with the image of the Palestinian as perceived by the public. In the words of the Israeli Palestinian writer Emil Habibi, these films are intended to show the public what a "real" Palestinian is.

WHY CINEMA IS WEAKER THAN TELEVISION

In order to believe that a compromise can be reached, it is crucial to be convinced that there is someone on the other side with whom it is possible to reach agreement. In other words, there must be awareness of the other as a human being. As was argued earlier (see chapter 9), television news, during the intifada, symbolically obliterated the Palestinians, showing them only in the role they play in the Arab–Israeli conflict, thereby reinforcing the perception of the conflict as a zero-sum-game, and strengthening the right wing in Israeli politics. Seen from our point of view the face of the Palestinian is hooded, both literally and metaphorically.

Obviously, as far as the chance of influencing public opinion in Israel is concerned, the cinema is in an inferior position to television. First of all, television is perceived by the public – though not necessarily by communications experts – as reflecting objective, external reality, while films depict subjective, imaginative stories which convey the film-maker's inner truth.

Second, while over 70 percent of the population was exposed on a continuous and daily basis to television's news-portrayal of the Palestinian, in the cinema he or she appears only rarely, and even then to an audience which is self-selected, with a relatively high level of education, and a special interest in being exposed to an image which could arouse cognitive dissonance.

Third, the ideological message underlying the presentation of "them" and "us" on the news is internalized and taken for granted as "real" by most viewers (who are not aware of the transformation rules whereby reality becomes the news). Movie audiences are far more aware of the existence of an author's intentions, and are hence more suspicious of what is perceived as a deliberate message.

Finally, it makes sense to argue that the point at which the author's ideology is revealed most clearly is the end of the story (Fiske, 1988). At the moment of truth, will the leader of the revolt choose to return to his family and abandon his friends, or will he continue to fight? At the end of the story, will it be the Israeli or the Palestinian who is still alive? The news-text does not have to confront that problem because it is never-ending and always interrupted. "A young man was killed in Gaza. The IDF is investigating." It is not yet clear what happened, who is to blame. There is even some relief in the fact that there is as yet no guilty party. It is almost certain that we shall never know. And yet the other side remains anonymous, often absent, almost always faceless.

THE BLURRING OF THE BOUNDARIES BETWEEN ROLE AND IDENTITY OF ENCODERS AND DECODERS

Critics, like film-makers, are confused as to what should be discussed. Should critics relate to the director who creates the character, or to the actor who plays the character? Should the director be required to give us a character who is psychologically convincing, or should he or she give us the real Palestinian? Should the actor be discussed in terms of his or her political and national identity (as an Arab actor "collaborating" in a Jewish film, for example), or in terms of his or her physical type (stereotype)?

Goffman's (1974) analysis of the confusion regarding the term "role" in reality and on the stage (in this instance, on the screen) helps to dispel some of this ambiguity. In real life an individual has an identity; it is continuous, it is his or her biography, his or her memory. Various skills and specific functions are brought into play in different situations. One can say that someone is a good plumber, a mediocre father, or a loyal friend. In the specific role of actor the same person takes on the role, or "part," of another person who is not "real," but who also has his or her own identity (granted, a fictional one), and who carries out specific functions; we use the term "role" to refer to all four.

Let us look at Muhammad Bakhri, for example. His identity comprises a body of skills and the following functions: family member – husband in a traditional society, where he is trying to come to terms with the demand for greater gender equality, and father of five (*Ha'aretz*, 26.3.92); national – a Palestinian who is also an Israeli citizen; professional – actor on the Israeli stage and in the Israeli cinema; a worker in the construction industry or salesman of vegetables when he is "resting" from freelance acting (*Dvar Hashavua*, 4.4.92); and political activist – he has been a member of the Hadash (Israeli Communist) Party since 1988.

Bakhri plays Palestinian leaders in both films under discussion. When he plays Isam (in *Beyond the Walls*) or Ziyad (in *Cup Final*) he is creating a fictitious identity which we perceive through the roles he plays – as a security detainee or terrorist leader (or, if you prefer, freedom fighter) fighting for the national rights of the Palestinians (whether in a political or a professional role, or as husband and father). In real life, whether acting in films made by Barabash or Riklis, on the stage of the Haifa Theater, or in a solo performance, he is working as an actor, and this is only one of his roles. But the choice of parts make the "real" and "on stage" identities particularly difficult to disentangle.

It is interesting to see how Bakhri presents himself to the Israeli public. In 1988 Bakhri appeared in a short election film for the Hadash Party. The camera pans in from behind on the silhouette of an actor on a stage. He begins to recite a poem by Israel's national poet, Bialik, but in Hebrew with an Arabic accent. Every Israeli knows that poem from school, and its opening line ("Hail to thee upon thy return, O lovely bird") symbolizes renascent Zionism. When he has finished the poem, Bakhri turns to the audience and explains that it is not so strange that he, too, knows the poem by heart. As an Israeli Arab he had to learn it at school. From being a symbol of the independence of the Jewish people, *To the Bird* has become a symbol of the Jewish state's suppression of another people's cultural identity.[1] The camera pans in on Bakhri's face until it fills the entire screen, contrasting the image of the Arab as portrayed in the election broadcasts of the two main parties – demonic, faceless figures (Likud) and the abstract "demographic threat" (Alignment) – with his own image, that of actor, Israeli citizen, head of a family and member of the Hadash party.

In other words, the Bakhri of the election broadcast is the antithesis of the masked Palestinian. He was chosen to appear in the election film for the Hadash party, first because of his European visage and "sex appeal," which make him "one of us." Second, as an actor, Israeli society accords him the same kind of legitimacy that it does to Arab football stars. And third, he is identified with the noble, human Palestinian heroes whose characters he has portrayed in a number of Israeli films.

When reviewing the two films mentioned earlier, the critics are not functioning solely within the framework of their professional capacity. Uri Klein explicitly reflects upon this in castigating *Cup Final*. He could have, says Klein, focused on the film's aesthetic properties, its pace, editing, or narrative, but he believes that is not the point. The relevant position to take is an ideological one.

In their role as political commentators, the critics refer, either alternately or indiscriminately, to Bakhri *the actor* who personalizes the other in the conflict ("doing his thing again"), to Bakhri the Israeli–Palestinian employed by Zionist Jewish directors, and to Bakhri whose blue eyes make him the anti-stereotype of the figure of the Arab. In each of those three aspects he may be judged positively or negatively in political terms.

The blurring of spheres in the production process also helps to cloud decoding by critics and the audience. Directors do indeed choose Palestinian actors to portray Palestinian characters, in order to attain maximal authenticity. Choosing the same actor to play similar roles in different films made by different directors also makes a contribution. For their part, the Palestinian actors contribute to the identity between the actor and the character by taking part in decisions about what happens to the character they play, and their involvement is politically motivated.

Thus, we learn from Ella Shohat that director Barabash planned for Isam to go home at the end of the narrative, but that Muhammad Bakhri refused, suggesting an alternative ending in which he goes out to his wife and little boy at the prison gate only in order to send them home, without him. Barabash, we are told, agreed to shoot the two alternatives, but gave in as soon as he realized that Bakhri's ending was the most powerful. Bakhri's justification for turning down Barabash's version was that he would not be able to look his (real-life) son in the eyes the morning after the screening of a film in which he had abandoned his Palestinian friends in jail. Three identities – Bakhri the actor (who found his own narrative solution to the story), Bakhri the father (in real life), whose family role led him to suggest the solution, and Bakhri the political leader in the narrative, whose role is fictitious but which is identified by his real-life son as his real role – combined to produce an argument whose logic was clear to both Bakhri and Barabash.

Obscuring the borders between an actor's real identity and the roles he plays on the screen, and/or stressing one aspect at the expense of another, serves the critic's ideological ends. Israeli film critics' interpretations of Palestinian characters can be defined in relation to the radicality of their positions. The minimalists – or perhaps romantics – regard the personalization of the Palestinian in films as a positive political act in itself, while those critics with higher aspirations – or perhaps expectations – treat the nature of the personalization more seriously. Dialectically, whichever of the two looks better is in fact worse.

CRITICS AS IDEOLOGISTS: ROMANTICISM VS DIALECTICS

It should not come as a surprise that two Palestinian critics, Emil Habibi (winner of the Israel Prize for literature) and Raja Shehada, author of *The Third Way*, are minimalists. Neither of them belongs to the narrow, elitist band of critics whose members write for one another. Habibi's and Shehada's reference group is the general Jewish public, and their political interest is pragmatic. The role of the Palestinian in films – regardless of whether as an actor or a character in the narrative – is to arouse the audience's empathy and emotional involvement, thereby helping to alter the way the Jewish public perceives the Palestinians.

THE MINIMALIST ROMANTIC APPROACH

For Habibi, the Palestinian characters in *Cup Final* contrast with "the character behind the mask" which official propaganda teaches the public to see as the real Palestinian. Shehada, on the other hand, criticizes the quality of the personalization in *Cup Final*. He claims that it is not effective because the Palestinians are removed from the context of their private lives, and cannot therefore arouse the audience's identification. If you are an Israeli you will not feel sorry when one of the Palestinians is killed. And because you cannot identify with the character, you remain the Israeli onlooker rather than a film-goer, to use Goffman's terms.

Some critics accept the idea of presenting the Palestinian as an admirable human being, whether they define the film as political ("political in the good sense of the word") or anti-political ("we're all human beings, and the political conflict is stupid").[2] Michal Peleg, a critic in the Jerusalem weekly *Kol Hair*, who believes in the value of personalization, criticizes *Cup Final* not only for failing to give the Palestinians a private life, but for creating asymmetry between the characters of the Palestinians and that of Cohen, the captured Israeli. The script gives Cohen more autobiographical background; we learn that he owns a boutique in Tel-Aviv, has a wife and two daughters, and supports the Likud. All this leads the viewer to identify with him and not with the Palestinians. This critic seems to be confusing our knowledge as Israeli viewers of Cohen in real life with what we learn about him from the script. On screen, Ziyad also discloses information about himself – he studied pharmacy in Italy, he has a wife and child who are waiting for him to come back. From our viewpoint, however, there is no symmetry between the two. It is enough for us to see the actor playing Cohen, Moshe Ivgi, to know who he is, and everything he says about himself is instantly applied to the Israeli reality with which we are familiar. Identifying with him as a human being is based on the evocation of other Cohens from real life. Not so for Ziyad.

Ironically, the absence from the screen of the Palestinians' private life echoes, in part, the attitude of real terrorists. They are not looking for that kind of identification from the viewers on the other side. Indeed, from a newspaper interview we learn that Eyal Halfon, who wrote the screenplay of *Cup Final*, actually interviewed prisoners released in the Ahmed Gibril deal. The interviewees refused to reveal any personal details, restricting their replies to their political activities. In contrast to Habibi and Shehada, but like the radical critics, real-life Palestinian terrorists oppose personalization because it de-ideologizes the conflict and obfuscates the real forces in control of the field. The politics of force cannot be translated into the characters of individual terrorists. Ziyad and his friends are themselves hostages, rather than representing the bosses in the conflict. The dramatization of their lives merely diverts the discussion from the problem as a whole to details whose relevance can be assessed only when anchored in a wider political context.

THE AMBITIOUS DIALECTICAL APPROACH

Critics with more radical demands analyze the authenticity of the image of the Palestinian in order to determine whether in political terms the film is a step forward or a false, illusory kind of progress which does more harm than good.

The demand for authenticity is made on two levels, in both of which the same question is asked – is it right to portray the Palestinian as being like us? On one level this refers to his external appearance (and whether it is desirable for a Palestinian actor to play a Palestinian), while on the other it refers to the socio-political context. In its most extreme version, the second level relates to the legitimacy of the production – do Israelis have a moral right to make a film about the problems of Palestinians?

The attempt to break physical stereotypes – by using a fair-haired, blue-eyed actor – has not gained the approval of the critics in Israel. The Palestinian hero who is like us is perceived as a stereotype in itself after two or three films. Worse, it is regarded as symbolically obliterating the identity of the Palestinian by granting him our identity, even if this is the identity of Jesus, as Ella Shohat contends.

Salman Matzlaha (*Kol H'air*) goes even further by claiming that until Jews are cast as Palestinians, the prejudices prevalent in Israel will not be eliminated. The next step after choosing a European-looking Arab will be to cast a Jew (possibly a Sephardi) in the role, thereby breaking the connection between the actor's origin and the character he portrays. (An attempt to achieve this was made by Bakhri and Tzadok when, in *Beyond the Walls 2*, they re-enact the story of *Beyond the Walls 1*, reversing roles.) Matzlaha's concern with the Jewish public's image of the Palestinian leads him to a conclusion which is opposite to Habibi's. Matzlaha would like to see the Palestinian portrayed as a true "other," different from us, without falling into the trap of depicting the other as the enemy or the native servant, as was done in early Hollywood and Israeli films. Matzlaha would like to see a Palestinian who, despite his otherness, arouses sympathy and respect.

Another problem critics have with the revisionist stereotype of the Palestinian is that it is not accompanied by an equivalent transformation of the character of the oriental Jew – Arnon Tzadok in *Beyond the Walls* and Moshe Ivgi in *Cup Final*. Barabash is attacked for this both by the radical left and the radical right. Ella Shohat claims that Beyond the Walls was made by Peaceniks who imagined themselves to be making a political protest, but in fact were simply serving establishment ends by romanticizing Palestinians and repressing oriental Jews. The film depicts Uri, the leader of the criminal prisoners, as if he is to blame for the fact that he has turned to crime. What does not come across, according to this argument, is that he represents the problems of oriental Jews, whose roots lie in the same social reality as that which created and perpetuates the Israeli–Palestinian conflict. At the other extreme, a *Maariv* columnist from the extreme right protests the fact that the oriental Jew is identified with crime in *Beyond the Walls*. As far as he is concerned, it is a film made by dangerous, left-wing, yuppie, bleeding-heart Ashkenazis who love Arabs and benefit from oppressing oriental Jews. Thus, the critics at both extremes of the political spectrum agree that the directors (because they are not left-wing enough, or because they are too left-wing) distort the character of the oriental Israeli.

The radical critics think that creating Palestinians who are "one of us" is an act of cultural imperialism. The implicit message is that Palestinians deserve self-determination because they are like us, they are "all right" because they are football fans, too. Uri Klein's contention, with which the Israeli viewer finds it harder to identify, is that the Palestinians deserve national rights because they are *them*. They must be respected even if, especially if, they are not like us. By superimposing a familiar identity on them in order to bring them closer to the viewers, Barabash and Riklis are symbolically eradicating their culture.

The contention is dialectical; it is in fact the attempt to bring them closer, to "tame" them, which coopts their culture and prevents the viewer from recognizing and respecting their true identity. The argument sounds familiar from radical feminist criticism of television portrayals of female characters.

Bizarre as this would seem, the presentation of an alternative image of the Palestinian was bound to evoke the type of criticism that was directed against alternative presentations of women (Iyengar, 1991; Van Dijk, 1987; Williamson, 1986). On the face of it, in Israeli society, women and Palestinians seem to have very little in common. The Palestinian as other in Israeli society is external, invisible, and does not belong. Women, on the other hand, are very much within, highly visible, and belong, perhaps even too much. The Palestinian is the other because he is perceived as a category (e.g. as a "demographic problem") rather than as a person. Women are possibly perceived *solely* on the personal level, thus their position of social inferiority is seen as natural, not as the problem of a social group or a minority. On the individual level the Palestinian was, certainly until the Oslo accord, regarded at best as a blurred figure seen through an opaque glass, and at worst as an enemy, threatening, faceless, and demonic. Nevertheless, attempts to "promote" the image of woman on American television meet with the same kind of criticism. In both cases radical critics claim that the attempt to offer equality through sameness is merely a neocolonialist distortion of the true nature of the other, thereby serving the dominant elite.

Unlike these feminists, who believe that there is a basic identity between the sexes which women have not yet had the chance to realize, some women critics believe that there is a unique female culture. They claim that presenting women as equivalent to male characters deprives them of their authentic culture and nature. The most extreme version of this view regarding the Palestinians' culture is that developed by the film and theater director, Yigal Burstein. He claims that the very fact that Israeli directors and producers take it upon themselves to depict Palestinians is itself neocolonialist, offering the Israeli establishment an opportunity to pat itself on the back for being so enlightened and self-critical. Another variation of shooting and weeping. Only Palestinians have the right to present and represent themselves. The problem then is that such representation may be too easily labeled as "minority art" (and ignored by the majority). A more systematic way of discussing the issue may be in terms of *who* is the work of art representing (minority/majority), *by* whom is it represented (member of the minority/majority), and *for* whom is it shown (minority/majority) (Gross, 1989).

COMPETITION AS METAPHOR: IS IT FAIR?

The way Palestinians are represented in these two films can also be discussed in terms of occupation and competition. Within the context of the occupation of the territories (*Beyond the Walls*) and of Lebanon (*Cup Final*), both directors seek to create a situation of competition, where the position of the Palestinian hero is compared with that of the Israeli hero. For the romantic, minimalist critics the metaphor of the rivals who support the same football team represents an achievement. Focusing on a competitive framework highlights the comparison between the opposing sides. There is no permanent victor in a competition, at times one side gains the upper hand, and at others the other. The rules of the game are the real winner.

The metaphor of the competition also creates a framework, a miniature model, which can contain the conflict and keep it under control. The interest they share puts the two rivals on the same side in the contest, creating empathy between them and arousing admiration in each for the expertise of the other.

The radicals perceive the presentation of both sides as equal as a distortion, because it postulates that the Palestinians constitute a genuine threat, an enemy who is on an equal footing (like calling the intifada a war, or equating the Gulf War with World War II). In the case of *Cup Final*, we do not forget that the IDF has conquered Lebanon and that the equality between the two sides is only momentary. The comparison is, as stated, distorted, representing the Palestinians as Israelis, depriving them of their culture, and depicting them as being detached from their personal, family, and political context. Every terrorist is perceived as being both powerful and doomed to failure; consequently, the films merely re-establish the hegemony of the Israeli establishment.

The problem seems to be how to avoid throwing the baby out with the bath-water. The battle over the way women are portrayed on television began with the claim that women were not portrayed at all, or solely in symbolic fashion. Once women began to be seen in prime time, that contention was superseded by the claim that their representation lacked authenticity. Women were shown on the screen, but their true culture was falsified by putting them in a setting where they had to play the game according to the rules of the men's world.

The representation of the Palestinian as a human being in the Israeli cinema was a step forward in view of his symbolical obliteration as a human being, sometimes his demonized portrayal, on television. It can also be claimed that by removing him from his family and personal context he becomes more political. The risk inherent in the demand that Palestinians be depicted as different is returning to square one. Because otherness on its own is simply not enough. What is needed is otherness that elicits empathy. So that the inevitable conclusion from the purist's perspective is that whatever one does is bound to fail.

Chapter 12

I and thou

How live broadcasts of Middle-East peace ceremonies wear out their welcome

Barring the attempts of ideologically committed artists and politicians, for most Israelis the Arab enemy remained a faceless or threatening "them" during the forty something years which elapsed between the founding of the state and the signing of the Oslo agreement. With one dramatic exception. In 1977, Anwar el-Sadat, in a psychologically insightful act that seemed unthinkable at the time, visited Jerusalem, offering Israel diplomatic recognition in return for territorial concessions. In contrast to prior negotiations with Arab leaders, which were conducted in secret, in disguise, and never got anywhere, the Jerusalem visit was broadcast live, every step of the way, with Sadat talking to Israelis "above the heads" of their (and his own) government. The Israeli public, starved for acceptance by its neighbors, reacted by falling in love with the Egyptian President. The strategy of addressing the enemy in the second person – replacing "them" with "thou" (Buber, 1958) – proved extremely effective, at least in this case. It provides a dramatic clue not only to the power of a face-to-face encounter, but for the potential power of television to transform the reality of conflict.

While staged peace ceremonies, broadcast live, have to be hegemonic almost by definition, they nevertheless constitute landmarks in media's construction of the other side, and as such have an important role in making reconciliation acceptable. Counteracting the routine coverage of conflict which, as we have shown, effaces, demonizes, and generally delegitimates the enemy, these events are designed to humanize, personalize, equalize, and legitimate. This is no easy task, and from the point of view of Israelis, some foes are more acceptable than others.

Making use of President Sadat's visit as a model for a successful transformative media event, this chapter asks why the later versions of the reconciliation ceremonies of 1993–5, with Yasser Arafat and King Hussein representing the Palestinians and Jordanians respectively, wore out their welcome.

On the face of it, television had an independent input into President Sadat's success in alleviating the suspicions of Israelis. A more realistic evaluation, moreover, would conclude that the political transformation (media strategy included) was initiated, planned, and carried out by the political establishment. In order to mobilize public support for a difficult, for some painful, policy change the political leadership (on both sides) wisely chose to enlist the press and the media, who, on their part, enthusiastically joined in. Far from a "naive" plea to the public for territorial sacrifice, Sadat's public appeal was delivered after he had already been promised the whole of the Sinai Peninsula (in a totally unexpected move from Begin's tough, right-wing new government). This was the same government which had engineered the Jerusalem visit, as a media event to create a liminal mood, and provide the public with emotional uplift in return for the very real concessions they were going to have to accept.

Thus, there was an evocative feeling of *déjà vu* on seeing the handshake between Israeli Prime Minister Yitzhak Rabin and PLO leader Yasser Arafat on the White House lawn, on live television, in September 1993. To many Israelis this moment of euphoria was reminiscent of the Sadat visit and signalled the transformation of the hundred-year-long conflict between Israelis and Palestinians. Yet, less than two years later, in the midst of a chain of the most massive terrorist attacks Israel had, to that point, known, the public signing of the Oslo agreement has lost its aura as a marker of transformation, to both Israelis and Palestinians. Some believed it could have succeeded had we progressed faster, others – that we should never have started down this road. But both would agree that the effectiveness of the public ceremony itself, regardless of how miraculous it seemed at the time, deserves to be reconsidered. Moreover, the crashing into tough reality of so many of the euphoric media events of recent years – in Eastern Europe and in the Middle East – leads to a reinterpretation of a media event as an unkept promise, a spectacle that had created more expectations than it could fulfill.

From the analysis, it will be obvious that assessments of long-term effects do not stand still; they have to be made repeatedly as time goes by. What is more interesting, however, is to ask whether the seeds of the future meaning of an event can be discerned, at least retroactively, in the ceremonies themselves.

This examination in hindsight follows Dayan and Katz's (1993) specifications of the conditions under which media events can be said to "work." Specifically, we ask when does an event "succeed" as a performative, as an affirmation of an immediate change of status by participants and viewers, and when does an event work transformatively, taking part in a long-lasting process of social and political change? With respect to both questions, we shall first recall the conditions of the Sadat case, and then go on to compare what we know of the subsequent cases.

ANWAR EL-SADAT'S VISIT TO JERUSALEM, NOVEMBER 1977

A heroic move

Israelis only knew the Egyptian President as the "hero of the crossing" of the Suez Canal in the Yom Kippur War, which had taken place only four years before the visit. As such he caused the worst collective trauma in the nation's history, and, at the same time (in spite of losing the war), restored the honor that Egypt had lost in the Six Day War (Katz, Dayan, and Motyl, 1983). This heightened stature allowed Sadat to reiterate his readiness to make peace with Israel (already stated in 1972), hoping, at the same time, to receive US aid for his economically ailing country. There seemed no chance, however, that Israel would accept his condition of total withdrawal from the Sinai.

On the Israeli side, the belated reaction to the Yom Kippur War, at least in part, brought the right-wing Likud Party to power for the first time in Israel's history. Prior to the election, Menachem Begin, the new Prime Minister, showed no hint of an interest in making peace. It was a complete surprise, therefore, when it was learned that Moshe Dayan, Begin's Foreign Minister at the time, had met secretly with Hassan Tohami, Sadat's emissary in Morocco, and had promised to yield the Sinai, whereupon Sadat announced again in the Egyptian Parliament that he might go to Israel for a visit of reconciliation. Katz, Dayan, and Motyl (ibid.) describe how, from that point on, events proceeded at a frenetic pace. Taking on the role of mediator, American television anchor Walter Cronkite, in a filmed telephone conversation, asked Sadat whether "It might be as little as one week?" and Sadat replied, "You could say so, Walter," making the rendezvous concrete. On Saturday night, at the expected hour, the plane arrived, the El Al stairway moved up to the Egypt Air plane, and Sadat emerged, followed by USA television star anchors – "A thrill ran through the crowd and a cheer went up at the airport, (and) echoed in every living room in Israel," while Bob Simon of CBS reporting from the ground, exclaimed "Will miracles never cease?" Next, Sadat walked down the reception line, greeting his Yom Kippur foes, as old acquaintances.

For the next three days, from their living-rooms, Israelis followed Sadat's every move – worshipping at the (Muslim) holiday service of the El Aqsa mosque, visiting the memorial to the (Jewish) Holocaust, laying a wreath at the tomb of the Unknown (Israeli) Soldier, receiving a standing ovation in the Knesset, accepting Golda Meir's gift "from a grandmother to a new grandfather," confessing that he used to refer to her as "the old lady." (In a book written by a senior Mossad agent eighteen years later, Sadat added "You know I could have been here years earlier.")

On television, Sadat presented himself as the hero who risked his life by coming, determined to extend a sincere and personal offer of peace to Israel.

From the minute he stepped off the plane, the Egyptian President made his visit into a grand gesture of sacrifice and reconciliation, offering his heretofore-unknown charismatic personality to the Israeli public, in order to overcome the psychological barrier (which, he claimed, constituted 70 percent of the conflict) and to turn suspicion into trust. In support of the idea that it was the exposition of his identity on television rather than a change in policy that transformed the relationship between Israel and Egypt is the fact that Sadat's political message remained unchanged. In his Knesset speech, delivered in Arabic, his terms remained uncompromising, which did not prevent the visit from proceeding as a process of romantic conquest in which what counted was the strange discovery by Israelis that an unknown enemy could be revealed as a new friend, charming generals and Knesset members, and capturing the hearts of Israeli viewers. In their hunger for recognition, Israelis seemed to be ready to give up all tangible advantages for a gesture of friendship.

Rhetorics of reconciliation

Sadat's Knesset speech packaged the bitter pill of his uncompromising conditions for peace in words and associations that evoked the potential sympathy of both Arabs and Jews. For Arab viewers, the words, symbols, and historical events mentioned by Sadat often signified meanings opposite to the one Sadat proclaimed. The most blatant example was his use of the word *salam* (the Hebrew *shalom*) for "peace." While Israeli Jews were overjoyed, Arabs knew that *sulch* is the Arabic term for "real" and complete reconciliation, while *salam* is a truce signifying temporary submission until conditions might be ripe for victory over the enemy. In prior speeches, when he explained the impossibility of ever making peace with the treacherous Jewish state, Sadat used the term *sulch*; now he chose to offer the temporary version of peace, *salam*, leaving the back door open (Liebes-Plesner, 1984).

In another passage, a peace treaty signed by the Prophet Muhamad and the Jews of Medina was evoked as a historical omen guaranteeing success to the current initiative.[1] For Muslim viewers, however, who know the unspoken end of the story, the evocation operated to throw doubt on the possibility of peace. The Jews of Medina, it seems, turned out to be traitorous; Muhamad killed them all, and pronounced that the Jews cannot be trusted. As in the case of *sulch*, Sadat himself, in other speeches, had often cited this story as "proof" that it is impossible to make agreements with the Jewish state.

Sadat made repeated use of this technique of "whitewashing" symbols. Thus, invoking Abraham, the ancient common ancestor of the Jews and the Arab peoples, Sadat directed his audience to consider that Abraham was ready to sacrifice his only son for a higher cause. Unspoken again was the Koranic version in which Abraham does not intend to sacrifice his son at all but goes on a pilgrimage to the sacred mountain as a pedagogic act in order to be publicly instructed by God not to sacrifice his son. By a sophisticated choice of symbols signifying common ancestry and history, by omitting the elements of competition, conflict, and contradiction, the Knesset speech clinched the meaning of Sadat's visit as a romantic conquest of the hearts of Israelis, and a wink of reassurance to the Arabs.

What did television do?

Dayan and Katz (1993) offer several reasons to explain why the live broadcast of the visit was crucial to its success. First, if recognition by an Arab leader was what the Israelis most wanted, what more tangible manifestation could there be? Recognition lies in publicity, as in the case of the declarations "You are married," or "Jerusalem is the capital of Israel," which become performative by virtue of their publicness. Thus, in accepting the hospitality and authority of the Israeli government and its Parliament, with the whole world watching, the senior leader of a major Arab state in the Middle East transformed Israel from an illegal squatter, a pariah state, into a legitimate neighbor, at the same time as Egypt was established as a trustworthy neighbor.

Second, live bargaining on television allowed Israelis to see for themselves that the Egyptian President was determined not to budge from his condition that every last grain of sand in the Sinai peninsula be returned. Had they been told these conditions of peace by their own leaders following the secret negotiations, they may have been left with a feeling that their government had not tried hard enough.

Third, in talking to Israelis over the heads of their political leaders, Sadat could present himself as making a huge sacrifice and taking enormous risks for the sake of peace, thereby gaining a moral right to demand an even greater sacrifice on the part of his hosts. In anthropological terms, says Daniel Dayan, he was performing the ceremony of "potlach" (Mauss, 1969), in which the chief of a neighboring tribe offers a gift which must be reciprocated with an even larger gift. Fourth, the visibility of the gesture exercised major pressure on the US to extend the aid it had promised in return for making peace with Israel.

If the success of a performative event is anchored in a kind of contract among three partners – principals, broadcasters, and public (Dayan and Katz, 1993) – it was impressively upheld on the Israeli side. The contract was much less apparent though for the Egyptian media and the Egyptian public.

Sadat's visit as a transformative media event

Dayan and Katz (1993) describe Sadat's televised visit as a series of identifiable phases that make it into a transformative event: from the *latency* of a chronic problem, to *signaling* that a solution is at hand,[2] to a miniature *modeling* of what the solution might look like, and to the *framing* of the event in speech. Framing was provided by Sadat, the "guest" leader, who carefully blended his proposal for an ultimate remapping of social reality into the gesture of the modeling phase, in which he mobilized the full force of his charismatic power.

The ensuing public debate that is meant to assess the impact and to construct the event's significance, the phase of *evaluating*, is regarded by Dayan and Katz as part of the event, except that it carries on in time far beyond the ceremony. Ultimately, it determines whether the event has indeed been the starting point for a historical and political transformation. On the Israeli side, the change in public opinion generated by the visit persisted and overcame the trauma of evacuating towns and agricultural settlements in the Sinai. The political right was disappointed, however, believing that the treaty with Egypt might ensure that the West Bank would stay under Israeli rule. On the Egyptian side, the event itself overshadowed the opposition at the time, although the reservations of intellectuals and other groups, such as the fundamentalists, were well known. This meant that the peace remained "cold," with one-way tourism, no collaborative projects, continuing criticism of the intellectual elite, and of the extreme religious fanatics who finally succeeded in assassinating President Sadat.

RECONCILIATION CEREMONIES, 1993–4

An attempt to apply the same criteria with which we examined Sadat's Jerusalem "conquest" to the ceremonies between Israel and the Palestinians, then Israel and the Jordanians, shows that important structural differences need to be weighed against the ostensible similarities.

Israel and the Palestinians: Rabin, Arafat, Clinton (Washington, 1993)

(1) **Coronation, not conquest**   Sadat, as hero, made use of his televised visit to confront Israelis with his conditions for peace, and to impress on them his sincerity and his determination. On television, he conducted political negotiation openly, using his personal charm in order to strike a tough bargain, with the pros and cons laid on the table for everyone to judge. There was still time to disagree. The (Oslo One) accord between Israelis and Palestinians, on the other hand, was reached *prior* to the White House signing, by unknown heroes, "in virtual hiding, not just from television cameras and journalists, but from almost everybody else in authority on both sides" (Katz, 1993). Washington was not a dynamic step in the process of *negotiation* but a seal of approval for what had been agreed. The drama is of marriage or engagement, not of courtship.

Sadat, on live television, made his visit a "conquest" of the hearts of

Israelis, while Arafat and Rabin, on the White House lawn, September 1993, in their first public appearance as a couple, were enacting a "coronation," which, however performative, celebrates the *conclusion* of an event, rather than portraying an event in the making, in *statu nascendi*.

Note, also, that the ceremony was conducted in the neutral domain of the go-between – not in Jerusalem or in Gaza, not even on the border. True, Sadat also came to Washington for the final signing after Camp David, but, at the crucial initial phases, he made his conquest in the heart of enemy territory. Israelis may have been ready to grant equality to Arafat in 1993 in Washington but not to invite him home to meet the family (which they had still not done by May 1995). It may also mean that, for Arafat, the invitation to the US was just as important (and less complicated) than an invitation to Israel, as his Palestinian constituency was the primary reference group from whom he was seeking legitimacy, no less than from the Israelis.

(2) Heroes Nevertheless, Rabin and Arafat do deserve recognition as heroes in their decision to acknowledge each other as partners to a mutual agreement. Both had to confront a strong "hawkish" opposition in their own communities, both had a long record as warriors, both risked their reputations. Unfortunately, their ambivalence and half-heartedness showed through in the ceremony. Rabin, said journalist Nahum Barnea, was forced into the ceremony, especially into the handshake. Arafat's entourage claimed that Rabin's signing in cheap ballpen showed his real attitude to Arafat. This ambivalence may also have spread the seeds of a possible self-destruction of the peace process. Ironically, the two leaders may yet pay the full price for celebrating something which they may not be able to carry out.

(3) Public and secret disintermediation Sadat and Begin reached over ("disintermediated," (Katz, 1988)) the hierarchy of officials surrounding them to make contact with the people. The Oslo team did something similar to the official teams of diplomats in Washington who believed for some months that they were charged with negotiating peace. But while Sadat and Begin went over the heads of their own establishment on television in full public view of both sides for all of three full days, the Oslo team undercut the official negotiators behind their backs, with no one watching. All that was left to do in Washington was to sign on the dotted line.

(4) Enter an unknown enemy/enter a well-known enemy While Sadat was almost unknown before his television debut in Israel, Arafat was too well known. For the Israeli public, Arafat had become identified, in the previous ten years, as the hero of the intifada, an identity coopted from the young local Palestinian leaders who started the spontaneous uprising, as a reaction to their sense of humiliation (Schiff and Yaari, 1990).

Having come to the signing, Arafat made a point of not changing his bizarre "veteran terrorist" getup – complete with the khaki uniform, the *kaffia* wrapped round the head (making spectators wonder whether he had had to hand over the pistol, usually stuck in his belt, for safekeeping). In the midst of men in dark suits and ties, he seemed to be gesturing that *his* battle is *not* yet over, almost signaling to Israelis and to Palestinians that he had not changed, that he had no choice but to participate while remaining true to his beliefs. This was far less subtle double-talk than Sadat's, and it alienated, rather than charmed, the Israelis.

(5) History (makes heroes), heroes (make history)   Media events represent the epitome of television's tendency to personalize history. Live on television, Sadat established his identity as the indisputable hero of the peace he was offering. Television convinced us that he made history, right or wrong. Did Rabin and Arafat, the heroes of Oslo, similarly convince us that it was they who changed history? Commentators at the time supplied a lot of context – it could not have happened without the collapse of Russian support for the PLO, or without the Gulf War in which the PLO backed Iraq (thereby shutting down the Saudi money taps, and remaining penniless), and without Arab fundamentalism which threatened to topple PLO leadership. The argument behind all these geopolitical reasons is that the accord would have happened whoever the actors. Television ceremonies, however, give us heroes. But, in this case, the result looked rather less heroic, and overdetermined, more like social science than ceremony.

Was the signing of the "Oslo One" accord a performative event?

Let us now consider the performative character of the event as a function of the concurrence of the three partners – public, principals, and media. Did each of these grant the ceremony its status as a media event?

The public   The participation of the Israeli audience, in the Oslo One ceremony, was tentative. Israelis were skeptical, as they had witnessed the failure of Rabin's negotiation team to deliver an agreement in Washington with the local Palestinian leaders, who were generally considered more moderate. This was added to the real reluctance of Israelis to agree to a major compromise over the territories, which is, ironically, why they had elected Rabin.[3] In addition, while Sadat was an unknown leader whom Israelis fell in love with at first sight, Arafat was perceived as a terrorist, and was disliked.

And yet Israeli public opinion did respond to the announcement of the Rabin government that there was going to be an accord and a mutual recognition, and, presumably, to the ceremony itself, with a radical increase in dovish opinion.[4] Some 40 percent of Likud voters supported the accord in addition to 95 percent of Labor and Left, for a total of 64 percent

(Levinsohn and Katz, 1994). The Palestinian public was especially approving (Gilboa, 1995).[5] But in terms of the transformative power of media events the following reservations should be noted:

1 The support of Israeli public opinion expressed a long-term trend of creeping dovishness, accelerated by the intifada.
2 The dramatic increase in support was already the result of the *announcement* preceding the ceremony, not only the result of the inspiration of the ceremony.
3 As the series of ceremonies continued, support declined on both sides (Gilboa, ibid.).

For Israelis this may be ascribed partly to the inflation in celebrations which eroded the effect, partly to Arafat's delivery of blatantly contradictory messages to different audiences (leading Palestinians in Gaza, in his homecoming ceremony, in rhythmic cries "in blood and fire we'll conquer Palestine," and explaining to Muslims in a South African mosque that the treaty is only temporary). But Israeli support waned mostly due to the increase in terrorist acts, in contradiction to the expectation of Israelis that the accord would bring about a decrease. A year later, less than half supported the agreement, and a majority opposed its extension beyond Gaza and Jericho.

The principals' ("organizers") participation in the contract, in the Oslo One ceremony, also seemed tentative. To begin with, there were two types of principals: the academics on both sides who had initiated the Oslo talks, and the official leaders. The academic team, heretofore unknown, was sponsored by foreign Minister Peres (Rabin's long-time competitor) and conducted negotiations away from the limelight of the official Washington talks, awaiting their moment. They received the go-ahead when front-line formal talks reached a dead end. Some were not even invited to watch the ceremony from the lawn. Instead, the official leaders, Yitzhak Rabin and Yasser Arafat, the heroes according to protocol, were invited to star in the celebration. This division into the "doers" and the "sources of authority" gave rise to the question who would come to sign (and to uphold the contract with the public)? The identity of the signatories remained undecided until the last day. On September 12, Israel National Radio announced that Nabil Shaat and Shimon Peres would go to Washington to sign. Rabin and Arafat were each awaiting the other's expression of readiness to walk together through the symbolic doorway. At the last minute, Rabin finally made up his mind, and Arafat followed suit. The true heroes had to make way for those in authority – and for the presence of the American President.

Once established, the two leaders had first to convince themselves to play the role prescribed by their seconds-in-command. Reporters watched closely for signs of regret, for hints of half-heartedness. "Will Rabin shake Arafat's hand?" was a major concern. The confusion about the identity of the "real" heroes remained throughout the following ceremonies. Will Peres be among the receivers of the Nobel Prize? Would Shaat also be nominated? As in Washington, this, too, was decided only three days before the ceremony – Peres yes, Shaat – no.

The ambivalence of Rabin and Arafat was revealed in various ways throughout the series of ceremonies. In Washington in 1993, Clinton was seen to help push the two together for the famous handshake, although it had been agreed. At the next ceremony, in Cairo, Arafat got last-minute cold feet, and, in mid-ceremony, live on television, he refused to sign the maps demarcating Israel's stage-one withdrawal. With the participants standing on the stage, some whispering furiously in Arafat's ear, it was finally President Mubarak who convinced Arafat that he could not shame him as host. Was this a misunderstanding? Was it a wish to show his loyalists that he was not selling them cheaply? Was it a new sign of growing resistance to the accord among Palestinians? Probably all of the above. But this argues that while Sadat, ostensibly secure in his own constituency, focused on transforming the Israelis, Arafat was more concerned with his own side, less concerned that he was fast losing his credibility with the Israelis. In Oslo, in his acceptance of the Nobel Peace Prize, Arafat spoke of promising his people, the ones who are "painfully carrying the keys to their houses" (the houses they abandoned in the 1948 war), that they would come home. Now he is looking at them and wiping a tear. This, he declared, is the first step in the battle of the brave... ending with "The holy places are holy for all of us." It was a touching speech, but it exacerbated the worst fears of Israelis. The accord, one may recall, did not promise return to the homeland, neither did it solve the problem of the holy places.

The media,   for their part, did accept the 1993 signing as a media event. The Washington broadcast was interposed with vignettes reporting live reactions from Jerusalem, Jericho, and Gaza, including Soha, Arafat's new wife, as commentator. Star reporters were flown in Rabin's plane to attend, and peak moments were repeated in slow motion. It was broadcast live to the world.

But subversive notes started to infiltrate the ceremonies that followed. The move away from the "priestly" function is seen, for example, in the producers' choice of commentators. Thus, the two commentators chosen to accompany the Nobel prize ceremony from the studios of the two Israeli television channels, were opposition leaders (Benny Begin and Dan Meridor), whose job, it appears, was to pour cold water over the celebration by commenting on "the gap between the celebration in Oslo and Israeli reality." In keeping with conventions of reporting on conflict, these commentators' opposition from the Israeli right was "balanced" with that of Palestinian opponents of the agreement. Thus, the Palestinian commentator in the studio, a member of the Popular Liberation Front, who spent seventeen years in an Israeli prison, regarded Oslo as an opportunity to declare to the Israelis that the Nobel prize had lost all its moral value. True media events do not leave room for such critical commentary.

All in all, can the 1993 ceremony in Washington (and Cairo and Oslo in its wake) be labeled performative? The answer is yes, as it granted equality to the Palestinians, and recognized their national aspirations. The Palestinians, in return, promised (but have not yet managed) to suspend the Palestinian Covenant, whose aim is to abolish the State of Israel. But rather than a "warm" reconciliation, Oslo may be perceived as a kind of coming-of-age party for Arafat, which, at the same time, is an occasion to get rid of him, as one does with a difficult relative. The performative act consists of saying, "You are now on your own," adding a farewell gift (in the form of a promise to raise money for his future).

Was the "Oslo One" accord a transformative event?

More important, have the Oslo peace ceremonies transformed reality? As in the case of Egypt, there was certainly a *latent*, long-standing problem. Moreover, the struggle between Israelis and Palestinians over the same homeland may be regarded as more crippling and incurable than Israel's conflict with its sovereign neighbors. Unlike Sadat's and Begin's instant drama, the *signaling* of a solution in this case was a gradual process of mutual recognition between Israel and the PLO, stretching over a number of years. It started at the Madrid conference (1991), in which the Likud government and Palestinians represented by local leaders agreed to negotiate, under heavy US pressure. The world was watching, and the PLO was granted the status of observer. Signaling continued during talks in Washington between representatives of Israel's Labor government and local Palestinian leaders, with Israel closing an eye to the Palestinians' commuting to Tunisia in order to receive instructions, and (as it turned out) with a competing Israeli team secretly talking with the PLO in Oslo. All this activity, indeed, culminated in Israel's public recognition of the PLO.

The symbolic enactment (*modeling*) of the new paradigm, was far less convincing than in the case of Sadat, as we have pointed out, with noticeably reluctant gestures on both sides. As Benny Begin noted on Israel television at the Nobel prize ceremony, Arafat received the prize ˏwearing his (terrorist's) uniform, and (even) wanted to wear his pistol." But Arafat and Rabin did stand on the same stage, did shake hands, and, as commentators have often observed, their political fates were tied together from then on.

While the gestures, if not effusive, did perform change, the *framing* of the situation painfully revealed the half-heartedness and ambivalence of the two leaders. Unlike Sadat's rhetoric, which, as we have shown, focused on turning the hearts of the enemy, Rabin and Arafat spoke mainly to their own publics, partly to the world, in an effort to convince that they were doing the right thing (partly because the other side was not doing its part in inspiring confidence).

In terms of transformation, the *evaluation* phase is the most shaky. To begin with, only 45 percent of Israelis were for giving up more than Gaza and Jericho. On the Palestinian side, the opposition soon increased in strength. Gradually, all the parties to the accord – Rabin, the Israeli right, and Arafat – converged on terrorism as the criterion by which to judge Oslo's success. The criteria that are applied in the case of Egypt – tourism (in spite of its one-sidedness), open borders, diplomatic relations – are not relevant to the Palestinian case. The only equivalent criterion, the assurance of US aid, took a long time to materialize in the Palestinian case.[6] Worst of all, Rabin and Arafat found themselves in a double-bind – Rabin felt he could not progress as long as Arafat did not prove he could stop terror, but not progressing meant that Arafat risked losing the support he still had among Palestinians. Thus, public approval on both sides had diminished.

Still, the public accord with the Palestinians has some transformative momentum. It is evident in that (1) the Israeli public was not totally surprised by the government of Israel's decision to retreat from certain areas in the West Bank, and may even be unsurprised if it decides to dismantle some settlements; (2) both sides are forced to start drawing maps, and to face the necessity of dividing territory between them; (3) the problem of the future of Jerusalem has been placed on the public agenda of the two communities. And, perhaps most important, (4) the Palestinian accord made possible the peace treaty with Jordan.

Israel and Jordan: Rabin, Hussein

The signing of a peace treaty between Israel and Jordan is the least problematic of the three cases. If the peace with Egypt meant an act of recognition, and the accord with Arafat was a form of legalistic, or greencard marriage – which both parties desperately needed, even if there is no love lost between them – peace with Hussein is an act of legalizing a common-law relationship. It is the celebration of a long-secret alliance, which heretofore the whole world knew about but could not or did not have to condemn (as a betrayal of the Palestinians, as it were), as it was not made formal. Formalization has the power of forcing the world to acknowledge the situation (or do something about it) (Lazarsfeld and Merton, 1948; Katz, 1981). This is the classic performative function of ceremonies such as marriages or declarations of war; it also means that by definition the only transformative function of the event is the making public of an existing situation.

As there is no real conflict of interest, no major sacrifice is demanded on either side. Jordan may have suffered a loss of face among its Gulf War allies, but the Oslo agreement, which presumably neutralized the Palestinian problem, allowed the more moderate Arab states to agree to an Israeli–Jordanian accord. True, the Jordanian Hashemite kingdom does represent nobility (however impoverished), and Israelis have a fascination with royalty, but Israel's role is not just that of a *nouveau riche* neighbor as it is by now better established in the region, and is still (as at the time of Sadat's peace initiative) backed by the same rich relatives who are pledged to help.

Unlike the tortuous struggle to formulate the awkward agreement with the refugee-cum-terrorist Palestinians – in an effort to create an entity (not a state!) in a territory that is geographically not coherent and almost impossible to determine – a peace treaty with Jordan is a dream diplomatic marriage with a real "Palestinian" state. There is no messy intermingling, and no embarrassing, sometimes violent, protestors; even the right wing Likud Party is in favor, in the hope that the Jordan agreement will subsume the autonomy agreement with the Palestinians.

Ironically, then, while the Oslo agreement made possible the peace with Jordan, in no time the two agreements became competing, with Jordan constantly overtaking Palestine. While Israeli politicians were busy declaring that neither agreement is on account of the other, they had repeatedly offended Arafat by assigning Jordan custody of the holy places, and by not inviting him to the signing ceremony in El Avrona, in spring, 1995, over which Clinton presided ("a tragic mistake" according to Ron Pundik, an Oslo team member). In Jerusalem, at the same time, the Palestinians demanded that their own religious leaders replace the Jordanian clerics on the Temple Mount, and, after being refused, installed their people anyway, leaving the Jordanians unemployed.

Was the contract among politicians, broadcasters, and public, upheld in the case of the Jordanian peace ceremonies?

From the *organizers'* point of view, the two leaders, not to mention Clinton in the role of overseer and guarantor, wholeheartedly carried out their share. Like Sadat, Hussein played an active part in the newly open relationship. He was sincere, profuse, sometimes embarrassingly emotional. He told his audiences that he regretted the lost years which had been missed, and that now he was in a hurry. Perhaps it was the economic crisis in Jordan, or the fundamentalist danger in the region (not unrelated), or perhaps it is more personal, having to do with the King's advancing age, his mortality, maybe his illness.

As in Sadat's case, the gesture and the declaration of intent came *before* the negotiation over details. Like Sadat, Hussein evoked symbols of the past – the desert as common origin of Jews and Arabs, of Abraham as common ancestor – connecting them with a utopian future. He even went a step further in choosing the location of the main ceremony as a (symbolic) metonymic object. Talking from a spot chosen somewhere in the Arava desert, he could be effective in saying that together, Jordan and Israel would make the desert – the actual sand on which they were standing – bloom.

As with Sadat, the ceremonies became part of the dynamics of making peace. Experts on water, borders, economic collaboration, etc., met under television floodlights, in the full diplomatic gear of dark suits and ties, in a tent in the Jordanian desert, at 40 degrees centigrade. They removed their jackets on live television only after a formal request was made by one of the negotiators. Negotiations began in Washington, then in the King's palace in Aquaba, a resort town on the Red Sea, then in El Avrona, on the border between the two countries, where a stadium-cum-television studio was specially erected. Rabin competed with Hussein in human warmth. He seemed to enjoy the ceremonies sincerely, perhaps as a moment of respite from the frustrations of the effort to implement Oslo and, as one sure achievement in which he could take pride. So did Clinton (who preferred El Avrona to electioneering for the 1992 Congress).

The media started by collaborating. It accepted the Rabin–Hussein–Clinton signing ceremony in Washington as a media event. The ceremonies that followed, however, were rather redundant. They were recycled as a movable feast – wandering from Washington, to Aquaba, to the Arava desert, to the Lake of Galillee. Instead of the electrifying experience of a unique encounter which characterizes media events, the peace with Jordan became one of a "mini-series" of coronations in which nothing new could be expected.

But beyond the broadcasters' weariness with reconciliatory events, regarding them as decreasingly attractive to the public, the effectiveness of the Rabin–Hussein encounters suffered from their being interwoven with the massive terrorist attacks of the Palestinian *Hamas* movement on Israelis. The story became a kind of juxtaposition of ceremonies signaling hope on the one hand, and human bereavement signaling despair on the other. Following El Avrona, *Yediot* had two color photographs on its front page – King Hussein kissing Queen Nur, entitled "tears of joy" and crying victims of an attack, entitled "tears of mourning."

Thus, the attack on a bus in the central square in Tel-Aviv, a few days prior to the glamorous ceremony in El Avrona, cast a heavy shadow on the event, raising doubts about the participation of President Clinton, and destroying the atmosphere of expectation in the media. Instead of focusing on the grandiose preparations of the organizers (who invented a site in the heart of the desert, complete with electricity, water, food, and a stadium constructed for the event), or on the arrival of the host of international press reporters, or on the proposed gowns (inadvertently identical) of the three first ladies, or on whether the Russian Foreign Minister would be allowed to speak – the media were occupied with the human tragedy of the Dizengoff Square victims. The planning of festivities seemed to carry a discordant note.

Ironically, the most memorable image from the El Avrona ceremony itself was a Muslim Sheikh, clad in a flowing white robe, who delivered a long prayer in Arabic, with monotonous, repetitive sounds, slow, unchanging, against all the rules of acceptable television, who, nevertheless hypnotized the audience in the desert and at home.

What do these latest examples of the genre contribute to the conceptualization of the role of live broadcasting of ceremonies of reconciliation? First, the peace ceremonies of 1993–4 illustrate the self-destructiveness inherent in overuse. The effectiveness of media ceremonies lies in their rarity, in the preciousness of their being one-off. Redundancy invites boredom, public devaluation, even cynicism, reminding us that television has the power to demystify political figures even if, under certain circumstances, it may allow them to enchant us. Second, in order to have a transformative potential, ceremonies need enough breathing space, enough freedom of action, without clashing with oppositional events, which, unfortunately, they themselves may trigger. Third, ceremonies may be bashed not only by non-ceremonial events but also by competing ceremonies. Such competition may destroy the effectiveness of one of the ceremonial events, or of both, in the process. Fourth, the process of public evaluation, which starts at a hopeful high (which relates to the relationship between the ceremonies and other events), should spiral upward, endowing it with increasing legitimacy, rather than lose momentum, in a downward spiral, legitimating oppositional readings. Which brings us back to the need for a supportive environment. Ceremonies are delicate plants which need nurturing in order to eventually bear fruit. Undermining them too early may squash the process.

Notes

2 BEDFELLOWS

1 Avneri was one of the journalists interviewed in order to gain insight into the evolution of the relationships between journalists and press editors and the political establishment from the perspective of the journalists themselves. The other informants were Tom Segev, ex-editor of *Koteret Rashit*, an elite weekly, and senior columnist in *Ha'aretz*, Yoram Peri, then editor of *Davar*, and member of the Editors Committee, Yehiel Limor, writer for *Maariv* and co-author of *The Mediators* (1992), Oren Tokatly, deputy head of the Public Authority of Channel Two at its creation.
2 Moreover, the willingness to refrain from publishing information which may be damaging to the Jewish community in Palestine had its roots in the Jewish attitude towards collaborators, internalized during generations of living as a minority under hostile regimes (Goren, 1979).
3 The choice to continue the committee also reflects, of course, the personal histories, temperaments, and ideological convictions of the press editors themselves. Mostly members of the ruling Labor party, with a strong need, duly noted and cultivated by the Prime Minister, to go on being in the know (Caspi and Limor, 1992, p. 178).

3 FOREGROUNDING CONFLICT

1 Some 75 percent of Israelis report that they discuss the news frequently or occasionally after viewing the Mabat news broadcast, as noted in Liebes and Ribak (1991).

4 INTERNALIZING CENSORSHIP

1 As decreed by Supreme Court judge Aharon Barak in the case of the Tel-Aviv weekly *Kol H'air*.
2 In its judgment on the case the court stated that any prohibition in the reporting of expected nomination for top army positions is not only illegal but is also damaging to the quality of the nomination, reiterating that publication can be stopped only if there is a close certainty of causing tangible damage to security.
3 The following editors, journalists, and legal experts were interviewed: Yoram Peri, then editor of *Davar*, Uri Avneri, founder and editor of *Haolam Hazeh*, a weekly, Shimon Schiffer, senior political correspondent of *Yediot Aharonot*, Moshe Negbi,

legal commentator on freedom of speech and on television and radio news, Natan Cohen, legal advisor of Israel Broadcasting Authority, Dr Amos Shapira, Professor of Law, Tel-Aviv University and member of the Israel Press Council, Nahum Barnea, senior columnist in *Yediot Aharonot*, and Orah Herman, news editor on Public Radio.

4 This paper, *Hadashot*, which was not in the Editors Committee, was threatened with closure a second time but negotiation prevented this (Caspi and Limor, 1992).

5 This weekly, *Koteret Rashit*, could not support itself in spite of its high journalistic quality and became one of a number of newspapers that had to close down when they were no longer subsidized.

6 Probably not by coincidence, until recent years the area of political journalism was strictly masculine, and women journalists were restricted to fashion, food, and human interest.

7 The story of the way in which Mordechai Vanunu – an Israeli who had been employed on Israel's nuclear reactor, sold secret information (including photographs) to the London *Times* in 1986, and was captured and brought to trial – was published for the first time in a local weekly in 1995.

8 *Kol Hair*, the Jerusalem weekly which belongs to *Ha'aretz*, is the most widely read paper in Jerusalem, overtaking the popular *Yediot Aharonot*.

9 The immediate excuse for which was a terrorist attack on the life of Israel's ambassador in England.

5 CONSTRUCTING SUCCESS

1 One way of understanding this distinction between professional and participant is in terms of the distinction, elaborated on by Alexander (1981), between the European model of the ideological political party press and the new commercial and public models of the "objective" electronic and printed press. Alternatively, it can be argued that the role of the independent press is to host a plurality of voices.

2 The texts we analyzed include video recordings of Israel Television coverage of the event during the first three days, and all stories in the two most popular newspapers – *Yediot Aharanot* and *Maariv* – during the week following the event.

3 Numbering and emphasis are mine. These phrases will be analyzed in the text.

4 The headlines which deal with the functioning of the army in the inner pages of the newspapers are also given over to army sources. In most headlines the IDF (the institution or its head) justifies army actions, as in *Maariv*: "IDF: We took a calculated risk in the decision not to evacuate the beaches" or in *Yediot*'s "The Chief of Staff at a press conference yesterday: 'It is impossible to close off the sea.'"

6 US AND THEM

1 The rhetoric was more accurate than the administration itself had believed, as was found out only in 1995, with the desertion of Saddam Hussein's sons-in-law to Jordan. Had the US army taken it more seriously at the time, it would have not stopped the war short of destroying this arsenal.

7 DOMINANT READINGS AND DOOMED RESISTANCE

1 This survey, and a parallel study in the Israeli Arab sector (in Nazareth and in Sakhnin), were conducted by the Guttman Institute for Applied Social Research during 1989. Detailed analyses of data are reported in Liebes et al. (1991), Liebes and Ribak (1991), and Liebes and Ribak (1992).

2 In half of the cases, a parent was asked to retell the news to his/her child "as if he/she didn't watch it," and in the other half it was asked of the child. In each case, the child or the parent in the role of a listener was asked to question, add, or correct what he/she was told. The reteller was then asked to mention the most important items on the newscast, and to "tell about them." In the continuation, the roles were reversed. Finally, all family members were asked to relate the item on the intifada, or to explain the intifada in more general terms, to a guest from abroad, who "doesn't know much about it."

3 On a five-point scale, 67 percent of the hawkish parents and only 13 percent of the dovish parents were found to reproduce their outlook in their children. Moreover, while hawks reproduced regardless of parents' education, doves needed higher education in order to transfer their political outlook to their children: whereas hawks of lower and higher education reproduced their outlook in 80 percent of the cases, doves reproduced in only 37 percent of the cases if they were less educated, but in 69 percent of the cases if they had higher education (see Liebes et al., 1991).

4 The other three types are (1) "Liberals," who believe in news-credibility and oppose censorship, (2) "Authoritarians," who do not believe in credibility and support censorship, and (3) "Cynics," who do not believe in news-credibility, but nevertheless oppose censorship. When relating this typology to doves and hawks, it was found that the types who demand censorship – the Authoritarians and the Deniers – were more likely to be associated with hawkishness: 51 percent of the Deniers and 70 percent of the Authoritarians tended to be hawks, unwilling to make any territorial concessions for peace. The types that were supportive of free expression were more likely to be doves: only 32 percent of the Liberals and 29 percent of the Cynics were unwilling to make territorial concessions. As the chapter suggests, it is not that news is easier for doves to accept, but rather, it appears that more doves than hawks are resolved to face it.

5 This is not surprising when remembering that even in the case of television drama, viewers mostly related to what they saw as real. In the study of the decoding of *Dallas*, only the minority of the statements referred to the character as "constructed" while mostly they were framed referentially. Moreover, viewers commuted from telling about television characters to discussing real-life situations.

6 In the study on the decoding of *Dallas*, and in the present study as well, we find that the same viewers commute between referential and critical decodings; we therefore prefer "decodings" to "decoders."

7 Advocating that the Arabs leave echoes the call of extreme nationalist parties (representing some 2 percent of the votes at the time of the intifada) supported to a large extent by young Israelis, for a "transfer" of the Palestinians to neighboring countries.

8 SOCIALIZING TO DOMINANT READING

1 Gouldner suggests in addition that journalists lose control of their readers, because even if they intend to hold up deviance as violation of norm, some readers may adopt the deviance as counter-cultural.
2 Many of the items do present clashes where soldiers, confronted with violent rioters, respond by firing rubber or plastic bullets, and sometimes live ammunition.
3 In a series of experiments, Iyengar (1991) shows that viewers' framing of social problems depends on the ways these problems are presented on the screen – i.e. as due either to social or individual responsibility. Although this approach is somewhat similar to ours, we have three reservations. First, as social psychologists have shown, the psychological statuses of the two kinds of explanations are not equal: people tend to explain the problems of the other dispositionally. Second, television's representations, we suggest, display this attribution bias. Third, not all viewers are affected in the same way – people differ in ideological outlook, which equips them with different degrees of critical distance. In an application of Iyengar's design to the case of the homeless, Power (1990) adds the notion of stigmatized presentation to the individual–structural dimension. We argue that restricting presentation of the socially deviant to their deviant role is stigmatizing in itself.
4 Schiff and Yaari (1990) offer a detailed account of the reasons leading to the uprising.
5 All family names were changed.
6 All the adolescents cited in this chapter, and most of the adolescents in the study, were born in Israel.

9 READING UPSIDE DOWN AND INSIDE OUT

1 The widespread tendency of Israelis not to distinguish Arab citizens of the state from Palestinians in the territories is exacerbated by occasional participation of Israeli Arabs in violent acts in support of the Palestinian uprising. We will have more to say about it later in our discussion.
2 The absence of Arab citizens from the screen certainly contributed to the findings that indicate failure to differentiate them from the Palestinians in the territories. Ironically, it is only since the change in government, when suddenly Arabs, and often controversial ones, are invited to talk shows in Hebrew, that one can realize the extent of their absence until then. In the first talk show to include an Arab interviewee, the Arab was juxtaposed with a Jewish nationalist who resides in the West Bank. The host justified giving more time to the Arab by pointing out that during the last ten years he did not interview any Arabs at all.
3 Data are taken from a survey of a representative sample of 400 Jewish and 200 Arab families, conducted by the Guttman Institute for Applied Social Research during summer 1988. The survey measured the political attitudes of parents and their adolescent children, the degree of ideological reproduction among nationalists and moderates in the two communities, and news viewing preferences and attitudes towards censorship and credibility of news. Detailed analyses of data are reported in Liebes et al. (1991) and Liebes and Ribak (1992).
4 The smaller number of Arab families – 15 as compared to 52 Jewish – is an expression of the relative isolation of the Israeli–Arab community and the hesitation to make statements which could be taken as political. In studying a minority which, until recently, was completely excluded from public opinion

polling in Israel, and one which is highly reserved and restrained in its relations with the authorities, it was difficult to find both interviewers and observers, and families, that would participate in the study.

5   Family names have been changed.

6   This may be contrasted with the case of fiction, in which decodings reveal at least some forms of critical ability (Liebes and Katz, 1993). What we find here, however, is that viewers in general, even those who do not accept the televised picture of the conflict, are unaware of the rules according to which social reality is transformed into news text, or that such rules even exist. Expecting the news to represent normal and normative reality, viewers are perplexed at the news' obsession with the deviant and argue against it in terms of mimesis and accuracy. Missing from their discourse is a literacy that consists of the recognition that news is all about the unusual, the exceptional, the violent; that it is a story, a simplified dramatic construction; that its content is intimately tied to available and accessible informants; and that for context one needs to rely on other items, other media, other sources.

7   The uniformity in this decoding of foreign news items stands out against the common interpretation among Jews, who typically point out the double standard in these countries' criticisms of Israeli policy in the territories. Rather than "all oppressed have a right to be free," Israeli Jews draw the lesson that everybody rules by force and that people in glass houses should not throw stones. Other countries which Arabs in Israel use in distancing the evidence are Syria, Lebanon, South Africa, Northern Ireland, and Chile. Jews focus their attacks on Jordan, Saudi Arabia, and India, among others.

8   Some Jews do go beyond this consensus to argue the Palestinians' right for self-determination. Such arguments, however, are not easily tolerated as the discussion in the Levi family illustrates; the daughter, Maya, continuously parallels the Palestinians' national aspirations to those of the Jews when struggling for the independence of the State of Israel. Family members, and father in particular, reject the comparison vehemently.

10 LYING LOW – SILENT WITNESSES FROM THE FIELD

1   No claim is made for the group's representativeness. The audiotapes of these interviews were transcribed and the analysis is based on detailed examination of all statements which relate to framing the conflict. For detailed socio-linguistic analysis see Blum-Kulka and Liebes (1993).

2   See Katriel and Nesher's (1986) analysis of the centrality of "cohesion" in Israeli education.

3   As suggested by psychoanalyst Amira Fletcher (personal communication).

4   That these soldiers were highly motivated to be interviewed can be explained by their regarding it as an occasion to express their anguish. To neutralize the emotional loading of the situation we notified interviewees in advance that this was a research interview, for which they were offered payment.

5   All names of interviewees are changed.

6   And compare with Stanley Cohen's (1988) analysis of the types of excuses and justifications which are invoked in Israeli society to account for the IDF's actions in the intifada.

7   Van Krefeld's (1989) "gangs" are a pejorative interpretation of the army psychologist's reference to officers who feel that they gain independence due to decentralization. See note 8.

8 An army study argues that many young officers – unlike our interviewees – may see an opportunity in the intifada to test themselves. Ben (1991) quotes former army psychologist Micha Popper who says, "the men said it strengthened them as officers."

9 Rhetorically, the descriptions of both David and Uri can be seen as two opposed patterns of mitigation (Frazer, 1980). Whereas David chooses distancing terms, such as doing "the job" "elegantly" and "correctly," to describe the activities of his unit, Uri plays it down by bringing it close to home. Beating up Arab boys is made to sound unserious, childish, by the image of fights among boys, thus smoothing over the inequality between the soldiers and the Palestinians. In terms of motivational account theory this example corresponds to the category of "denial of injury" (Cohen, 1988).

10 For Kelman and Hamilton (1989), the type of relationship with authority, i.e. the possibility of asserting rather than denying responsibility, depends on the manner in which one perceives one's place in the system: defining one's task as compliance by the rules is derived from a sense of helplessness, on the assumption that by refraining from mistakes one will avoid punishment and gain security. Defining one's task in terms of enacting a role leads to obedience through identification with the job and a motivation to fulfill system-specific expectations of the army. Only that form of coping which is based on self-direction, that is, the type that values internalization, allows for critical evaluation of one's behavior and self-questioning based on the assumption that policy should reflect basic values.

11 As Kelman and Baron (1968, p. 679) propose "Inconsistency-maintenance is motivated to the extent that the two goals to which the two inconsistent elements are linked are independently important to the individual, particularly if they are of more or less equal importance.... Inconsistency reduction would require a sacrifice in at least one of the elements, a resolution which he would prefer to avoid. He is thus highly motivated to find some way of handling the discomfort generated by the inconsistency that would, at the same time, permit him to keep the two inconsistent elements intact."

12 Ultimately it can be argued that the function of this imbalance at a reflexive level is nonetheless gratifying. Zillman and Bryant (1986) provide an analogous example in their discussion of the moral approval (pleasure) we give ourselves in enduring the pain of viewing tragedy. In their analysis of the pleasure of viewing tragedy, Zillman and Bryant make the point that one may give moral approval to one's ability to endure the narrative.

11 THEM AS US – PALESTINIANS ON ISRAELI CINEMA

1 Ironically, the poem has now been adopted by the Palestinians to explain nascent Palestinian nationalism.

2 The three critics referred to here are Yair Hai, Ben-Dror Yemini, and Hadas Lahav, who represent several Israeli newspapers.

12 I AND THOU

1 Interestingly, for better or worse, the State of Israel is conceived as a direct continuation of the ancient Hebrews as in Ben Gurion's rhetorics.

2 The signaling gave rise to speculation (what will Sadat ask in exchange? Will Israel return the whole of the Sinai peninsula? Is peace with Israel what Sadat wants?)

and to the suspension of disbelief in confronting the paradox of "how can an offer of peace emanate from our worst enemy?"

3 As it was assumed within the Labor Party that, as a known compromiser for peace, Shimon Peres had no chance of winning the elections, he lost the Labor Party leadership to Rabin, a "tougher" and therefore more "electable" politician.

4 Compared to surveys just months earlier, the accord led to a substantial increase in the proportion of Israeli Jews willing to cede at least some territory for peace and in the percentage willing to consider the prospect of a Palestinian state (from 25 percent to 40 percent). Support for the autonomy plan rose to 57 percent following the accord and to 61 percent immediately following the ceremony.

5 Among Palestinians, support for the accord went from 65 percent before the ceremony to 69 percent immediately afterwards.

6 The reason for the delay in fulfilling the promise was the American demand that the Palestinian Authority provide proof of "transparency" – an open and coherent institutional structure which would be in charge of administrating the funds.

Bibliography

Alexander, J. (1981) "Mass news media in historical, systemic and comparative perspective," in E. Katz and T. Szecsko (eds) *Mass Media and Social Change*, London: Sage.

Anderson, J. A. and Meyer, T. P. (1988) *Mediated Communication: A Social Action Perspective*, Newbury Park, CA: Sage.

Back, K. W. (1968) "Equilibrium as motivation: between pleasure and enjoyment," in R. Abelson, E. Aronson, W. McGuire, and P. Tannenbaum (eds) *The Cognitive Consistence Theories*, Chicago: Rand McNally.

Back, K. W. and Gergen, K. J. (1963) "Apocalyptic and serial time orientations and the structure of opinions," *Public Opinion Quarterly* 27: 427–42.

Bar-Tal, D. (1990) *Understanding the Psychological Bases of the Israeli–Palestinian Conflict*, Tel-Aviv: The International Centre for Peace in the Middle East.

Barthes, R. (1975) *The Pleasure of the Text*, New York: Hill and Wang.

——(1977) "The rhetoric of the image," in J. Heath (ed. and translator) *Image, Music, Text*, London: Fontana.

Ben, A. (1991) "I.D.F. Junior officers in the intifada," *Ha'aretz*, January 12.

Ben-Ari, E. (1989) "Masks and soldiering: the Israeli army and the Palestinian uprising," *Cultural Anthropology*, 44: 372–89.

Bennet, L. (1983) *News, The Politics of Illusion*, New York: Longman.

Benyamini, K. (1982) "Society and youth in Israel and expressions of social narcissism from crisis to chance," in *The Conference Book of the Israeli Social Workers*, Tel-Aviv, 164–7.

Blum-Kulka, S. and Liebes, T. (1993) "Frame ambiguities: narrativization of the intifada experience by Israeli soldiers," in G. Wolfsfeld and A. Cohen (eds) *Framing the Intifada: Media and People*, Norwood, NJ: Ablex.

Buber, M. (1958) *"I" and "Thou"*, New York: Charles Scribner and Sons.

Carey, J. (1989) *Communication as Culture: Essays on Media and Society*, Boston: Unwin Hyman.

Carragee, K. M. (1990) "Interpretive media study and interpretive social science," *Critical Studies in Mass Communication*, 7: 81–96.

Caspi, D. and Limor, Y. (1992) *The Mediators: The Mass Media in Israel 1948–1990*, in Hebrew, Tel-Aviv: Am Oved.

Cohen, A. A., Adoni, H., and Bantz, S. R. (1991) *Social Conflict and TV News*, Newbury Park, CA: Sage.

Cohen, A. A., Adoni H., and Drori, G. (1983) "Adolescents' perceptions of social conflicts in television news and social reality," *Human Communication Research* 10: 203–25.

Cohen, S. (1988) "Criminology and the uprising," *Tikkun* 3: 60–2.

Cooper, J. and Fazio, R. H. (1984) "A new look at dissonance theory," *Advances in Experimental Social Psychology* 17: 229–59.

Crain, R., Katz, E., and Rosenthal, D. (1969) *The Politics of Community Conflict: The Flouridation Decision*, Indianapolis: Bobbs-Merrill.

Curran, J. (1991) "Rethinking the media as public sphere," in P. Dahlgren and C. Sparks (eds) *Communication and Citizenship*, London: Routledge.

Dahlgren, P. (1985) "Media, meaning and method: A Post-rational perspective," *The Nordicom Review of Nordic Mass Communication Research* 2.

Davison, W. P. (1983) "The third person effect in communication," *Public Opinion Quarterly* 47: 1–15.

Dayan, D. and Katz, E. (1993) *Media Events: The Live Broadcasting of History*, Cambridge: Harvard University Press.

Dewey, J. (1954) *The Public and Its Problems*, Denver: A. Swallow.

Diamond, E. (1975) *The Tin Kazoo: Television, Politics, and the Press*, Cambridge, MA: MIT Press.

Edelman, M. (1988) *Constructing the Political Spectacle*, Chicago: University of Chicago Press.

Eiser, J. R. (1983) "Attribution theory and social cognition," in J. Jaspers, F. D. Fincham, and M. Hewstone (eds) *Attribution Theory and Research: Conceptual Development and Social Dimensions*, London: Academic Press.

Elizur, J. and Katz, E. (1990) "The theatre of redemption: Israel's images and their functions." Paper presented at the colloquium of the Faculty of Social Sciences, Hebrew University of Jerusalem.

Entman, R. (1989) *Democracy Without Citizens: Media and the Decay of American Politics*, New York: Oxford University Press.

Epstein, E. (1973) *News From Nowhere*, New York: Random House.

Fish, S. (1980) *Is there a Text in this Class? The Authority of Interpretative Communities*, Cambridge: Harvard University Press.

Fiske, J. (1988) *Television Culture*, London: Methuen.

Fiske, J. and Hartley, J. (1978) *Reading Television*, London: Methuen.

Frazer, B. (1980) "Conversational litigation," *Journal of Pragmatics* 4: 341–50.

Gal, R. (1985) "Commitment and obedience in the military: An Israeli case study," *Armed Forces and Society* 11: 553–64.

Galtung, J. and Ruge, M. H. (1970) "The structure of foreign news," in J. Tunstall (ed.) *Media Sociology*, London: Constable.

Gamson, W. (1992) *Talking Politics*, New York: Cambridge University Press.

Gamson, W. and Modigliani, A. (1989) "Media discourse and public opinion on nuclear power: A constructionist approach," *American Journal of Sociology* 95: 1–37.

Gans, H. (1980) *Deciding What's News*, New York: Random House.

Gerbner, G. (1992) *The Triumph of the Image: The Media's War in the Persian Gulf – A Global Perspective*, Boulder: Westview Press, 1992.

Gilbert, G. N. and Mulkay, M. (1984) *Opening Pandora's Box: A Sociological Analysis of Scientists' Discourse*, Cambridge: Cambridge University Press.

Gilboa, E. (1995) "Israelis and Palestinians: Public opinion and peace making." Paper delivered at the annual conference of the International Communication Association.

Gitlin, T. (1980) *The Whole World is Watching*, Berkeley: University of California Press.

Glasgow University Media Group. (1976) *Bad News*, London: Routledge and Kegan Paul.

Glasser, T. L. (1991) "Communication and the cultivation of citizenship," *Communication*, 4: 235–48.

Goffman, E. (1973) *The Presentation of Self in Everyday Life*, Woodstock, NY: Overlook Press.

——(1974) *Frame Analysis*, New York: Harper and Row.

Goren, D. (1979) *Secrecy and the Right to Know*, Ramat Gan: Turtledove.

Goren, D., Cohen A. A., and Caspi, D. (1975) "Reporting the Yom-Kippur War from Israel," *Journalism Quarterly*, 52: 199–206.

Gouldner, A. (1975) *The Dialectics of Ideology and Technology*, New York: Oxford University Press.

Graber, D. A. (1984) *Processing the News: How People Tame the Information Tide*, New York: Longman.

——(1990) "Whither research on psychology of political communication?" Paper presented at the annual meeting of the International Society of Political Psychology, Washington.

Griswold, W. (1987) "The fabrication of meaning: Literary interpretation in the United States," *American Journal of Sociology*, 92: 1,077–117.

Gross, L. (1989) "Out of the mainstream: Sexual minorities and the mass media," in E. Seiter, H. Borchers, G. Kreutzner, and E. Warth (eds) *Remote Control*, London and New York: Routledge.

Hall, S. (1985) "Encoding/decoding," in S. Hall et al. (eds) *Culture, Media, Language*, London: Hutchinson.

Hallin, D. (1985) "The American news media: A critical theory perspective," in J. Forrester (ed.) *Critical Theory and Public Life*, Cambridge: MIT Press.

——(1986) *The Uncensored War: The Media and Vietnam*, Berkeley: University of California Press.

——(1991) "The first casualty revisited," in *The Media at War*, New York: A Gannett Foundation Report.

Hallin, D. C. (1994) *We Keep America on Top of the World: TV Journalism and the Public Sphere*, London: Routledge.

Hallin, D. C. and Gitlin, T. (1993) "Agon and ritual: The Gulf War as popular culture and as television drama," *Political Communication* 10: 411–24.

Hallin, D. C. and Mancini, P. (1984) "Speaking of the president: Political structure in American and Italian news," *Theory and Society*, 13, 829–50.

Horowitz, D. and Lissak, M. (1973) "Authority without sovereignty: The case of the National Centre of the Jewish Community in Palestine," *Government and Opposition* 8 1: 48–71.

Iser W. (1991) *Framing Effects in Politics: Television and Political Responsibility*, Los Angeles: University of California Press.

Iyengar, S. (1991) *Is Anyone Responsible? How Television Frames Political Issues*, Chicago: University of Chicago Press.

Katriel, T. (1985) "Griping as a verbal ritual in some Israeli discourse," in M. Dascal (ed.) *Dialogue: An Interdisciplinary Approach*, Amsterdam: John Benjamins.

——(1991) *Communal Webs: Communication and Culture in Contemporary Israel*, Albany: State University of New York Press.

Katriel, T. and Nesher P. (1986) "Gibush: The rhetoric of cohesion in Israeli school culture," *Comparative Education Review*, 30: 216–32.

Katz, E. (1971) "Television comes to the people of the book," in I. L. Horowitz (ed.) *The Use and Abuse of Social Science*, New Brunswick: Transaction Books.

——(1981) "Publicity and pluralistic ignorance: Notes on the 'spiral of silence,' ' in H. Baier, H. M. Kepplinger, and K. Reumann (eds) *Offentliche Meinung und Sozialer Wandel* (Public Opinion and Social Change), Darmstadt: Westdeutscher Verlag.

——(1988) "Cutting out the middle man," *Inter Media* 16: 30—1.
——(1989) "Journalists as scientists," *American Behavioral Scientist* 33: 234–8.
——(1992) "The end of journalism," *Journal of Communication* 42: 5–12.
——(1993) "Television, diplomacy and Israeli opinion on the Palestinian peace accord." Paper delivered to the Faculty of the Annenberg School of Communication at the University of Pennsylvania.
——(in press) "And deliver us from segmentation," in K. Jameison (ed.) *Annals of the American Academy of Political and Social Science* 546: 22–33.
Katz, E. and Gurevitch, M. (1976) *The Securalization of Leisure: Culture and Communication in Israel*, London: Faber and Faber.
Katz, E. and Haas, H. (1994) "Twenty years of television in Israel: Are there long-run effects on values and cultural practices?" *Stiftung Lesen* 52: 80–91.
Katz, E. and Levinsohn, H. (1988) "Too good to be true: Notes on the Israel elections of 1988," *International Journal of Public Opinion Research* 1, 2: 111–23.
Katz, E., Dayan, D., and Motyl, P. (1983) "Television diplomacy: Sadat in Jerusalem," in G. Gerbner and M. Seifert (eds) *World Communications*, New York and London: Longman.
Kelman, H. C. and Baron, R. M. (1968) "Determinants of modes of resolving inconsistency Dilemmas: A functional analysis," in R. P. Abelson, E. Aronson, W. McGuire, T. Newcomb, M. Rosenberg, and P. Annenbaum (eds) *Theories of Cognitive Consistency: A Sourcebook*, Chicago: Rand McNally
Kelman, H. C. and Hamilton, V. L. (1989) *Crimes of Obedience*, New Haven and London: Yale University Press.
Kepplinger, H. M. and Roth, H. (1979) "Creating a crisis: German mass media and oil supply," *Public Opinion Quarterly*, 43: 285–96.
Keren, M. (1988) *Ben-Gurion and the Intellectuals: Power, Religion and Charisma*, Beer Sheba: Ben Gurion University.
Lahav, P. (1985) "Israel's press law," in P. Lahav (ed.) *Press Law in Modern Democracies*, New York: Longman.
Lazarsfeld, P. and Merton, R. (1948) "Mass communication, popular taste and organized social action," in L. Bryson (ed.) *The Communication of Ideas*, New York: Harper.
Lederman, J. (1992) *Battle Lines: The American Media and the Intifada*, New York: Henry Holt.
Levi, S. (1992) *Indicators of Social Problems in Israel in 1979–91: Society and State*, vol. 2, Jerusalem: Guttman Institute of Applied Social Research.
Levinsohn, H. and Katz, E. (1994) "Stability and change in attitudes towards the peace process," report 1236, Jerusalem: Guttman Institute of Applied Social Research.
Liebes, T. (1989a) "On the convergence of theories regarding the role of the viewer," in B. Dervin and M. Voigt (eds) *Progress in Communication Studies*, Norwood: Ablex.
——(1989b) "Negotiation of political identity through the interaction of family, peers and television." Third report to the Spencer Foundation, Jerusalem: Guttman Institute for Applied Social Research.
——(1996) "Notes on the struggle to define involvement in television viewing," in J. Hay et al. (eds) *The Audience and its Landscapes*, Boulder: Westview Press.
Liebes, T. and Katz, E. (1993) *The Export of Meaning*, Cambridge: Polity Press.
Liebes, T. and Ribak, R. (1991) "Democracy at risk: A reflection of political alienation in attitudes toward the media," *Communication Theory* 1, 3: 239–52.
——(1992) "The contribution of family culture to political participation, political outlook and its reproduction," *Communication Research*, 19: 618–41.

Liebes, T., Katz, E., and Ribak, R. (1991) "Ideological reproduction," *Political Behavior*, 13: 137–52.

Liebes-Plesner, T. (1984) "Shades of meaning in President Sadat's Knesset speech," *Semiotica* 48: 229–65.

Limor, Y. and Nossek, H. (1995) "Military censorship in Israel: Anachronism in a changing world or modern model of coexistence between press and government in a democracy," in M. Lehmstedt and L. Poethe (eds) *Leipziger Jahrbuch Zur Buchgeschichte*, vol. 5, Leipzig: Leipziger Arbeitskreis zur geschichte des buchwesens.

Lipstadt, D. (1986) *Beyond Belief: The American Press and the Coming of the Holocaust, 1933–1945*, New York: Free Press.

Livingstone, S. (1990) *Making Sense of Television*, Oxford: Pergamon Press.

Manoff, R.K. (1986) "Writing the news (by telling the story)," in R. Manoff and M. Schudson (eds) *Reading the News*, New York: Pantheon Books.

Mauss, M. (1969) *The Gift: Forms and Functions of Exchange in Arabic Society*, London: Cohen and West.

Merton, R. (1957) *Social Theory and Social Structure*, Glenco: The Free Press.

Molotch, H, and Lester, M. (1974) "News as purposive behaviour," *American Sociological Review* 3, 101–12.

Morley, D. (1980) *The "Nationwide" Audience*, London: British Film Institute.

——(1987) *Family Television*, London: Comedia.

Moscovici, S. (1984) "The phenomenon of social representations," in R. M. Farr and S. Moscovici (eds) *Social Representations*, Cambridge: Cambridge University Press.

Murdock, G. (1973) "Political deviance: The press presentation of a militant mass demonstration," in S. Cohen and J. Young (eds) *The Manufacture of News*, London: Constable.

——(1988) "Talking about terrorism: Television and the context for political discourse," in P. A. Bruck, (ed.) *The News Media and Television*, Carlton: Carlton University, The Center for Communication, Culture and Society.

Negbi, M. (1986) "Paper tiger: The struggle for press freedom in Israel," *Jerusalem Quarterly* 39: 17–32.

——(1995) *Freedom of the Press in Israel: The Legal Aspect* (in Hebrew), Jerusalem: The Jerusalem Institute for Israel Studies.

Nir, R. and Roeh, I. (1993) "Covering the intifada in Israeli Newspapers," in G. Wolsfeld and A. A. Cohen (eds) *Framing the Intifada*, Norwood: Ablex.

Nisbett, R. E. and Ross, L. (1980) *Human Inference Strategies and Shortcomings of Social Judgment*, Englewood Cliffs: Prentice Hall.

Noelle-Neumann, E. (1985) *The Spiral of Silence*, Chicago: University of Chicago Press.

Nossek, H. (1994) "The narrative role of the holocaust and the state of Israel in the coverage of salient terrorist events in the Israeli press," *Journal of Narrative and Life History*, 4: 82–101.

Paletz, D. L. and Entman, R. M. (1981) *Media, Power, Politics*, New York: The Free Press.

Power, J. G. (1990) "Mass communication of otherness and identification." Unpublished doctoral dissertation, University of Southern California.

Roeh, I. (1989) "Don't confuse me with facts: Storytelling in the news," *American Behavioral Scientist*, 33: 234–9.

Roeh, Y. and Nir, R. (1990) "Covering the intifada in the Israeli press: Popular and quality papers assume rhetoric of conformity," *Discourse and Society*, 3: 22–36.

——(1991) "The passing on of speech in the Israel radio news: Rhetorical strategies and ideological limits," *Hebrew Li*, 31–2: 79–93.

Russett, B. and Shye, S. (1993) "Aggressiveness, involvement and commitment in foreign policy attitudes: Multiple scaling," in D. Caldwell and T. McKeont (eds) *Diplomacy, Force and Leadership: Essays in Honor of Alexander E. George*, Boulder: Westview Press.

Scannell, P. and Cardiff, D. (1991) *A Social History of British Broadcasting*, Oxford: Basil Blackwell.

Schenk, R. C. and Abelson, R. P. (1977) *Scripts, Plans, Goals and Understanding*, Cambridge: Cambridge University Press.

Schiff, Z. and Yaari, E. (1990) *Intifada: The Palestinian Uprising – Israel's Third Front*, New York: Simon and Schuster.

Schiffrin, D. (1984) "Jewish argument as sociability," *Language in Society*, 13: 311–35.

Schudson, M. (1986) "When? Deadlines, datelines and history," in R. K. Manoff and M. Schudson (eds) *Reading the News*, New York: Pantheon Books.

——(1989) "How culture works," *Theory and Society* 21:357–381.

Shakow, A. (1995) "Swapping stories: News narratives and professional ideology in Palestinian coverage of the occupied territory." MA thesis, Hebrew University, Jerusalem.

Shohat, E. (1989) *Israeli Cinema: East/West and the Politics of Representation*, Austin: University of Texas Press.

Siebert, F., Peterson, T., and Schramm, W. (1972) *Four Theories of the Press*, Levington, MA: D. H. Heath.

Tuchman, G. (1978) *Making News*, New York: Free Press.

Van Dijk, T. A. (1987) *Communicating Racism: Ethnic Prejudice in Thought and Talk*, Newbury Park, CA: Sage.

——(1988) *News as Discourse*, Hillsdale, NJ: Erlbaum.

Van Krefeld, M. (1989) "The future battlefield is the intifada," *Ha'aretz Magazine*.

Wetherell, M. and Potter, J. (1989) "Narrative characters and accounting for violence," in J. Shotter and K. Gergen (eds) *Texts of Identity*, London: Sage.

White, H. (1980) "The value of narrativity in the representation of reality," in W. J. Mitchell (ed.) *On Narrative*, Chicago: University of Chicago Press.

Williams, R. (1974) *Television: Technology and Cultural Form*, New York: Schoken Books.

——(1977) *Marxism and Literature*, Oxford: Oxford University Press.

Williamson, J. (1986) "A Woman is an island: Femininity and colonization," in T. Modlesky (ed.) *The Uses of Entertainment*, Bloomington: Indiana University Press.

Wolfsfeld, G. (1988) *The Politics of Provocation: Participation and Protest in Israel*, Albany: State University of New York Press.

——(in press) *Media and Political Conflict: News from the Middle East*, Cambridge: Cambridge University Press.

Zanna, M. P. and Cooper, J. (1974) "Dissonance and the pill: An attribution approach to studying the arousal properties of dissonance," *The Journal of Personality and Social Psychology* 29: 703–9.

Zelizer, B. (1991) "CNN, the Gulf War and journalistic practice." Paper delivered to the Speech Communication Association convention, Atlanta.

Zillman, D. and Bryant, E. (1986) "Exploring the entertainment experience," in E. Bryant and D. Zillman (eds) *Perspectives on Media Effects*, Hillsdale, NJ: Lawrence Erlbaum Associates.

Index